R. A. DICKEY of the Toronto Blue Jays is one of the premier pitchers in baseball. In 2012 while playing for the New York Mets, he became the first knuckleballer to win the National League Cy Young Award, major league baseball's highest honor for a pitcher. He has also written for the *New York Times* and is working on a young adult version of *Wherever I Wind Up* as well as two children's books. When not on the road with his team, Dickey lives in Tennessee with his wife and children.

WAYNE COFFEY is an award-winning journalist for the *New York Daily News* and the author of more than thirty books, including *The Boys of Winter*, a *New York Times* bestselling chronicle of the 1980 U.S. Olympic hockey team. A three-time Pulitzer nominee, he has long been regarded as one of best sports feature writers in the nation.

Praise for *Wherever I Wind Up*

"It might be the finest piece of nonfiction baseball writing since *Ball Four*. Perhaps above all, it's a classic epic quest, a flawed hero's unlikely odyssey to the major leagues and to discovering the mystical pitch that helped him get there."

—L. Jon Wertheim, *Sports Illustrated*

"An astounding memoir—haunting and touching, courageous and wise." —Jeremy Schaap, bestselling author, Emmy Award–winning journalist, ESPN

"Gripping . . . Searingly personal . . . To know Dickey is to root for him."
                                        —Tyler Kepner, *The New York Times*

"Compelling . . . Dickey credits his faith with overcoming myriad trials both personal and professional, but it never feels as if he's preaching. . . . The author emerges as one of baseball's good guys, and someone who can write as well as he pitches. Dickey has set a new standard for athlete autobiographies."
                                        —*Publishers Weekly* (starred review)

"R. A. Dickey's book is unlike any other professional athlete's autobiography you have ever read. And that is a very good thing."
                                        —Mike Bauman, MLB.com

"A wonderful and powerful new memoir."   —Jim Caple, ESPN

"Nobody in baseball has overcome more obstacles than R. A. Dickey, and nobody writes about them with more honesty and insight. R. A. doesn't want to be called a hero, but he is exactly that, and when you read about his life's journey and his courage, you will agree with me. This is an awesome book by an awesome man."
                                        —Orel Hershiser, ESPN *Sunday Night Baseball* analyst,
                                        former MLB All-Star

"I can't recommend *Wherever I Wind Up* enough."
                                        —Gary Cohen, SportsNet New York (SNY)

"A baseball story that is unlike anybody else's."
                                        —Buck Showalter, manager of the Baltimore Orioles

WHEREVER I WIND UP

MY QUEST FOR TRUTH, AUTHENTICITY, AND THE PERFECT KNUCKLEBALL

R. A. DICKEY

with

WAYNE COFFEY

A PLUME BOOK

PLUME
Published by the Penguin Group
Penguin Group (USA) Inc., 375 Hudson Street,
New York, New York 10014, USA

USA | Canada | UK | Ireland | Australia | New Zealand | India | South Africa | China
Penguin Books Ltd, Registered Offices: 80 Strand, London WC2R 0RL, England
For more information about the Penguin Group visit penguin.com

First published in the United States of America by Blue Rider Press, a member of
Penguin Group (USA) Inc., 2012
First Plume Printing, 2013

Copyright © R. A. Dickey, 2012
All rights reserved. No part of this product may be reproduced, scanned, or distributed in
any printed or electronic form without permission. Please do not participate in or
encourage piracy of copyrighted materials in violation of the author's rights.
Purchase only authorized editions.

 REGISTERED TRADEMARK—MARCA REGISTRADA

THE LIBRARY OF CONGRESS HAS CATALOGUED THE BLUE RIDER PRESS EDITION AS FOLLOWS:

Dickey, R.A.
Wherever I wind up : my quest for truth, authenticity and the perfect knuckleball /
R.A. Dickey, Wayne Coffey.
p. cm.
Summary: "A memoir written by baseball pitcher R.A. Dickey"— Provided by publisher.
Includes bibliographical references and index.
ISBN 978-0-399-15815-5 (hc.)
ISBN 978-0-452-29901-6 (pbk.)
1. Dickey, R.A.   2. Baseball players—United States—Biography.   3. Pitchers (Baseball)—
United States—Biography.   I. Coffey, Wayne R.   II. Title.
GV865.D46A3 2012
796.357092—dc23
[B]   2012001700

Printed in the United States of America
1   3   5   7   9   10   8   6   4   2

Original hardcover design by Nicole LaRoche

PUBLISHER'S NOTE
While the author has made every effort to provide accurate telephone numbers, Internet
addresses, and other contact information at the time of publication, neither the publisher
nor the author assumes any responsibility for errors, or for changes that occur after
publication. Further, publisher does not have any control over and does not assume any
responsibility for author or third-party Web sites or their content.

Penguin is committed to publishing works of quality and integrity.
In that spirit, we are proud to offer this book to our readers;
however, the story, the experiences, and the words
are the author's alone.

For Anne and the kids

—R.A.D.

For Denise, Alexandra, Sean, and Samantha

—W.C.

Dum spiro, spero.

—Latin proverb

(Translation: While I breathe, I hope.)

CONTENTS

THE WORST NIGHT
I EVER HAD

I remember details. I've always been able to remember details. I will never be a Hall of Famer and will never lead the league in strikeouts, and am in no imminent danger of joining the 300 Victory Club. But my memory—that I will put up against anybody's.

I can tell you about the little wagon wheels on my red comforter when I was four years old, my phone number and address—247 Timmons Avenue—when I was in kindergarten, and the smoky haze that hung in my mother's beat-up Impala when I was six, a sorry heap with a gas gauge that was habitually on "E." I can give you a foot-by-foot description of my boyhood bedroom, highlighted by the Larry Bird photo I tore out of *Sports Illustrated* and taped on the wall—I loved Larry Bird—and can still see my first glove, a brown synthetic $12 model from Kmart. It was called the Mag. I have no idea why. Maybe it was short for "Magician," or "Magnificent," or "Magadan," as in Dave. I used the Mag when I played shortstop for Coach Teeter, my first Little League coach, who gave us yellow iron-on stars after we did something positive or had a good game.

I got my share of yellow stars, but they never made it onto my uniform. My mom had a lot going on.

I can give you every detail you want, and plenty you don't want: about the dark times in my life, about the saloons I went to with my mom, and the empty houses I slept in as a teenager, a wayward kid in search of soulless shelter, and about the most traumatic summer of my life. It came when I was eight and it included a new babysitter, and a game with a tennis ball out in the country, on the roof of a garage. Then things happened—horrible things. I remember the smells and colors and feelings, and the pile of the carpeting. I remember it all.

I wish I didn't.

When I think of that summer, and so many dysfunctional seasons that followed, the details threaten to go on forever. The inner warfare that gripped me the day I went from baseball bonus baby to baseball freak—the Pitcher Without an Ulnar Collateral Ligament—and lost almost three-quarters of a million dollars in the process. The blue flip-flops I wore when I tried to swim across the Missouri River, one in a long line of unfathomably stupid risks I've taken. The orange-red hues of the autumn of 2006, when, eleven years into my professional baseball career, I thought about taking my life because of the mess I had made of it.

I remember the tiniest nuances from events, big and small, through the thirty-seven years of my life. That's why it's strange that I don't have even a vague recollection of the time when I stopped being a phenom.

The word "phenom" has been in the baseball lexicon forever, or at least since 1881, when it was used to describe a pitcher for the Boston Red Stockings named James Evans "Grasshopper Jim" Whitney. Grasshopper Jim was twenty-three years old and went

31–33 and threw 552 innings and 57 complete games that year (this was the pre–La Russa era), his performance undeniably phenomenal. Soon the "-enal" was left off the end, and Grasshopper Jim simply became a phenom—a word that anoints you as the embodiment of hope, someone whose youthful gifts are going to bring joy and victories for years to come.

A word that means you are special.

It is during my seventh-grade year at Montgomery Bell Academy, in Nashville, that people first notice me. I strike out twelve in six innings and pitch our team, the Big Red, to a league championship, and a year later I make the varsity, and before long people start making a fuss over how I throw. By the time I'm a sophomore, big-league scouts begin to come to my games, and they seem to talk not only about my arm but about my makeup, how I'm a kid who knows how to compete, who you want to have on the mound in a big game. As much as I love throwing the ball and hearing it smack into the leather of the catcher's glove, I love the pure competition of pitching more than anything, bringing a street fighter's sensibility to the mound with me, treating every at-bat as a duel at sixty feet six inches.

You may hit me. You may knock me around and knock balls out of the park.

But I am always going to get back up and keep coming at you.

The scouts keep coming too. I am the Tennessee state player of the year as a senior in 1993 and an All-American at the University of Tennessee and a starter for Team USA in the 1996 Olympics in Atlanta. The Texas Rangers select me with their number one pick in the June free-agent draft. Everything is falling into place, my map to the majors laid out before me, as precise as anything a cartographer could draw.

And then it all goes haywire. Five years pass before I make the big leagues, a cup of coffee so brief I don't even have time to add cream and sugar. I spend seven years—seven!—as a member of the Triple-A Oklahoma City RedHawks, and some people in town are seriously suggesting I run for mayor. I tell them I don't want to be a mayor, I want to be in the majors. But I am going in the wrong direction. I start losing velocity, and don't get nearly enough people out. I give up conventional pitching at the urging of Buck Showalter and Orel Hershiser, my manager and pitching coach at the time, and become a full-time knuckleball pitcher. We live in thirty-one different places over a ten-year span. My wife, Anne, who graduated at the top of her class at the University of Tennessee, takes on a series of jobs she is way overqualified for, just to help us make ends meet and support my dream. She teaches aerobics to senior citizens. She works as a salesperson at The Limited in a mall in Port Charlotte, Florida.

During one of our years in Oklahoma City, she gets a clerking job at a big-chain bookstore. I visit her one day and, after sifting through the *Stars Wars* section (I am a total Tatooine geek) and the Tolkien shelf, I meander over to sports and see what new baseball books are out. I peruse the classics—*The Natural* and *The Long Season* and *The Boys of Summer*—and leaf through *Ball Four* and *The Glory of Their Times*. I keep walking and come upon one of those preseason prospectus books.

This should be interesting. I wonder who they're predicting big things from.

I look up the Texas Rangers section. Why not start with my own organization? The authors roll out half a thesaurus to praise the Rangers' power-laden lineup, Alex Rodriguez and Juan Gonzalez and the rest. They talk about Pudge Rodríguez being the best catcher in the game and rave about a kid named Michael Young. I keep reading. They don't do nearly as much raving about the Rangers' pitchers or their pitching prospects. I scan farther down, seeing if I am in there at all.

Finally, I find my name at the bottom. It is in bold type, like the other names. I can't tell you I remember the exact text a decade later, but this is within a few words of verbatim:

> *In the farm system, the Rangers' alleged prospects include former first-round draft pick, R.A. Dickey, a marginal right-hander who has given no indication that he's ever going to amount to anything.*

I consider throwing the book, but don't. I close it and put it back on the shelf.

Marginal. This is what I have been reduced to, at least in the estimation of the authors. A *marginal* right-hander. It's a hard word to read. A brutal word to read. But are they wrong?

You tell me.

When you spend seven seasons in the same minor-league location, when you log almost fourteen years and three hundred games in the minors overall, you're not on what you'd call the fast track. You are not on any track at all.

You may get called "has-been" or "never-was" but you can be fairly certain that you are not anybody's idea of a phenom anymore.

Doing all that minor-league meandering tends to leave you in one of two camps. You either resign yourself to never getting out, to just playing out the string until your skills erode or you've had it with the back roads and bus rides. Or you go the other way and convince yourself that you absolutely still have a chance to make the big leagues, even if all available evidence suggests otherwise. You keep finding a way to hold on to hope, keep waiting for the Call, and if and when it comes, you make darn sure that you don't give the club any reason ever to send you back down.

I am in Camp Number Two. And hanging on by a fingernail of hope is exactly where I find my non-phenom self in the early spring of 2006, when the Texas Rangers hand me number 45. It is the fourth day of the season. We are playing the Detroit Tigers at home, at the Ballpark in Arlington, as it was then called. Against considerable odds, I have made the Rangers' starting rotation out of spring training and am beginning my first full season as a knuckleball pitcher. The pitch is still a work in progress, some days good, more days not so good, but if Buck Showalter thinks I'm ready, what am I supposed to do, decline?

Say, "Thanks, Skip, but I think some of the kids are more deserving"?

No. I wasn't going to do that.

I am thirty-one years old and darn tired of being mediocre. Anne and I have two young daughters and a baby boy on the way. I am living in a Hyatt and getting around on a borrowed bicycle because I don't want to spend money on a rental car. One part retread, one part restoration project, I am a decade removed from my years studying English lit at Tennessee, forgetting a lot of Faulkner and firing a lot of fastballs. I have become the quintessential "4A" pitcher—baseball code for a player who is too good for Triple-A but not good enough to stick in the majors. I had already spent two full, extremely undistinguished years in the big leagues. I know that I cannot reasonably expect to get another shot if this doesn't work out.

You want to know how desperate I am? I have turned myself into the baseball equivalent of a carnival act—maybe not a two-headed turtle or a bearded lady, but close. I am trying to make a living throwing the ugly stepchild of pitches, a pitch few in the game appreciate and even fewer understand. Almost nobody starts out planning to be a knuckleball pitcher. When was the last time you heard a twelve-year-old Little Leaguer say, "I want to be Hoyt Wilhelm when I grow up"? You become a knuckleball pitcher when you hit a dead end, when your arm gets hurt or your hard stuff isn't getting the job done. Tim Wakefield was a minor-league first baseman with a lot of power and a bad batting average; that's when he made the switch. I made mine when the Rangers told me, in the middle of 2005, that I was going nowhere with my regular stuff—an assessment that I could hardly argue with.

I'd been going nowhere for a long time, after all.

AT 3:45 P.M. on Thursday, April 6, I walk out of the Hyatt, hop on the bike, and pedal to the Ballpark for the most important start of my baseball life. I cannot view it any other way. I roll up to the park after a ten-minute ride. It's time for my far-flung odyssey to stop, for some measure of stability to start.

I know the only way that's going to happen is by getting big-league hitters out.

After eating a turkey sandwich in the players' lounge, I head for the video room to watch a tape of Wakefield pitching against the Tigers the year before. I'm not looking for specific strategies on how to attack Pudge Rodríguez (he left the Rangers via free agency after the 2004 season) or Magglio Ordóñez so much as reassurance that major-league hitters can be retired with the pitch. It's a positive-imaging exercise for me, balm for an insecure soul. I have zero confidence in myself, and in the consistency of my knuckle-ball. I don't really want to send R. A. Dickey out there against the Tigers. I want to send out Tim Wakefield, the most successful knuckleball pitcher of the 1990s and 2000s.

If it works for him, maybe it will work for me.

Ninety minutes before game time I take a shower, spending most of it visualizing myself going after every Tiger batter. When I am finished, I say a prayer out loud. I put on my uniform and go out to the outfield with the bullpen catcher, Josh Frasier. I start throwing and I feel good. I have a pretty good knuckler on flat ground. After a few minutes we move onto the bullpen mound, and I am throwing it even better, the ball fluttering, my confidence building to unaccustomed levels. When you throw a knuckleball, you want to have the same release point every pitch. You want your arm and your elbow at the exact right angle, and you want your nails biting into the horsehide the same way. The ball is moving well and I have good control over it. I am locked in.

The PA man announces the lineups. It's almost time.

I walk in from the bullpen and sit on the bench. I run a towel over my face and take a swig of water. I wonder how Nate Robert-son, the Tigers starter, is feeling at this very moment. As I prepare to go out to the mound, I pray for confidence, for good health, for the courage to get after them.

"Be glorified, Lord," I say.

I remind myself to stay positive. It all feels good.

The Tigers' leadoff hitter is Brandon Inge, their third baseman. Inge is not a typical leadoff guy; he strikes out often and is not in-clined to be patient, but he does have a lot of pop in his bat. I throw him a knuckleball for a strike to start the game. I wind and deliver the 0–1 pitch, a knuckler that tumbles slowly toward the inner part of the plate. It feels okay coming out of my hand, but it has too much rotation. Rotation is the mortal enemy of knuckleballers, the thing we spend years working to eliminate. When knuckleballs rotate, they don't move. They sit up and often disappear. As the ball nears the plate, I can actually see Inge's eyes grow wide.

He swings and puts serious wood on it, driving the ball deep to left. I follow the flight of the ball, and watch it go over the fence.

Two pitches into the game, I am already down a run. Not the start I had in mind. At all.

I get the next two guys and then Ordóñez steps in. On a 1–0 pitch, I float another knuckleball toward the plate. He coils and takes a rip. A loud thwack fills the park, and then another ball disappears over the left-field wall. Two-nothing is the score, and .500 is the Tigers' batting average against me, and even in that moment I know why.

I had prayed for confidence but the fact is I don't have any. Once there are real live hitters at the plate, I turn into a completely different pitcher than I was in the pen. I am afraid to make a mistake. I'm not going after the Tigers hitters, and the upshot is that not only are my knuckleballs not confounding the Tigers, they are coming in looking like beach balls.

I get Dmitri Young to ground out to end the inning. I come into the dugout, and try to forget about it. Pitching coach Mark Connor—we call him "Goose"—comes over and pats me on the back, and reminds me that plenty of pitchers get roughed up early on before settling into their rhythm.

You'll be fine. Just keep battling, Goose says.

We get two hits but don't score in the bottom half, and now I am back on the mound.

One hitter at a time, I remind myself. It may be baseball's oldest cliché, but I've learned that a lot of clichés gain currency for the best possible reason: they work.

The first Tigers hitter in the top of the second is Chris Shelton, a power-hitting first baseman. Ahead, 1–2, I throw another knuckler that sits up. Shelton waits. He takes a huge slugger's cut at it and an instant later the ball is in orbit, another knuckler leaving the premises—quickly. I try not to think that I've already given up 1,200 feet worth of dingers. Shelton isn't three steps out of the box when I ask the umpire for a new ball. I am not going to watch him round the bases. What would be the point? I know what his destination is. I stand on the mound and rub up the ball and look vacantly toward the sky. I can't fathom what is happening. I turn around and look at the blank faces of my infielders, shortstop Michael Young and first baseman Mark Teixeira, and feel terrible that I am letting them down, letting the whole team down. The infield is as quiet as a library.

Forget it. Go get the next hitter, I tell myself. *This can still be a quality start if you stop it right here.*

I retire the next three guys and manage to get through a bumpy third inning, despite a long fly and two line drives. It isn't pretty, but it is scoreless, and that constitutes progress. The first batter in the fourth is Dmitri Young. I strike him out, my first strikeout of the night. I am happy Dmitri is in the lineup. Then it is Shelton's turn again. I go up on him, 1–2, just as I did the last time.

Don't make the same mistake, I tell myself. *If you miss, make sure you miss down.* If I get him, I'll be an out away from a second straight scoreless inning. I can maybe salvage this start and show something to Jon Daniels, the general manager, and Showalter, the men who had given me this opportunity.

Except that on my next pitch I throw another beach ball up in the zone and Shelton crushes it to left, way over the fence, farther than any of the others. Goose comes out to the mound. He looks like an undertaker, only sadder. Goose knows me as well as anybody on the club. He lives in Knoxville, about three hours from me. All winter long, I'd drive to see him and throw to him, and then drive home. He wants me to succeed as much as I do, and one look at his face tells me he is feeling every bit of my pain.

Hey, R.A., let's just take a breath right now, okay? he says. Let's slow the game down right here. Just keep fighting. Keep grinding it out. Don't fold up. Take a breath and give us some innings.

Goose is right in everything he says. It feels reassuring to hear his words. I take the breath. I tell myself I am going to stop the carnage here, once and for all, and get out with no further damage. The next hitter is Carlos Guillen, the shortstop. I walk him, and that brings up center fielder Craig Monroe, who swings at the first pitch, one more knuckleball that does almost nothing. Monroe hits it halfway to El Paso. Now it is 6–0, and a full-blown debacle. I could take breaths until the 162nd game and it isn't going to change the hideous truth: the biggest start of my life has turned into the worst start of my life.

The next hitter is Marcus Thames, the left fielder. No matter what, I am not going to let him hit a knuckleball out of the park.

Instead, I throw a fastball. And he hits *that* out of the park. It is my sixty-first, and last, pitch of the night.

As Thames circles the bases, I look up into the half-filled stands and listen to boos rain down on me. It's hard to get baseball fans in Texas to boo you, but I have done it, with a pitching line that isn't just bad, but epically bad, tying the post-1900 record for most home runs given up in a start. My line is 3⅓ innings, 8 hits, and 7 runs. Buck is on his way out to get me now. The whole scene is completely surreal, as if I were at the center of a slow-motion highlight reel, Tigers swinging, Tigers slugging, balls flying out of the park, a home-run derby come to life. It seems as if it takes Buck a half hour to get to the mound. I stand there and wait and feel more alone than I ever have on a ball field.

It feels very, very familiar.

How long have I felt alone? How long have I been fleeing from my shame and my secrets, bobbing and weaving through life, terrified about people finding out about where I'm from and what I've been through?

In a strange way, as I wait to hand Buck the ball and get out of there before any more Tigers can take me over the wall, I realize that I've spent my three and a third innings doing the same sort of bobbing and weaving.

I'd trusted myself and pitched with conviction during my warm-up. I'd thrown good knuckleballs, and thrown them with a purpose—knuckleballs that had big movement, late movement, the kind that could make even the best hitters look silly. I was fully in the moment. And then the game started, and I hid. I pitched with fear, pitched like a wimp, doubting whether I was good enough to beat the Detroit Tigers and letting that doubt rob me of any shot I had at succeeding. As I let each pitch go that night, I had voices in my head saying, *Please, let it be a strike* and *Please don't let them hit it.*

It is no way to pitch, no way to live.

As I walk off the mound, I take in all the details of the scene around me: the vitriol of the fans; the little white lights telling the hideous truth on the scoreboard; the grim reality that I am indeed a marginal big-league pitcher. I want to believe that God has better things in store for me, and that this is not how my baseball life will end. I want to hold on to hope. I look out at the outfield walls that couldn't contain the Tigers.

There is still hope for me. Isn't there?

CHAPTER ONE

PLASTIC SPOON

Harry Lee Dickey and Leslie Bowers got married on May 29, 1974, wearing jeans in the Davidson County Courthouse in Nashville, Tennessee. It was the anniversary of the day when Abraham Lincoln said, "You can fool some of the people all of the time, and all of the people some of the time, but you can't fool all of the people all of the time." I don't think that had anything to do with their choice of day. I think they picked May 29 because there was a judge available and a clerk to fill out the certificate. My father was twenty-two years old, my mother nineteen. They had met eighteen months earlier through a mutual friend at a school in town called Aquinas Junior College. Things moved quickly.

My parents didn't get married because they were hopelessly in love. They got married because my mother was pregnant with me.

So life begins as an accident. It begins with a lot of strife and the predictable money problems, and a dump of an apartment in a complex called Natchez Trace on Nolensville Road, a part of town teeming with pawnshops and used-car lots and fast-food joints, including one named Taco Tico. Nolensville Road is your go-to neighborhood if you want to sell a ring and eat cheap nachos. The rent in the apartment is $175 per month and my parents get what they pay for. The paint is peeling and the walls are dingy and the cockroaches have the run of the place. My mom does battle with them as best she can, standing on a chair and squishing them with a towel, but they keep coming in nocturnal platoons. You don't win against cockroaches. You just move and hope the next place doesn't have them.

Our apartment has another problem. A neighbor problem. He lives downstairs and his name is Pitt. The centerpiece of his apartment is a pyramid of Coors Light cans that almost goes to the ceiling. When he isn't working on his aluminum skyscraper, Pitt, a skinny man with long, shaggy hair, keeps to himself and keeps away from bathing. My parents don't have much to do with Pitt, other than keep their distance. When they scrape together enough money to move out, they pity the next person who has to deal with Pitt, until something terrible happens.

Did you hear the news about Pitt?

No, what happened?

He died of a drug overdose.

Oh, that's too bad.

He didn't look too good, so you had to figure he was on something.

My mother works as a receptionist at a supply business. My father works construction by day, operating heavy machinery, and at the Davidson County Juvenile Delinquent Center by night as a security guard. One of the perks of his night job is access to jeans, which are standard issue to the delinquents upon admission.

After the delinquents wear them, my father brings them home

for him and my mom. You know they're from the JD Center because the pockets are cut out of them.

My parents learn how to get by, but not always how to get along. They almost never kiss or hold hands or have an arm around each other. When I watch Luke Skywalker and Princess Leia kiss in *Star Wars*, it's the first time I see people being affectionate. Maybe my parents are too busy or too tired from work, or maybe they just don't belong together and they both know it. They grit it out for as long as they can. People in my family are good at gritting things out. But when you fight a bunch and you don't kiss at all, all the grit in the world isn't going to get you through.

The marriage doesn't last five years.

My father is a big, strong man, a quality athlete at six feet one inch and 205 pounds, a guy with shoulders that go on forever. He's a man who doesn't complain about anything, the sort of guy who could have a gaping wound in his leg and might—*might*—ask for a Band-Aid. There are people who specialize in high drama, making mountains out of every available molehill; my father specializes in no drama. He's had surgeries that he hasn't even talked about until he was back home. My mother is the same way: no drama at all. Together they'd make for a terrible reality TV show.

I spend my early years in Betty Waters's day care center in Nashville, playing with toys and getting my diaper changed in the basement of Betty's house. Mom picks me up one day after her shift is over. She is driving a Chevy Vega that has a 50 percent chance of starting on any given day; she's constantly opening the hood and jiggling the wires in the distributor cap to get it going. On the way home that day, the Vega breaks down about a half mile down the road from Betty's, so my mom leaves it on the shoulder, puts me on her hip, and starts walking back to Betty's to call for help.

She's about halfway there when a big German shepherd comes out of nowhere, running right at her, barking and baring his teeth. She keeps walking and tries not to act scared, even though she is terrified. She shifts me to her left arm, away from the dog, which keeps growling at her. She takes a few more steps, hoping he'll give it up, but he's all over her and now he's biting her leg. She yells and tries to shake free, but her mobility isn't great with Baby Dickey in her arms. The dog gets another couple of bites in. She yells again and just keeps holding tight to me, telling herself over and over: *Don't let him get my baby.*

Finally, the dog retreats and my mom continues on her way to Betty's.

If you are a mother, you protect your children no matter what, my mother says. Nothing gets in the way of that, no matter what the story is.

My father's story, meanwhile, takes him all over Aquinas Junior College. He is an A student who gets his grades with minimal effort. He is an actor in the school's theater group whose work draws favorable notices. Most of all, he is a star in baseball and basketball, an athlete who big-league scouts like as a pitcher. Everybody calls my father Horse. People say he could've had a pro baseball career, especially after his impressive tryouts for the Cubs, the Reds, and the Cardinals. The Reds are the most interested and offer him $2,000 and a bus ticket to Plant City, Florida, to join their Florida State League team. It is a dream opportunity for a promising young pitcher.

But it is also 1974, the year I am born, which screws up everything.

I want to finish my education, my father tells the Reds. I can't see leaving school to go down to Plant City to see if I can be the one-in-a-thousand ballplayer who makes it to the big leagues.

I don't know if the Reds tried to change his mind or if my father agonized over the decision. He has never talked to me about his baseball dreams or about how he felt when the door on them closed. He has never talked about how hard it was to be a young father, or about why he went from being a dad who would do everything with his son to a dad who more or less checked out.

My dad's approach to problems and emotions is to not say a word about them, to lock them away. It's a skill I perfected, too, getting me through a lot of rough times as a kid and causing me a lot of rough times later.

He could throw the highest high pops in the world, my dad. We'd have a catch and he'd fire them up in the sky and I'd chase after them, wobbling around and trying to get under them and trying my best to have them wind up in my glove. My favorite days in school were when an announcement would come over the loudspeaker at Glencliff Elementary School:

"Robert Dickey to the main office... Robert Dickey to the main office."

My dad would write down some little lie in the book, like a doctor's appointment, sign me out, and then off we'd go to Harpeth Hills Golf Course. Maybe my mom knew about my father aiding and abetting me in playing hooky. Probably not. My dad would let me drive the cart and drink pop and knock the ball around. I wanted to play thirty-six holes.

Everything my dad and I did revolved around sports. He'd take me to Nashville Sounds games and we'd get $2 tickets and I'd root for Don Mattingly, the first baseman, and chase foul balls into the parking lot. I loved the way the horsehide of the ball smelled, the way it felt in my hand.

Look what I got, Dad, I'd say, showing the ball to my father.

Way to go, Little Horsey, he'd say. "Little Horsey" is what he always called me.

I'd spend a big part of the game down the left-field line, where the other kids and I would play a game of "cup ball," batting around a crumpled up soda cup. I dreamed about playing in Herschel Greer Stadium one day, with my dad—the best ballplayer who ever lived—watching me. More than anything, I wanted to throw like my dad. When I won the beanbag toss competition at field day, it was the best day of the school year.

My dad and I spent the most time of all, though, at the Green Hills Family YMCA, playing basketball. Although baseball was his best sport, my dad wasn't a shooting guard to mess with. He could bury outside shots all night, and his range was legendary.

Twenty-five feet? Thirty feet? Horse would start looking at the basket just a few steps inside half-court. I loved watching him play, and watching him referee games when he started doing that to make a little extra money.

Money was always an issue. I won't tell you that I grew up hungry, on the bad side of a trailer park, but every day was a battle to get by. My dad's car would run out of gas every other week. I wore my uncle Ricky's hand-me-downs and if I absolutely needed something new, I'd get it at Kmart. We didn't go out to eat much, but if we did, it would be Western Sizzlin or some other place with a buffet where the food was cheap and you could load up your plate as often as you wanted. Western Sizzlin was where my parents got their first silverware. Not service for eight, just a few forks and knives and spoons they smuggled back to Natchez Trace.

After my parents split up, my younger sister, Jane, and I would sometimes visit our dad in his new place in a nearby section of Nashville. It wasn't very nice or big, and didn't even have a kitchen. Kind of like camping out, minus the campfire. He'd make us macaroni and cheese on his hot plate. There was only room for one bed, so that's where the three of us slept.

Whatever we did and wherever we went, my father's advice to me was the same:

Keep doing the work. You always have to keep doing the work.

He never elaborated, but he liked saying those words. He liked language in general, liked the sound and texture of written and spoken English. He taught me one of my first grown-up vocabulary words: "enigma."

You know what that means? he asked.

No, I don't.

It means mystery. As in: "He's always been an enigma to me."

My mom played sports, too, and played them well. She was a star shortstop in softball. I had more catches with her than I did with my dad. I thought it was cool that my mom could make a play deep in the hole and gun a runner out, and that she'd slap a ball the other way and run the bases and hook-slide into home. One of her teams was Joe's Village Inn. She worked there as a cook, a waitress, and a bookkeeper, but got most of her attention for the way she could pick up grounders. I'd go to her games on the weekends, and sometimes we'd be at the field until the early evening. Then the whole team would head over to Joe's, a little roadside place on the corner with air that reeked of smoke and beer, with a big table in the back where all the old-timers hung out. Joe's wasn't a mean place; on the contrary, it was a friendly, Cheers-like place. But people acted different in Joe's. I noticed that from the first time I went there when I was five. They were louder, happier. Sometimes much, much louder and happier. Joe's had a bowling game by the door and a whole video arcade in the back. The bartender's name was A.V. We had a routine.

Hey, A.V., you got any quarters? I'd say.

Here you go, Robert, he'd say, and give me a stack of coins.

Off I'd go to video heaven, to race make-believe cars and shoot make-believe guns or blow up make-believe planets.

My mother spent a lot of time at Joe's, and at Amber III, another Nashville tavern bar she played for. The team would gather at one bar or another after games. Nobody wanted to leave, least of all my mother, who her teammates described as the life of the party.

I got very good at Pac-Man.

Miller Lite was my mother's beverage of choice. It surprised me how thirsty she would get from playing softball. A.V. kept filling up the pitchers of Miller Lite, and my mom and her teammates kept pouring them into glasses. I lost count how many times this went on. My mother acted silly after a while—a little loopy—and then we'd drive home in the Vega or the beat-up Impala with an ashtray overflowing with cigarette butts.

Joe's Village Inn was fine at the beginning, but as much as I liked playing Pac-Man and getting the infusion of quarters from A.V., I knew it was a place Jane and I didn't belong. Of course we didn't belong there. Joe's was a bar and we were little kids.

Even at Joe's, though, my mom was always loving and nurturing. The safest place in the world was being in her lap or her arms, and they were always open. Always. She gave so much comfort, so much kindness. On the sofa at home, she would lie on her side and bend her legs at the knee behind her, and I would hop in the little cubbyhole between her heels and her rear end. It was the best spot on earth to watch television.

We'd spend hours cuddled up that way during the week, but slowly the Miller Lites began to intrude. The empties would pile up fast in the garbage. Sometimes my mom would fall asleep as soon as she got home. She was still loving, just not so available. She did her best to keep up with my teachers to see how I was doing in school, but she wasn't much for helping with homework or getting to games or activities. She was a single mom who worked hard and was beginning to drink hard. With my dad already gone from the house by the time I was in kindergarten, I learned to be by myself, and to seek diversions. I was good at that. I loved Luke Skywalker, because he was brave and ventured out in the world even though he didn't have a mother or father. I loved how Luke was his own person, and how boldly he lived. I even named my dog, a German shepherd/golden Lab mix, after him. The canine Luke and I spent a lot of time lying down in the front yard, with my head on his belly, in our own little world. If I wasn't there, I was with Lowell Dillon, my best pal. He lived right across from us when we moved to our little house on Timmons Street. Lowell and I were constantly playing football or war, the Cold War still enough in play that the object was always to get the Commies.

I made sure to be busy, because it was always better to be busy. I'd eat Cap'n Crunch and watch the Braves on TBS and try to imitate Dale Murphy's stance, going into a deep crouch and wagging the bat back and forth, just like the Braves' center fielder. I'd retreat to my room and play with baseball cards or cut out photos from sports magazines and tape them to the wall. This was my gallery of heroes, my own Wall of Fame. I liked cutting up those photos. I liked the safety of my room.

....

MY FAVORITE TIME of year was Christmas. The whole family would gather at the home of my grandparents, MeeMaw and Granddaddy, in the Green Hills section of Nashville. It had a big yard and sat at the crest of a hill, and we'd go sledding down it if we were lucky enough to get snow. It was so much fun, being around my aunts and uncles and cousins. I would get my bundle of presents and take it to a little alcove area in the corner of the living room, and while all the other kids were ripping into their stuff, I would sit back and wait. And wait. I'd open one. Then I'd wait a little more and open another one. When everybody else was tapped out of presents, I'd still have a pile of unopened ones.

I liked having the discipline to hold off. I liked having so much to look forward to.

The only trouble was, you just didn't know what to expect from Granddaddy.

Granddaddy was the first knuckleball pitcher in the family. He fiddled around with it as a kid and got the hang of it, and got so good at it that he once struck out sixteen batters in a six-inning game. He showed me a newspaper clipping to prove it. He probably would've kept up with his knuckleball after his school days, but he got into a fight when some guy insulted MeeMaw, decking the guy but busting up the knuckles of his right hand in the process.

Most everybody in the family agreed that Granddaddy was like two different people. He loved to cook breakfast and dance around the kitchen with his apron on. He'd make me poached eggs and crispy bacon and he'd always keep fudge graham cookies in the refrigerator for me. He was the most organized person I ever met. He put adhesive-tape labels and rubber bands on everything. He had a can of King Leo peppermints that had PEPPERMINTS in big letters right on the packaging. He taped a piece of adhesive over it anyway, writing PEPPERMINTS in his own hand.

Granddaddy was a big drinker in those days. A whisky drinker. MeeMaw would join him starting around five o'clock in the afternoon. Things were okay for awhile, but when Granddaddy was on his second or third glass, something happened. He'd get ornery and angry and everybody would get on edge. He'd start yelling at MeeMaw and could be real hard on the seven kids, my mom and her twin sister, Lynn, being two of them. When he was deep into the bottle and really angry, Granddaddy would sometimes holler for hours on end and make my mom and her siblings sleep under the bed.

If the kids ever tried to protect their mom, things would escalate in a hurry. My aunt fired a football right at Granddaddy's glasses one time, breaking them in two. I didn't see that fight, but I sure did see the one on Christmas when I was nine years old.

Granddaddy had his whisky in hand and he was really getting worked up about something, getting on MeeMaw and his kids. My uncle Ricky, the youngest of the seven, had seen this too many times before. Uncle Ricky was one of my heroes, maybe the best athlete in the family, an uber-competitive guy who was a five-foot-nine-inch All-American basketball player at David Lipscomb University and one of the hardest-hitting 150-pound safeties in the annals of Nashville prep football. If you were playing a game or going into battle, Ricky Bowers was the guy you wanted on your side. And the guy you least wanted to see on the other side.

Now Uncle Ricky had reached his limit.

He and Granddaddy were face-to-face in the kitchen. Uncle Ricky's face looked hot and red, his jaw set. Granddaddy wasn't but a few feet away, wobbly and defiant. I was peering around a swing-ing door between the kitchen and the den, having come upon the scene by accident. Granddaddy would always take a ruler and pen-cil and carefully measure the height of his grandchildren and put a line with a name and date next to it right in this same doorway.

Daddy, knock it off, Uncle Ricky said. This is no way to act on Christmas Day.

The kitchen was completely silent for a minute. Granddaddy glared at his son.

You don't tell me what I can or can't say in my house, Grand-daddy said. Who are you to tell me how to act?

If you weren't being out of line, then I wouldn't. But you've been drinking and you're mistreating people, and I'm sick of it, Uncle Ricky said. I am really sick of it.

Granddaddy cussed at him and Uncle Ricky cussed back, and then it was on, Uncle Ricky slapping Granddaddy hard across the face, knocking him back against the oven, down to the floor, and sending his glasses twirling off his face like a helicopter blade.

I couldn't bear to look anymore. These were two of the people I loved the most in the whole world. I hurried back to the couch in the den. I heard loud noises and hollering and lots of commotion. I didn't want to know anything about it. I didn't want to be there at all.

After my uncle Ricky and Granddaddy had their Christmas Day scuffle, my mom and sister and I went back home to Timmons Street. Nobody said much. It was the worst Christmas of my life. I walked around the neighborhood and looked at the twinkling Christmas lights and the neon Santas and the Three Wisemen at the crèche, awaiting the arrival of baby Jesus. I had nothing to look forward to, nothing at all.

I didn't know what went on in other families. I didn't know what normal was. I just knew what I saw that day made me scared of my family and scared of who I was. I had so many questions.

Would Granddaddy and Uncle Ricky hate each other from now on? What would happen the next time we got together? Would I be safe?

I made a promise to myself then and there:

I would never drink alcohol. I would never touch the stuff. All it does is cause problems. I've seen it at Joe's Village Inn and the Amber III and now I've seen it at Granddaddy and MeeMaw's house. I've seen people slurring and stumbling and smacking each other, and seen good, gentle people morph into monsters.

And for what? A buzz? A short-term escape from long-term pain? A way to medicate unpleasant feelings?

As I went to sleep on Christmas night, all I could think of was Granddaddy's glasses helicoptering off his face and Uncle Ricky standing over him, a scene that was now seared on my brain. It made me so sad to think about. The only thing that made me sadder was that I couldn't figure out a way to stop it.

CHAPTER TWO

SUMMER OF '83

t is a hot night in the middle of a hot summer, the air as sticky as cotton candy. It is July 1983. I am eight years old, approaching nine. I'm begging every relative I can think of to take me to see *Return of the Jedi* on the big screen. I'm heading into fourth grade. I've spent the whole summer doing summer things: going swimming. Staying up past my bedtime. Losing baseball games.

I am on a baseball team that stinks so bad we make the Bad News Bears look good. The team is the Twins and we play in the Lipscomb–Green Hills Little League. We're bad at hitting and even worse at fielding. If we lose by ten runs instead of fifteen, it is a moral victory; and if we lose by five, we want to go for pizza. I leave the field in tears most of the time. My season with the Twins teaches me how much I loathe losing.

The Twins are their usual hapless selves one Saturday, and when I get back home my mother tells me she is going out that night and is leaving my sister and me with a babysitter.

Which one? I ask.

It's somebody new. I think she just started babysitting, but she's supposed to be very nice, my mother says.

We drive over to a condominium and my mother introduces me to the new sitter. She is thirteen years old, a tall girl with an athletic physique and fair skin and long brown hair. You never know what you are going to get with babysitters, but she does seem nice. I've actually met her before, but this is the first time she is sitting for me. My mother goes over the basics—bath, bedtime routine, and the rest—and lets her know what time she'll be back.

The babysitter and I are alone in the foyer, getting reacquainted.

How old are you now? she asks.

Eight, I reply.

What school do you go to?

Glencliff Elementary.

Oh, I know that school. I have some friends who have gone there.

The condo has a den with a television and stereo equipment and toys. She puts on some country music. I find a big, bulbous set of headphones and put them on, even though they dwarf my skinny face, and bop around the room to the strums of "Elvira" by the Oak Ridge Boys. Twenty minutes, a half hour, I'm not sure how long we listen to music. I take off the headphones and sit down on the sofa to watch TV. I check the listings. I feel like watching a cartoon, maybe *The Jetsons*, something like that.

I feel like laughing.

Why don't we go upstairs? the girl tells me. I like it in the den, but okay, she's the babysitter. She's in charge. She leads me by the hand. Her grip is firm, as if she were a mother taking her child to a private place for disciplining. It feels a little bit strange. The staircase is dark and leads to a narrow hallway, with soft orange-brown shag carpeting underfoot. She takes me into a bedroom with a four-poster bed and bunch of pillows and stuffed animals scattered around on top of it.

The bedroom is pink and frilly. Not a Larry Bird photo in sight. *What are we doing here? Did she bring me up here to play hide-and-seek or something?* I think.

She is wearing a white cotton outfit, a top and shorts with little pink flowers. I don't know what I am wearing.

The whole thing is getting stranger and stranger, the way she's leading me around. No babysitter I've ever been watched by has ever acted like this. I wish we were back in the den, watching cartoons. I wish I still had the headphones on.

Downstairs in the living room, the babysitter's mother and my mom and a group of friends are having drinks and talking before they go out. I can hear laughter and the clinking of glasses through a heating vent in the floor. The grown-ups are supposed to go out for the evening, but they haven't left yet. They seem to be having a good time.

The babysitter chucks the pillows and stuffed animals out of the way on the four-poster bed. She peels back the covers. Now she's acting as if she's in a big hurry. She looks straight at me and says, Get in the bed.

It's not even close to bedtime yet. I don't know why I have to get in bed, but I do as she says.

Take off your top, she says.

She speaks with whispered urgency, different than the way she spoke in the den. Her voice is hard and almost robotic. There are no niceties, no explanations, about as much warmth as an ice pack. I am confused and afraid.

I am trembling.

What is happening? Why is she asking me to take off my top? I start to sweat. She tells me to take off my shorts. Everything is going so fast. She tells me to take off her top and shorts, and I watch them fall on the floor, pink flowers on the shag carpet. Her skin feels like porcelain but touching it isn't pleasurable.

Touching it is terrifying.

Now the orders start coming faster, in the same robotic cadence. I hear more clinking through the vent and pray with all my might that somebody will come upstairs and save me from this girl. That somebody will do something.

I think about running away or saying no. I think about yelling "Help!" into the vent. I do nothing except follow her orders of how and where to touch her.

Sweat is coming out of my every pore now. I pray for this to stop, for me to be anywhere in the world but on this four-poster bed with this girl. Beneath the covers she presses herself into my face. The odor is overpowering, assaulting my nasal passages.

Finally, she is done with me. She tells me to go to the room where I'm supposed to sleep.

I feel discarded, like a piece of trash. She acts as though she is mad at me, as if I hadn't followed her orders properly. I lie on a bed by myself wondering if what just happened is real. I am still trembling, still sweating.

I feel paralyzed, my limbs leaden.

The babysitter has her way with me four or five more times that summer, and into the fall, and each time feels more wicked than the time before. The venues shift to the bathtub and other places. I try to cover my private parts with bubble bath but that doesn't work. With each encounter, my goal was simply to get it over with as quickly as possible. I couldn't control what was happening, but I figured I could control the duration.

Every time that I know I'm going back over there, the sweat starts to come back. My mouth gets dry. I sit in the front seat of the car, next to my mother, anxiety surging in me like a hot spring. I don't know if my mother notices. I never tell her why I am so afraid. I never tell anyone until I am thirty-one years old.

I just keep my terrible secret, keep it all inside, the details of what went on beneath the hot, sticky sheets of a Tennessee summer, of the orders and the odor and the hurt of a little boy who is scared and ashamed and believes he has done something terribly wrong, but doesn't know what that is.

I TRY TO jam the memory of what happened on the second floor of the condo that summer as far back in my brain as it will go. I try not to think about what will happen if a grown-up finds out about it or if someone confronts me about what went on. I become good at compartmentalizing things, boxing them away into secret places forever.

Much better that they stay boxed away forever. Things are safe in boxes.

Weeks pass. I start fourth grade and like my teacher, Mr. Hazen. We read *The Adventures of Tom Sawyer*, and I think about what it would be like to go down the Mississippi River. The more time that goes by, the more comfortable I am with the idea that my boxes are in a place where nobody can get at them.

In the waning days of September, my mother, sister, and I drive into the country to visit with family, as we often do. It's a few hours outside of Nashville and a completely different world, a place with farms and barns and one-room schoolhouses, the kind of place where you don't make a playdate; you just go out and play. I am out in the yard, throwing a tennis ball off a roof behind a dilapidated garage, an area with a little knoll and a tomato garden. A kid from the neighborhood is there. I've seen him before but don't know his name. He's sixteen or seventeen years old, tall and wiry. He lives somewhere nearby. He doesn't talk much. He seems to be interested in my game with the tennis ball. He walks closer and I'm thinking he wants a turn, tossing the ball on the roof, seeing if he can catch it.

Maybe we can make a contest out of it and see who gets the most catches, I think.

I turn around and see him unzipping his pants.

No.

I don't know what he's doing but that's my first thought.

No.

I start to run but he grabs me. You ain't going anywhere, kid, he says. I am back on the bed with the babysitter, except this time there is physical force involved.

A lot of force.

I struggle to get away, but it is no contest. He is rough and strong, and he forces himself upon me, overpowers me. This time there are no words, no vents or clinking glasses. There is just submission and so much sadness. I can't do anything. I close my eyes and wait for it to be over. When people ask me how I got the scratches and bruises on my face and lip, I have a ready answer.

I fell down in the garage, I say.

On the ride back home, I say nothing and try to forget, but there is no forgetting. I try to distract myself by counting the yellow dashes along the center of the road. It doesn't work. I feel filthy and bad, like the scum of the earth, only worse. I have been stained and it can never be cleaned up. There is no helping me or my shame. It feels as though it is choking me to death. Mile after mile, the car keeps moving, but there is no escaping the beat-up garage on the knoll. It is so much worse than the babysitter. I don't know why and it doesn't matter why. There is no hope for me and no help for me. I have no options. No place to go. The car rolls on to Nashville, to my house. I think of my room and my photo of Larry Bird. I want to get in my bed and pull the covers up over my head and not wake up for a long time.

Please, God, let me be safe.

Port St. Lucie, Florida

First impressions are important, and in his first full meeting with us as the Mets manager, Terry Collins makes a really good one. We are in a conference room in Digital Domain Park. Everybody is there—Sandy Alderson, the new general manager, his assistants, the players, the coaches, the trainers, the clubhouse manager, and even our two cooks. We go around the room and introduce ourselves. Sandy speaks first. "The expectations for this club outside of this room are very low," he says. "I know you guys expect more of yourself, and I expect more of you too." Sandy is not a rah-rah guy, and his approach is low-key but very compelling. "The goal of any professional sports franchise is to win, and that's why we're here."

When he's done, he turns the floor over to Terry, who says, "Sandy stole my speech." Everybody laughs.

Terry has no notes. He speaks from the heart. I've heard a lot of these first-day speeches, and believe me, it's more common than not for them to seem formulaic, straight off boilerplate. This is not like that at all. Terry is intense, fiery, and enthusiastic. I never get the feeling he is saying things for effect. It seems so authentic, the way he makes contact with everybody in the room and jacks up the decibel level. Even when he dabbles in clichés—"We're going to do things the right way"—you can't help but feel his passion and energy. Terry is a small man and doesn't have an imposing presence when you first see him, but he is powerful nonetheless. The essence of his talk is simple:

"Everybody says we're going to stink. I hear it over and over. I think they've got it all wrong. You want to come along as we prove them all wrong?"

Terry talks for twenty minutes or so, and by the time he is done, all I can think of is: This is a guy I'm really going to enjoy playing for.

· ·

CHAPTER THREE

FAITH ON WALNUT

Some kids are fighters. Other kids are scrappers. I am a scrapper. I spend two extremely scrappy years—fifth and sixth grades—at St. Edward School, and the trend continues into the seventh grade at Wright Middle School, where the kids are bigger and stronger than me, but not too many have less regard for their bodies. I don't worry about pain or getting hit or getting knocked down. I just get back up and come back at you like a boomerang. My goal when I fight is simple: I want to give more than I receive. This doesn't make me proud. It's just what it takes to survive, and in seventh grade survival is what I'm all about.

Fights aren't an everyday occurrence in my neighborhood, but I seem to have more than my share of them. I fight to defend myself, to right a wrong, or to settle a dispute. I'm not picky. I figure out early that in a school where smoke billows out of the bathroom and pregnant girls walk the hallways, you don't want people thinking you are wimpy.

So I learn to act tough when I need to, and sometimes when I don't need to—which gets me into trouble. In the lunchroom one day, I get up from my seat. You have assigned seats at Wright at lunchtime, and strict rules about leaving them, the school's effort to prevent the cafeteria from turning into WrestleMania. But I need to get a homework assignment from a classmate, so I get up and walk across the lunchroom.

A monitor corrals me and says, Get back to your seat.

He's kind of nasty about it. I don't appreciate his tone. I cuss under my breath. Not loud, not a bad cussword, but an audible obscenity, no doubt.

Now he doesn't appreciate *my* tone.

Come with me, young man. You are going to regret your garbage mouth.

He's right—I *am* going to regret it—because this is Tennessee in the mid-1980s and corporal punishment still rules the day. The monitor escorts me down to see Mr. Tinnon, the assistant principal in charge of paddling. He conveniently keeps the paddle by his desk.

Bend over, Mr. Tinnon says.

He wallops me hard on the butt three times, then informs me that I have been suspended for three days.

Three days? For one little whispered cussword?

I don't think the punishment fits the crime—I know kids who had full-scale brawls in the hallway who didn't get suspended for three days—but my viewpoint does not get a forum.

Three days, he says.

I serve my sentence, but whether I learn any enduring lesson from it is far less clear. I have my first fight in seventh grade two weeks later. It's against a big, fat kid whose name I never learned. I have no idea how or why we wind up in the Wright parking lot behind the school, but somehow he crosses me, or I cross him, and there we are, a couple of dopes with our dukes up, ready to rumble.

I follow my usual strategy, which is to barge right in and see what the guy's got, and watch carefully to see if he closes his eyes when he throws a punch. Most kids do. And when they do, I know I have an opening to hit them. This kid hits me with a few minor punches when I charge in on him, and he closes his eyes with every punch. I take a step back and when he begins to throw another one, I rip an uppercut into his jawbone. Blood spurts out of a gash in his face and he goes down on the pavement. He isn't moving.

I take a look at him, lying there in a bloody heap, and at my blood-splattered right knuckle, and then pick up my stuff and head for home as casually as if we'd met for afternoon tea. I return to the usual empty house, have a bowl of Froot Loops, and climb the poplar tree in the front yard. I think about the kid again, wonder if he is still laid out in the parking lot. I can't believe how little I care.

I never mention the fight to anybody.

The next time I fight, I use the same full-bore approach. We are playing a tackle football game a couple of streets over from my house, and this older kid, strong and sinewy, takes me down hard.

Too hard.

What do you think you're doing? I say, scrambling to my feet.

What's your problem, punk? Can't take a hit?

We square off and I wade in on him and he drives a fist into my temple and knocks me almost to the ground, doubled over, and finishes the job with a kick to the gut with what feels like a steel-toed boot. I am done. TKO in the first round. The other kids disperse. This time I am the one left on the ground. Some boomerang.

A stray dog comes over and sniffs me. I slowly get to my feet, mad at myself that I couldn't take the kid's punch, furious at him that he used a kick to end it.

I never mention this fight to anybody, either.

....

IN THE SPAN OF four years, I go from Glencliff Elementary to St. Edward School to Wright Middle School. Whatever my address, I keep finding my way into tangles and still don't care about pain. I don't care about lots of things. At St. Edward's, my uniform consists of dark green chino slacks and a collared shirt. I wake up late one day and have to dress in a hurry. I really have to go to the bathroom, which is downstairs, and I really don't feel like going downstairs. It will take too much time, so I just go ahead and pee right in my pants, which are now just a little darker. I finish getting dressed and walk to school. A block into the walk, my legs start getting chafed by the wet pants.

What am I doing? Why didn't I just change my pants? I think, *Do I really care so little about myself?* When I finally get to school I head for the bathroom and stuff a wad of paper towels inside my pants to blot up some of the wetness. It doesn't help much.

I spend the whole day in urine-soaked pants.

It's not that big a deal, I tell myself. *They'll get cleaned up the next time my mother goes to the Laundromat.*

WHEN I TURN THIRTEEN, I am on the move again, in more ways than one. I have been admitted to a prestigious all-boys school, Montgomery Bell Academy, or MBA, as everybody around Nashville calls it. My uncle Ricky went to MBA and it changed his life. My parents don't have all that much communication with each other, but they both want my life to change, too, so, one year removed from wetting myself and being a low-level troublemaker, I find myself taking a long and intensive MBA entrance exam. I don't make the cut. A year later I take the test again and this time I do make the cut. When MBA generously offers me a full package of financial aid and my parents agree with the school's plan for me to repeat seventh grade, the deal is sealed.

MBA was founded in 1867 and ever since has been educating Nashville's elite, a demographic group I know nothing about. Many MBA students have parents who set them up with six-figure trust funds. I have parents who smuggle flatware from Western Sizzlin. It's not a great socioeconomic fit. I may not be the only kid from the other side of the proverbial tracks, but we're not exactly taking over the school, either.

By the time I hit my new, hoity-toity hallways, most everybody I know is calling me R.A. It stands for Robert Allen. I was Robert for most of my life, but people in the family call Granddaddy R.G., for Robert Green, and now they've taken to calling me by my initials too. The only person who continues to call me Robert is my mother, though it's remarkable she's not calling me much worse.

I am giving my mother a hard time—about everything. I'm an adolescent brat running amok. Cleaning up my room, hanging up my coat, taking out the trash—I battle her over the most mundane of household tasks, and work hard every day to find new ways to be defiant and beat her down with my unruliness. As my time at MBA approaches, I go for the jugular.

I'm going to go live with Dad, I tell her. I don't ask her permission. I tell her this is how it's going to be.

My mother is sitting in her blue La-Z-Boy recliner. She couldn't have been more stunned if I'd told her I was quitting sports to take up the cello.

What's wrong with living here with me, where you've always lived?

Nothing, I just want to live with Dad.

I have custody of you, Robert. You can't just decide you are living with your father.

I'm going to live with him. That's what I want. I want to do the things I used to do with him. He only lives ten minutes away, so it's not like it's that big a deal.

She tells me that it's not my choice, but I don't hear her; I've already turned and left the room. I don't know why my mother doesn't just bring down the hammer and tell me that it's not my decision and I'm not going anywhere. My mother is a functioning alcoholic, but her drinking is getting worse and she's down a lot and probably ashamed that her life hasn't turned out differently. She probably doesn't feel entitled to stand up for herself.

I see an opening and seize it.

A couple of weeks later, moving day arrives. I pack up a duffel bag and head downstairs. My mother is again in the blue recliner. I hear my father's car pull up. I don't hug my mother or kiss her or thank her for everything she has done over the first twelve years of my life. I behave, quite honestly, like a completely self-involved teenage punk. I just walk out the door and get into my father's car. The last sound I hear when I walk out of 247 Timmons is my mother sobbing. They are the big, heaving, gasping-for-air kind of sobs. I can still hear her out in the driveway.

I'm a child of divorce who is learning on the fly how not to feel pain—or anything else. It's been that way since the babysitter and the kid behind the garage.

I can't believe how little my mother's sobs bother me.

All I am fixated on is getting close with my dad again. That's the whole point of my power play. It's not about getting away from my mother's drinking or about the towels she wants me to pick up. It's not about having more independence. It's driven entirely by this yearning to be back at the Green Hills Family YMCA and chase foul balls at Sounds games again and drive a golf cart next to my father, hoping to play thirty-six holes.

That's what I want to do with my dad. That's what I want more than anything in my life. I want to hear him call me Little Horsey and have everything be the way it was before he left, before the divorce and all the instability.

It'll be great, Dad, don't you think? That's what I want to say to my father, but I never do.

THERE ISN'T ANY part of MBA that I'm not intimidated by in the beginning. I don't know the buildings, the teachers, or where the bathrooms are. Everywhere I look I see kids wearing their collared Ralph Lauren Polo shirts, with the familiar logo of a man on a horse with a polo mallet. We can't afford them, so I dress in the knock-off Knights of the Round Table shirts, with a less familiar logo of a man on a horse with a flag. It doesn't bother me, and nobody mocks me for my clothes, but I am in a whole different orbit, and it's strange. I've never heard of a school having a motto ("Gentleman, Scholar, Athlete"), and I've never heard of having to adhere to an academic honor code, either. Every time I submit an assignment or paper, or take a test, I write these words and sign my name beneath them: *On my honor as a gentleman, I have neither given nor received aid on this work.*

But the biggest difference is the splendor of the place itself: the columned brick buildings and towering trees and wide porches, and old stone walls that seem to go on forever, low gray guardians of Southern gentility. In the main courtyard are two Civil War cannons. Not facsimile cannons: real Civil War cannons. They have authentic history at MBA, and I've parachuted right into the rock-ribbed thick of it, leaving grit for grandeur, beaten-up linoleum for buffed marble. I feel like a Wookiee at a White House dinner, without question, and yet there's something that warms me about MBA, no matter how much social climbing I do to get there. I like the order, the discipline, the nurturing. I feel cared for there. I complain about the rules, but privately I relish them. People pay attention to me and listen to me and are trying to help me. That doesn't happen in all that many places. Not in the same way. I know my mother loves me, but she has problems now. My stepmother, Susan, is awfully nice to me and drives me all over Nashville, to this practice and that game, but she is not my mother and I don't let her forget that. I feel adrift, torn between two parental poles and not getting what I need from either. I feel alone at home. I don't feel quite so alone at MBA.

As the first days of the seventh grade turn into weeks, I get to know an eighth grader named Bo Bartholomew. I am not one who makes friends easily. I am much more comfortable sitting in the back, observing, calculating and measuring my options, a kid who has a hard time with trust. A kid who has secrets. What terrifies me more than anything is that those secrets could somehow be uncovered.

But something about Bo feels different, safer. He is a big blond-haired guy who plays on the school football team with me and wrestles in the winter, and one look at his muscular torso makes me hope that MBA kids don't fight the way we did on the other side of town. Smart and strong and handsome, Bo has a perfect smile above a perfect chin, and looks as if he stepped right out of a J.Crew catalog. You look at a guy like Bo Bartholomew and you think you might as well give up because you'll never be as gifted or as good-looking.

Bo turns out to be much different than other kids I've been around. He is kind, generous, and concerned with the welfare of others. He treats me as a complete equal. He invites me over to his sprawling colonial on a dead-end street in Belle Meade, the swankiest part of Nashville, and the first person I meet is his mother, Vicki Bartholomew. She was Miss Tennessee in 1966, the runner-up to Miss America, and she looks it even now, twenty-two years later, a pretty, slender woman with blond hair and a welcoming spirit. She offers us a snack and we head upstairs to play Duck Hunt on Bo's Nintendo. I have never seen a Nintendo. I could get used to it. We play Duck Hunt for an hour and then decide to go out to throw the football, and as we turn the corner into the den to head outside, I am startled.

I am captivated.

It is my first memory of ever being captivated.

On the couch, curled up with her homework, is Bo's younger sister, Anne. She has thick, blond hair, with curls and waves, something approaching a lion's mane. She has a green sweater on over a white collared shirt. She has green eyes and she is beautiful.

Bo introduces me.

Nice to meet you, says Anne, a seventh grader at the Ensworth School.

You too.

The words have barely left my mouth when I start beating myself up.

That is the best you can do? *You too?*

Bo and I go toss the football, but all I can think about is Anne and how ridiculous I must've come across with my caveman vocabulary.

Hanging out in school the next day, I want to talk to Bo about his sister and Bo wants to talk to me about a meeting. It's on Thursday night, a group called the Fellowship of Christian Athletes. He invites me to join him.

I'm a three-sport athlete—football, basketball, and baseball—and anything to do with sports I'll try at least once.

What is it? I ask.

It's just what the name says. It's a fellowship of guys who are honest with each other and care about each other, and get together to share about their faith in God.

But I don't know much about God. The only times I've been to church, really, have been with my grandmother, and that hasn't been very often.

Bo assures me that there are no entrance exams or prerequisites. It is simply a time to be around people who care. I have some big doubts about it, but I tell Bo I'll give it a try.

I get to the meeting early. It's in the Roberts Room, right off the gymnasium. I grab a seat in the back. I have a good bit of courage as I enter the room, but it dissipates rapidly with every new face that comes through the door. There are at least thirty boys here.

What if they ask me to pray or to share about myself? What do I say? What if they throw me out for being an impostor?

If they could see under my jacket, it would look like I've just gone swimming—that's how much I am sweating. How did I let Bo talk me into this? Is getting to know his sister really worth all this?

I take three deep breaths and the meeting starts. It opens with a prayer and with guys talking about their lives and their struggles and how a relationship with God through Jesus Christ has been a pillar of peace and stability for them. I listen to those words and find myself somehow drawn to them, warmed by them.

Peace and stability.

They sound noble. They sound nice. They sound like something I want.

The meeting goes for about ninety minutes, and I enjoy it. I go back to more meetings, and my self-consciousness abates and I begin to get a greater sense of who Christ is, and what a relationship with Him would be like. I continue to observe the people in the room, and Bo too. There really does seem to be a difference in their behavior, the way they treat people, and the way they deal with adversity, owning up to their mistakes and not looking around for someone to blame.

One Friday afternoon, Bo invites me to spend the night at his house. I eagerly accept, hoping to ask him more questions about his faith and maybe to see Anne again.

When we get there after football practice, we play outside for a while before we move upstairs for more Duck Hunt.

I have a few questions for you, Bo, I say.

Sure.

It's about becoming a Christian.

Shoot.

How do you do it? Where do you start? I don't even have any idea how to do it.

Well, it's nothing more complicated than asking.

What do you mean, "asking"?

When you feel you are ready, you just invite Him into your life.

You are basically saying with that invitation that you believe Jesus Christ is the son of God and that He ultimately died for you on the cross and rose again so that you can have eternal life with Him.

It's a lot to take in. I'm trying. I hear Mrs. Bartholomew coming up the stairs. She overhears Bo's answer to my question. I'm uneasy at first, because I don't know her very well yet, but it's clear that she wants to guide me and reassure me.

God cares about you and God loves you, R.A., she says. So much so that He wants to have a very personal and intimate relationship with you, and that is why He sent His son Jesus to Earth.

This is all so new and uncharted for me. Over the past few weeks, I have heard words that speak to my core, but that I have no personal connection with: "Peace." "Stability." "Intimacy." "Forgiveness." They sound good, but they seem totally beyond me, as if I'm trying to hold the ocean in two cupped hands. How am I supposed to do that?

I don't know. But when Mrs. Bartholomew finishes talking, I want to try. I am beyond my doubts. I clasp my hands and look up and clumsily blurt out:

I want a relationship with Jesus Christ.

So on a fall Friday in an upstairs bedroom on Walnut Drive in Nashville, Tennessee, I get on my knees with Bo and his mom and ask Christ to come into my life. I tell Him that I believe He is the son of God, and I want to trust Him with my life. I secretly ask for forgiveness for what seems like a galaxy of sins and guilt and shame.

When I am done speaking, the room is completely still. I feel relief. A lightness. It's not the sky opening up, or angels singing, or lightning bolts striking the big magnolia in the front yard. Nothing grand and God-like. It's much more subtle, like the best deep breath you could ever take.

What do I do now? I ask.

You learn, Bo says. You study. You read the Bible and try to soak in every word. Remember, you're going to make mistakes. Being a Christian doesn't mean that you all of a sudden stop making mistakes, or that your problems magically disappear. It's actually the opposite. You are admitting that you are not perfect. You can never be perfect. That is why you need a perfect savior, and you trust that what Christ did on the cross for you is enough.

The rest of the night is a blur, but I smile a lot and feel light, comforted by the knowledge that I have a perpetual Companion who loves me and wants to be with me, secrets and all.

CHAPTER FOUR

THE WOLF OF GREEN HILLS

P eople around town like to poke fun at MBA and its blueblood heritage. Our nickname is Big Red but kids from other schools are more apt to call us Momma's Boy Academy or the MBA Silver Spoons. I don't get worked up about it; thankfully, I left my fighting days back at Wright Middle School. What's a bigger issue for me is demerits. You get demerits if your shirttail is out or you are late for class or you miss an assignment. When a teacher spots an infraction, he or she calls you on it and you are demerited on the spot. I rack up demerits the way Mariano Rivera racks up saves. I lead the school in them, getting fifty of them in one year alone, most of them because of my unruly shirttail.

Every demerit earns you a half hour in Saturday school. My weekends get pretty tied up.

Discipline is not my greatest strength as a student, either, especially in English. I don't like to be bothered with punctuation or spelling or to get hung up on subjects and predicates, which explains why I routinely get papers handed back to me that are halfway to Hades with red. I care about stories. I love telling stories, but the fine points of grammar bore me. I am the king of sentence fragments. Dangling participles. Run-on sentences. Sentences that slither snakelike and are overly ambitious and try to do too much and are sometimes excruciatingly overwritten and almost always leave the reader gasping for air, waiting breathlessly for the verbosity to end and the period to arrive.

Miss Brewer is trying to rein me in. She is one of my English teachers, a petite woman with short brown hair, and one of the few instructors I have who thinks I have some ability with language and is willing to look beyond my grammatical train wrecks. She has a calm voice that is as flowing as the long skirts she likes to wear, and a gentle, nurturing way about her, always encouraging students to take on new challenges as writers. She asks me to stay after class one day.

R.A., there's a region-wide poetry contest coming up and I'd love to see you enter it. I think you have a gift and it would be nice if you would share it.

Thanks, Miss Brewer, but I have written a total of about four poems in my life. I don't want to embarrass myself.

Oh, trust me, you won't. You have an original mind and an appreciation of language. Being creative is all about taking risks, anyway. Why not do it?

I grudgingly agree to write a couple of poems, and Miss Brewer submits them to the competition, which is called St. Cecilia Fine Arts Assembly. One of the poems is in traditional iambic pentameter and the other a haiku. I actually enjoy writing them, but I don't tell her that.

A few weeks later, we gather in the auditorium and the results are announced. The master of ceremonies says: And the winner of the St. Cecilia Fine Arts Assembly poetry contest is . . . R. A. Dickey.

There must be some mistake. Was I the only one entered? I am flabbergasted as I walk up to the stage and shake the emcee's hand and get a certificate, much more sheepish than proud. Miss Brewer, who is thrilled, tells me later I won the competition for the haiku. It reads this way:

> *Lifelike buttercups*
> *Sway in graceful unison*
> *With the midnight breeze*

More than even writing or poetry, my greatest creative outlet at MBA is art. For years, I study under an inspiring teacher named Rosie Paschall, who is the wife of the headmaster, and whose singular gift is the way she can tug art out of her students—even students who are reluctant or scared or overly self-critical. She makes it safe and makes it stimulating, whether you're composing pottery or working with oil on canvas. As a senior advanced-placement art student, I want to do something extra meaningful before I leave Rosie's art room for the last time.

I have an idea for my last work, and I hope you'll like it, I tell her.

I'm sure if you put your creative soul into it the way you always do, I am going to love it, she says.

I spend a month working on the piece, a charcoal on large canvas. It shows a young boy eating an ice cream cone as he leans against a barn door, the picture of innocence. Behind him is a large face, an adult face, looking menacing and intent on evil, with its vacant eyes and angry mouth.

Rosie loves it. I never talk about where the idea came from.

....

TOMMY OWEN doesn't go in for the nurturing that Rosie and Miss Brewer do, but what do you expect? He's a football coach. Everybody in the school knows him as Coach Owen, even in the classroom, where he teaches history, his principal subject being World War II—something he knows because he lived it, serving as a navigator on a B-24 Liberator. Coach Owen teaches me about the Luftwaffe and Hitler's propaganda machine and the Normandy invasion, and then after 3:00 p.m. we head out to the football field, where the lessons switch to post patterns and play-action passes. I am the quarterback, and he has a lot to teach me. Coach Owen is an original tough guy. His body is as taut as a cable, his voice deep and raspy, straight out of central casting for drill sergeants, though he doesn't use it much when he's really angry; he much prefers to just bore a hole through you with his stare.

Of all the things Coach Owen loathes on the football field, lack of discipline and mental mistakes top the list. I accomplish both in a single play against Hillwood High School, dropping back to pass at their twenty-five-yard line one Friday night as Hillwood rushes everybody but Davy Crockett, the blitz coming from everywhere. I start to scramble, retreating and dodging and retreating some more, channeling my inner Favre. I am all the way back at midfield, trying to keep the play alive, when I hear Coach Owen hollering, "Throw it out of bounds!" I keep scrambling and he keeps hollering, but I finally see an opening and start going forward, running left. At the forty-yard line, I see a receiver, Mark Fuqua, in the clear near the end zone. I throw the ball against my body, all the way across the field, a semi-wobbly ball that isn't pretty but gets there.

Mark grabs it and scores the game-winning touchdown, and we all start celebrating and jumping around. When I get to the sideline, Coach Owen grabs my face mask and snaps my head straight. His face is an inch or two away from the bars of my helmet. The glare is on.

When I tell you to throw the ball out of bounds, son, you throw the ball out of bounds, he says.

Coach Owen teaches me a ton about discipline, and helps me grow up by not going in for hand-holding. We beat a tough team from inner-city Nashville, Pearl-Cohn Comprehensive High School, one time, and we are walking back across the campus to our bus. I have my helmet off and I'm not far from Eric Crawford, our fullback, when all of a sudden we are pounced on, a gang of kids ambushing us. Eric gets slugged in the side of the face and falls hard. Just as I get ready to help him, I feel something smash into the back of my head. I go down to a knee and look behind me and see the assailants running away. On the ground next to me is their weapon of choice, a brown bottle that somehow did not break on impact with my skull.

The coaches hurry us up and we get on the bus without further incident. As we pull away, Coach Owen walks back to my seat and gives me the glare again.

That's why you always keep your helmet on, he says, and then he turns and goes back to the front of the bus.

WHILE I'M LEARNING to navigate my way (and keep my shirttail tucked in) at MBA, my mother is graduating from Miller Lite to vodka. Her drinking is getting worse, her denial starting to crack.

I hear it in her voice when I talk to her, and I sense her guilt too. Once I walked out, it all began to pile up for her, like cars in a NASCAR wreck. She thinks she has failed as a mother, beating herself up for all the ways she has let my sister and me down, starting with the times she hauled us with her to Joe's Village Inn and Amber III. My mom is in acute pain, and the time-honored way to medicate pain in her family is to drink.

I am so occupied with sports and my new life that, honestly, I do not pay much attention to my mother's problems. I talk to her every week or two, and that's enough. The more I immerse myself in MBA's athletic culture, the more it appeals to me, because it insulates me from everything else: my mother's increasing alcohol problem and my father's increasing aloofness problem. I trust baseball and I trust football and basketball; I trust my ability to play them and I trust that the games and competition will follow a proscribed order, even if you don't know who's going to win. I do not have the same trust in my own mother and father. My relationship with my mother has become more and more distant. My father is becoming a man I don't understand. I think he comes to my football games, but I'm not sure, because I never see him afterwards. I don't get to ask him what he thinks about how I played, or what advice he has, or get to celebrate with him. I don't even know where he is. While most of my friends meet with their parents and go out for dinner or dessert, I am a tagalong.

Sports, on the other hand, are much more reliable. They never check out. There's always another game, another season.

Game days and game nights are the best times of my life.

The ball fields and gyms of Montgomery Bell Academy become my sanctuary.

On her way home from work one day, my mother asks God to lift her compulsion to drink. She happens to be going by a liquor store at the time and the car almost feels as if it's turning itself, making a hard left turn into the store parking lot. My mother doesn't understand. She says a prayer for her compulsion to lift and in the next instant it as if Satan is all but hijacking her and demanding that she go into the liquor store.

Isn't it supposed to go the other way? Isn't the idea to *stop* drinking?

She buys a fifth of vodka and heads for home. She gathers her stuff and walks up to the house, already thinking about how good it will be to be in her blue recliner with a Bloody Mary alongside her. As she fumbles in her purse for her keys, the bag with the vodka slips from her grip and smashes on the porch, twenty-five ounces of Smirnoff trickling into the bushes. She watches the rivulet of spirits and smells the alcohol and feels a deep sense of relief.

In His own time and His own way, God answers my mother's prayer.

Broken and distraught, my mother cries out for help. She knows she can't continue on the course she's on and is finding the courage to get off it. She calls me.

Robert, I have to go away for a while, she says.

What do you mean?

I need to get help. I've got to work on me and make some changes in my life.

The help is coming from a rehabilitation facility called Cumberland Heights, on the Cumberland River, west of Nashville. The treatment program lasts for thirty days. My mother is fifteen days in and I keep coming up with excuses why I can't go see her. My guilt finally gets the better of me and I show up one afternoon. I drive through a stone entry gate and see vast expanses of land and white split-rail fences. Wisps of fog hang over the surrounding hills. It looks as if my mother is getting her treatment at a horse farm.

I walk into the main building and I feel my anxiety build. I am afraid and resentful. I do not want to be there. I do not want to see my mother in a rehab. I want her to get the help she needs and get better, but I am apprehensive about the whole visit, a feeling that is only heightened when I sign in and get a whiff of that unmistakable antiseptic smell of a hospital. I wonder where my mom is, and whether she's going to be escorted out by two guys in white jackets who won't let her handle anything sharp.

I wait in a large room with clusters of tables and chairs and ashtrays every three feet, all of them spilling over with cigarette butts. After a few minutes, my mother walks out with an orderly. She is wearing sweatpants and a T-shirt. She looks good. Her eyes are clear. We go for a walk around a pond, and she talks about how great the program is, how she is facing hard truths about her own family background and learning to accept her powerlessness over alcohol and to own her behavior. She is praying to receive God's strength and mercy. I don't fully grasp the concept of alcoholism being a disease or the challenges of recovery, but I see a difference in my mother already, after just a couple of weeks. I see someone who doesn't seem so beaten down by life anymore, who wants to find a different way. I know what she's doing is hard work, and as sad as it makes me that she has to be in there, I'm proud that she has the guts to do that work.

What will she be like when she gets out? Will she really change her life? Will she be someone I can fully trust again? I don't know.

I hug her and tell her I love her, hopeful that she seems to be getting better and proud of her courage to go right at her problem. As I drive out of the stone gate, my guard is a little bit lower than it was when I drove in.

LATE ONE FRIDAY NIGHT in my junior year, after a Big Red victory, we go to our usual postgame hangout, Dalts Classic American Grill, for good food and high-quality milk shakes (I go for chocolate). When we finish, it's almost eleven o'clock. We have practice in the morning. My dad's house is twenty minutes away, across town.

I don't feel like making the trip, knowing I have to be back at school first thing. Often I crash with friends who live right in Green Hills, kids like David Fitzgerald or Tiger Harris or Mike Anderson, my catcher in baseball, but I feel funny asking them if I can stay over again. I don't want to wear out my welcome. I also don't want to go home tonight. It's a strong feeling. Home doesn't feel like home. It's where my father and Susan live, but it's not a place I feel connected to. When I walk up the steps and open the door, I am not happy to be there. I don't feel that I've reached a place of refuge and safety. I've just reached a place, four walls and a roof. I'm not saying it's their fault. Maybe it's mine. It just doesn't feel that it's where I belong.

Home, to be honest, is a place where there is no tending to the heart. We don't have many meals together, or play board games together, or do much of anything together. My father seems to be there in body only, as if he's got something much bigger on his mind. I don't know what that something is. An enigma? Yes, that's what it is. An enigma. There are no rules or discipline, no curfews or consequences. I just come and go as I please. I am a kid who is crying out for limits, and getting none.

The nomad checks back in, my father says when I come home after a few nights away. He doesn't ask where I've been or what I've been up to. I could've been stealing cars or dealing drugs, for all he knows. I want to believe my dad is proud of me and that he loves me, but it's rarely spoken. I want him to tell me. I want him to hug me. It's not that I'm angry with him so much as I miss him. I want it to be the way it used to be. I want him to be the most important man in my life.

Can you do that for me, Dad? I want to ask, but again, I never do.

More and more, I spend time at places like the Bartholomews' and the Fitzgeralds' and with my aunt and uncle, Billy and Lynn Caldwell, whose doors and hearts are always open. I don't tell anybody, but this is what I want. What I crave. I want to be in a place where hearts are open. I want to sit around the dinner table and listen to people talk about their day and share their feelings and concerns. I want to pray together as a family. Now that I am a Christian, I want more. I don't want to be a tenant in my own house.

I drive around Green Hills, trying to think of my options. I could sleep in my car, I tell myself. No, that wouldn't be comfortable. I wouldn't get any sleep. I've got a warm sweatshirt in the car and a couple of towels in the backseat. What about sleeping outside, on the golf course? Nah, I'm not a sleep-under-the-stars kind of guy, and besides, the grounds guys will start mowing and raking traps at five in the morning.

All through Green Hill this goes on. I keep driving, thinking, *What am I going to do?* Ahead on the right I see a sign: FOR RENT. I slow up and pull over. It's a brick home with a nice fenced yard. The house is dark and appears empty.

Dueling voices fire up in my head.

VOICE ONE: *Maybe you can stay here tonight. Who would ever know? You won't damage anything. You'll sleep and leave. No harm, no foul.*

VOICE TWO: *You can't break into somebody's house and sleep in it. Are you out of your mind? That's a crime. That's the most ridiculous idea you've ever had.*

VOICE ONE: *It'll be fun. It'll be an adventure. It's just one night.*

VOICE TWO: *Stop it already. It's insanity. You are not doing this.*

I park up the road a bit and walk back to the house and do some minor reconnaissance, peering through the windows. I don't see an alarm or a dog or furniture. The house is vacant. I decide that if I can find a key, this is where I am spending the night.

Voice One wins.

Now I have to find the key. It's probably under the mat or on the doorframe. Real estate agents aren't that imaginative when it comes to hiding keys. I poke around for a few minutes, but no luck. I contemplate breaking a window, but my vagrancy has limits. I go around to the back of the house. There is a single pot on the back porch containing a half-dead fern. I lift up the pot and there is a single key amid sprinkles of fern dirt. I feel like Bilbo Baggins in the Misty Mountains when he stumbles on the Ring of Power. I put the key in the lock and, after a quarter turn to the right, I am in.

I walk into the darkness, tiptoeing. I'm in the kitchen, I think. My heart is throbbing and I realize I would be a terrible criminal. I move slowly into different rooms just to confirm the house is empty. Voice Two, the Voice of Reason, resurfaces.

What if I am arrested? Or caught by the owners and turned in to MBA? What will happen? I'll be a goner from MBA, that's what'll happen. This is reckless, stupid. Yes, it is. There is still time to turn around and get out before trouble arrives. So get out now.

All valid points. I ignore them. I decide: *This is where I am spending the night.*

I head to the car to retrieve my sweatshirt and towels, the extent of my supplies. I brush away a few dead bugs and lay the towels down in a corner of the bare living room floor and build a terry-cloth bed. I put on my sweatshirt, lie down, and look at the water stains on the ceiling.

They may want to check that out, I think. *It could explain the vacancy.*

My heart settles down. My breathing is even, rhythmic.

I go to sleep quickly.

The next morning, I gather my towels and head out the back door as if it were my own house. I lock it up and put the key back under the fern. I head to football practice.

I sleep in vacant houses another half dozen times over the next two years, and I get much better at it. On nights when I think it might be a possibility, I go to the library and look at the classifieds. I find places that are close to school and scout them out. I look for quiet streets with ample parking and make sure I have a sleeping bag and pillow in the trunk of my car at all times, just in case. It gets easier, breaking into other people's houses. I enjoy the hunt for the key, the rush of being somewhere I'm not supposed to be. I don't know why. Other than speed limits, I have never broken a law. I like the danger, the independence, and maybe, most of all, the power to choose. I am still lonely, but it is a loneliness of my choosing. And that makes a big difference.

BY THE TIME I'm a senior at MBA, I've stayed at a lot of different houses, both occupied and vacant, and played a ton of ballgames, as a quarterback, shooting guard, and pitcher/shortstop. Some Division II and Division III schools offer me scholarships for football and basketball, but I know by now that baseball is my game. The first man to impress that upon me is Fred Forehand, whose name suggests he should be coaching tennis, but who is in fact the MBA baseball coach. He's a small guy who seems much bigger than he is because of his personality, and who perpetually wears a maroon-and-white MBA warm-up suit. In the winter in my eighth-grade year, Coach Forehand tells me he wants me to try out for varsity.

You've got a chance to be our shortstop, he says.

Starting shortstop for a really good high school baseball team? In eighth grade? I can't believe Coach Forehand thinks that much of me that he'd give me a shot at that. His faith empowers me, makes me feel like somebody. I may be a nomad and I sure have my secrets and I've gotten good at not letting anybody get close to me. But now I finally have an identity:

I am an athlete.

You can't be in the running for the MBA shortstop in eighth grade if you aren't an athlete.

The competition for the starting job comes down to a freshman named Brett Miller and me, and the last day before our games start. Coach Forehand has a fungo bat in his hand and he's running a situational drill, with a guy on first and two out, and a batter running from home. He smacks a grounder in the hole between third and short. It rolls up the third baseman's arm and bounces off his shoulder. I am behind him and catch the ball off his shoulder, deep in the hole. I gun the ball to first.

My throw beats the runner by a half step.

The next day I am the starting shortstop, and I stay there for four years, except when I am pitching.

Through good games and bad, Coach Forehand is right there for me, a kind and fatherly constant. All I want to do is be around him. I ask him about two hundred questions every day. He starts calling me Lapdog, because I am practically in his lap all day long. The other guys pick up on it and soon everybody on the team is calling me Lapdog. The day the uniforms arrive, Coach whispers to me in an almost conspiratorial voice: *Go pick out the one you want, Lapdog, before the troops arrive.*

Coach Forehand does thoughtful little things like that all the time. One day he motions to me to meet him on the side of the field. I run over to him from shortstop, with the Mag, my old $12 glove from Little League, in tow. I've never done a survey but I'm sure the Mag is the oldest and worst glove on the team.

Just in case you are thinking about getting a new glove, Poe's Sporting Goods is a good place to go, Coach Forehand says. Mr. Poe has real nice gloves and he's a friend of MBA and he'll give you a good deal.

Okay, thanks. It's probably time I get an upgrade on the Mag.

Granddaddy takes me down to Poe's, off Highway 100, west of

Nashville. There's a wall of beautiful gloves, and the whole place smells like leather. I could stay there and smell it all day. I try out a few gloves, and then come upon a Wilson A2000. It's black and has a beautiful, deep pocket. It's the nicest glove I've ever seen. I want it desperately. I look at the price tag.

Oh, jeez. One hundred dollars. No way we can afford a $100 glove.

I put the glove back and keep looking. Mr. Poe comes over and says, That A2000 is a beauty, isn't it?

Yeah, it is, but we can't afford it.

He pulls the glove off the shelf and puts it back in my hands. I'm not sure what he's doing; I just finished telling him we couldn't spend that much.

Mr. Poe says: The cost of the glove has been taken care of, young man. Now go play some ball with it.

Excuse me, what did you say?

The glove is yours. It's all squared away.

Squared away, as in mine? To keep?

I can't even take it in. Somebody just bought me the best glove in the world? Is this for real? I thank Mr. Poe again and again and shake his hand, and leave the store with the A2000 on my hand.

It wasn't until years later that I found out that Granddaddy and Mr. Poe were in cahoots to get me the glove. And of course Coach Forehand was in on it, too, because he steered me to Mr. Poe in the first place. He'd seen enough of the Mag, that's for sure.

Midway through my senior year, 1993, Jeff Forehand, Fred's son, asks if he can talk to me for a minute. Jeff, a former second baseman for nearby Belmont University, is an assistant coach for MBA.

What's up, Jeff?

I don't know how to put this, but we just found out my dad has cancer, and it's at a pretty advanced stage. He doesn't want to make a big deal out of it and doesn't even want to tell the team, but I wanted you to know.

Oh, no. I am so sorry, Jeff.

He's starting chemo right away, so we just have to hope and pray for the best.

Your dad's going to have every prayer I've got, I promise you.

Coach Forehand goes through chemo and radiation and keeps right on teaching and coaching. By the time our season starts he looks more gray and gaunt with each passing week. Everybody on the team knows what's going on but Coach still never talks about it, never alludes to it, never complains. He just keeps running himself out there, directing drills and hitting fungoes and getting us ready to play, doing it all with a colostomy bag attached to his abdomen.

We win our district and region and make it all the way to the state championship game, against Germantown at Middle Tennessee State University. Coach Forehand looks thin and weak, the months of treatment having taken a huge toll, but he's not stopping now and neither are his players. In the span of three days, I pitch twenty-one innings and give up one run. The title comes down to a single final game. I come in the game in relief in the fifth with the score tied, 1–1. It stays tied into the ninth. With pinch runner Ted Morrissey on second, Trent Batey, our shortstop, lines a shot over the Germantown left fielder's head and within moments, we are all in a pile on the field, hugging Ted and Trent and anybody else we can find. It's bedlam, a tangle of maroon-and-white uniforms everywhere you look, and right in the middle of it all I see is

Coach Fred Forehand and his colostomy bag. He has a smile on his face and the game ball in his hand, and a single tear running down his right cheek. I walk over to him. Now I have a tear running down my cheek. I give him a hug and hold on to him for a long time, and say the only thing I can think of:

I love you, Coach.

SATURDAY, FEBRUARY 26, 2011
Port St. Lucie, Florida

Boys will be boys, and ballplayers will always be arrested ado-
lescents at heart. The proof comes in the mid-afternoon of an
early spring training day, when 40 percent of the New York
Mets' starting rotation—Mike Pelfrey and I—hop a chain-link
fence to get onto a football field not far from Digital Domain.
We have just returned from Dick's Sporting Goods, where we
purchased a football and a tee.

We are here to kick field goals. Long field goals.

A day before, we were all lying on the grass stretching and
guys started talking about football and field-goal kickers, and
David Wright mentioned something about the remarkable
range of kickers these days.

I can kick a fifty-yard field goal, Pelfrey says.

You can not, Wright says.

You don't think so? You want to bet? You give me five tries
and I'll put three of them through.

One hundred bucks says you can't, David says. This is going
to be the easiest money I ever make.

I am Pelf's self-appointed big brother, always looking out
for him, and I don't want him to go into this wager cold. So I
suggest we get a ball and tee and do some practicing. We get back
from Dick's but find the nearby field padlocked, so of course
we climb over the fence. At six feet two inches and 220 pounds,
I get over without incident, but seeing Pelf hoist his big self

*over—all six feet seven inches and 250 pounds of him—is much
more impressive.*

*Pelf's job is to kick and my job is to chase. He sets up at
the twenty-yard line, tees up the ball, and knocks it through—
kicking toe-style, like a latter-day Lou Groza. He backs up to
the twenty-five and then the thirty, and boots several more from
each distance. Adding the ten yards for the end zone, he's now
hit from forty yards and is finding his range. Pretty darn good.
He insists he's got another ten yards in his leg. He hits from
forty-five, and by now he's probably taken fifteen or seventeen
hard kicks and reports that his right shin is getting sore.*

We don't consider stopping.

*Pelf places the ball on the tee at the forty-yard line: a fifty-
yard field goal. He takes a half dozen steps back, straight behind
the tee, sprints up, and powers his toe into the ball ... high ...
and far ... and just barely over the crossbar. That's all that is
required. I thrust both my arms overhead like an NFL referee.*

He takes three more and converts on a second fifty-yarder.

*You are the man, Pelf, I say. Adam Vinatieri should worry
for his job.*

*That's it, Pelf says. I can't even lift my foot anymore. My shin
is killing me.*

*We hop back over the fence, Pelf trying to land as lightly as
a man his size can land. His shin hurts so much he can barely
put pressure on the gas pedal. He's proven he can hit a fifty-yard
field goal, but I go into big-brother mode and tell him I don't
want him kicking any more field goals or stressing his right leg
any further. I convince him to drop the bet with David.*

The last thing you need is to start the season on the DL because you were kicking field goals, I say. Can you imagine if the papers got ahold of that one?

The wager just fades away. David doesn't mind; he gets a laugh at the story of Pelf hopping the fence and practicing, and drilling long ones.

CHAPTER FIVE

VOLUNTEERING FOR DUTY

Ten years is a long time, but it's not so long that I forget the babysitter. The summer after I graduate from MBA, I'm gearing up to enroll at the University of Tennessee when I make an impromptu visit to see my mother's family. Next thing I know the babysitter and her mother are walking through the front door.

It takes a millisecond for my insides to seize up, like an engine without motor oil.

Oh, my Lord, it's her.

How long has it been exactly? I don't know. I don't want to know. I haven't seen her since the last time she abused me. I forget whether that was in the bed or the tub. I try to remember which and then scold myself. *Who cares? Why waste one second thinking about that?*

She's all grown up, done with college, with the same long brown hair, as tall and athletic-looking as ever. The seized-up feeling gets worse the closer I stand to her, my heart racing. My insides feel as if they've been freeze-dried. I wonder how many other boys she was supposed to babysit who she wound up violating.

I think I might vomit.

As much as I want to stop it from happening, I can't: the sight of her instantly transports me back to the summer of 1983 and all the sensations that came with it—the sweat and the smell, the trembling and the terror that went through me when she took off her white outfit with the flowers and climbed on me.

If we happen to have a private moment, I debate whether I should take her down Nightmare Lane. Wouldn't it be nice to let her know that I remember everything—and let her know what I think of her for doing what she did? I know I am supposed to forgive as a Christian, just as God forgives me.

I am not much of a Christian at the moment, I am afraid.

People move into the next room. We are alone. Nightmare Lane, here we come.

Remember those times when you babysat me? I ask.

She looks at me, puzzled.

I don't really remember much about them, no, she says.

Oh, really? You don't remember what happened? I can remind you, because my memory is crystal clear about what happened. Remember the four-poster bed in the room at the end of the hallway?

I'm sorry, but I don't know what you are talking about. Could you be thinking about another babysitter?

Oh, no. That's not possible. There was only one babysitter in my whole life who did what you did.

She stares at me blankly, almost dismissively.

I'm sorry. I don't know what you are talking about, she says. She looks excruciatingly uncomfortable.

Good, I think.

I can see this is going nowhere, that she is not going to cop to anything, and finally drop the subject. I say good-bye to my family and head to Billy and Lynn's. The next few days, predictably, are awful, the worst kind of emotional relapse. It's almost as if I'm reliving the abuse again and again, with an extra measure of humiliation brought on by her refusal to acknowledge anything, triggering an appearance by toxic old friends in the back of my head saying: *Did it really happen the way I remember? Did she really do all these things, or did I dream it?*

The helplessness, the shame—it all comes back in a torrent. It's almost a week before it begins to recede, and I don't feel seized up anymore. In a few weeks I head off to college in Knoxville.

I never see the babysitter again.

GIBBS HALL is the athletic dormitory at the University of Tennessee, conveniently located near the Volunteer sports facilities. I arrive in Room 329 of Gibbs in the fall of 1993 with two duffel bags stuffed mostly with sweatshirts and sweatpants and with the mindset of a walk-on. I am a top recruit, I guess, but I never want to think of myself in those terms. It's the main reason why I couldn't stand the recruiting process, which is basically Smoke Blowing 101. They tell you how great you are and have pretty girls escort you around campus on your official visit, and then they have you meet with some of the players, who want to take you out for a night on the town, as if this were all part of a typical day at the University of Tennessee.

I don't want to be fussed over or gushed over, and I sure don't want a night on the town. I just want to take some interesting

English classes and play baseball and compete at the highest level possible. I am not there long before I get a glimpse of one of the best ballplayers I've ever seen. His name is Todd Helton.

Helton is recruited to play football and baseball at Tennessee. He's the backup quarterback to Heath Shuler in his first two years, and then the backup to Jerry Colquitt, who waited years to get a chance to play, as a junior. In the season opener, Colquitt rips up the ligaments in his knee, and Helton takes over. Three weeks later, Helton bangs up his own knee and gets replaced by a kid named Peyton Manning.

Helton knows his future is in baseball, and after people see Manning play, he isn't getting the job back anyway. Helton eventually quits football, but in the fall of my freshman year, he is still playing. We're having a baseball workout just down the hill from the football practice field and one day I see Helton walking toward the ball field during a break in football practice. He is wearing his orange football jersey and football cleats and has his helmet in his hand.

Can I jump in and get a couple of swings? Helton asks the coaches. They say sure. He puts down his helmet and grabs a wooden bat and gets in the cage. He hasn't had a single warm-up swing. He eschews aluminum in favor of good, old-fashioned lumber. On his second swing, he crushes a ball far over the right-field fence.

That's good, thanks, Helton says, picking up his helmet and going back to football practice. I tried not to stare.

Helton is one of the greatest clutch hitters I've ever seen. During the NCAA regionals my freshman year, we are down four in the eighth inning against Arizona State when he comes up with the bases loaded. One swing later, the game is tied. Helton comes through again and again with his bat, but he is also a phenomenal left-handed relief pitcher, once putting together a string of forty-seven scoreless innings. He still holds the school save record (twenty-three).

Helton is something to watch, but the truth is that Peyton Manning puts on the best show in Knoxville, Saturday after Saturday. Peyton and I become friends, and I'm a sideline spectator at Neyland Stadium—one of the perks of being an athlete—for almost every Tennessee home game. The more I study him, the more I appreciate what he brings to the field. Peyton is a good, accurate passer, but he doesn't have an arm that totally wows you; it's not as if I watch him throw and think, *That is the most beautiful ball I've ever seen.* He's got nowhere near the arm that Heath Shuler had, or even the arm that Brandon Stewart, a quarterback who transferred to Texas A&M, had. Peyton even throws his share of ducks, but it doesn't matter, because everything else is so out of this world that it overrides any little flaw he might have. His decision making, his presence, his gift for leading and making others around him believe—they are all without peer. He is the guy you want in charge, a guy who has been around the game his whole life and it shows. I learn so much from observing him, because it's a reminder that the best pitchers are not necessarily the ones who throw the hardest or have the scouts salivating over their natural arm strength. The best pitchers are the guys who have a plan and know how to execute it—who know how to compete and never stop doing it.

AS MUCH AS I am in awe of Todd Helton's two-way talents and Peyton Manning's quarterbacking stature, they are not my inspiration during my freshman year at Tennessee. My inspiration is a softball pitcher from Nashville named Jane Dickey.

My little sister. The sister I left behind when I moved in with my father—something I've felt guilty about for a long time.

Before I go to college, Jane gets involved in a relationship with an older guy. She gets pregnant at fifteen years old. She's a superb student and first-rate athlete at a private school in town, and you can imagine what she's dealing with at such an age, when she's not much more than a child herself. Everybody has an opinion about what to do. More than a few people privately advise her that if she goes ahead and has a baby now, she might as well say good-bye to every goal and dream she has ever had. Officials at her school tell her that if she decides to get married, she will not be welcome back. So now her education is on the line too.

Amid all this noise and pressure and a society that sometimes wants to treat childbirth as an inconvenience, Jane says, I am going to have this baby.

She says, I didn't plan on getting pregnant and the timing is terrible, but I have a human life to nurture now and that is what I am going to do, and nobody is going to change my mind.

My parents completely support her decision and do what they can to help her.

So Jane has the baby and gets married and gets tossed out of school and winds up living on an army base with her husband. She graduates high school through a GED program. She loses her last two years of high school, and college, and a good piece of her childhood. Eventually she has to get out of a marriage that probably never had a chance. It is some load of freight, but my sister carries it with grace and dignity.

Jane's reward for doing the right thing is a beautiful daughter, Abby, who is now eighteen years old and makes everything worth it a million times over. Abby is the pride of my sister, and a young woman who is cherished by the whole family. Jane's strength and courage as a teenage mother is something I draw on and admire, not just in my freshman year at Tennessee, but for years beyond.

THE FIRST START of my college career is against the University of Miami, one of the top programs in the country. It's even more special because Anne Bartholomew surprises me by flying down for the game from Davidson College in North Carolina where she's spending her freshman year—and with no small effort: she goes around dormitories singing Christmas carols in exchange for donations. Her renditions of "O Holy Night" and "God Rest Ye Merry, Gentlemen" are so well received that she earns two hundred dollars and books a plane ticket using cash.

I battle hard in the game, but we're down, 3–1, in the middle of the seventh, at which point everything stops, and not just for "Take Me Out to the Ball Game." Lazaro Collazo, the Miami pitching coach, is standing behind home plate in his baseball uniform, alongside a clergyman and a woman in a wedding dress. They proceed to walk beneath a canopy of upraised baseball bats, a sixty-foot-six-inch procession to the pitcher's mound.

I have seen a lot of things happen on ball fields. I have never seen a wedding during the seventh-inning stretch.

I am happy for the newlyweds but not happy for me, because—for better or for worse, for richer or for poorer—my start is over. By the time they exchange vows and rings and get the bats back in the bat rack, almost a half hour has passed.

You're done, R.A., Bill Mosiello, the pitching coach, says. I don't want to send you back out there after such a long delay. I try to argue, but probably don't do it strenuously enough. I make a point to remember that.

Even as a freshman, I become the staff workhorse, and the owner of a fast-changing body. I had never lifted a weight in my life before I enrolled in Tennessee; now I'm lifting all the time, having Creatine before every workout, and adding slabs of muscles to my quads and hamstrings and deltoids. I go from 175 pounds to 210 pounds, and my fastball jumps from the 87- to the 89- to the 93- to the 94-mile-per-hour range. I'm still not a prototypical, strike-out-the-side power pitcher, but I can bring enough heat that it makes my breaking pitches and changeup more effective.

I wind up winning fifteen straight games after the Collazo nuptials, and we make it to the regional finals. I throw seven innings in a victory over Northeastern on Thursday, then come back on Sunday against Arizona State, another huge baseball power. I go ten innings and throw 140 pitches, losing on an opposite-field single by Antone Williamson in the tenth. It is a brutal defeat, but the pain gets put in perspective in a hurry. I go over and shake hands with Jim Brock, the legendary Arizona State coach. He is gravely ill with cancer. His body is so full of chemotherapy that his eyes are yellow.

Congratulations, Coach Brock. Good luck in the College World Series. I will keep you in my prayers, I say.

Thank you, young man, Jim Brock says. Arizona State goes on to beat Miami, but then is eliminated by Oklahoma, the ultimate winner. Coach Brock dies four days after the College World Series ends.

I MAKE ALL-AMERICAN as a freshman, and do my usual sticking and moving in Gibbs Hall and around campus, just the way I used to in Green Hills. I flit around the dorm, alighting here and there, making friends and being cordial but making sure nobody gets too close. As long as you don't let anyone get close, you can't get burned, can't get hurt. I don't think that consciously; I just live that way, a fugitive who doesn't know what he's running from.

The one thing I don't run away from is work. Indeed, I want to pile it on. I want to be the most committed, hardworking guy on the team, an attitude that is only reinforced by my freshman experience, which underscores to me that, short of having Sandy Koufax–caliber stuff, the greatest attribute a pitcher can have is a willingness to compete. Without an out pitch, a weapon I can turn to again and again when things gets stressful, I have to be aggressive with my fastball and inventive with my other pitches, and refuse to give in. I have to be a bulldog, which isn't so much a pitching strategy as it is a pitching mentality.

You know how hitters talk about never giving away an at-bat? I don't ever want to give away a single pitch. Even if I'm getting belted around, I want every pitch to have conviction behind it. I want it to be a pitch I'm bringing as a personal challenge to the hitter: *Let's see what you can do with this.* I've always believed talent is over-rated and will is underrated. Or, as Uncle Ricky used to tell me over and over: "The mental is to the physical as four is to one." I'm learning that he is right again.

....

AT THE END of my sophomore year, we need to win two games in the regional finals to advance to the College World Series. Dave Serrano, my pitching coach, gives me the ball Thursday and I go seven innings before he pulls me with the victory in hand.

We're going to need all you've got on Sunday, the coach tells me. Our opponent in the regional final is Oklahoma State. A record crowd of 5,086 turns out at Lindsey Nelson Stadium, our home field. (Lindsey Nelson, a UT grad with an affinity for outlandish sports jackets, later became the legendary first voice of the New York Mets.) We score in the third to go up by a run before Oklahoma State ties it up in the bottom of the eighth. I've thrown about 150 pitches by then. Serrano comes up to me on the bench.

Great job, R.A. Really great job. We're going to let the bullpen take it from here.

I look right back at him and say, You are not taking me out of this game. Serrano walks away. I go out for the ninth. After the ninth he approaches me again and says, That's it. You are done.

I am capable of being a complete idiot when it comes to leaving games. I can be a totally obstinate, impenetrable donkey, refusing to listen to reason or heed authority figures. This is exactly how I behave in the Lindsey Nelson Stadium home dugout that day.

I am not coming out of this game, I tell him. Serrano tells me later that I look at him like a guy in the middle of war who refuses to put his gun down.

I retire Oklahoma State in the tenth, and when I come into the dugout, Serrano collars me right away and tells me again, more emphatically, that my day is done. He is losing patience now. He tells me he has never been a win-at-all-costs guy and isn't going to start now.

You've pitched your butt off but I'm not going to risk hurting your arm. You've got a lot of years ahead of you in this game.

He starts to walk away and I hold him there. My anger is starting to rise. I am not going to let him entrust this game to somebody else. I'm just not.

I don't care what you say. I am going back out there and I am finishing this game, all right? This game is mine. Nobody else's. I feel fine, feel great. I'm going as long as it takes.

Serrano comes right back at me and tells me I'm not in charge and now we are nose to nose, bumping into each other. There isn't going to be a dugout rumble, but there *is* a major confrontation in the biggest game of the year.

I walk away and tell him again: I am finishing this game. That's it. It's mine.

Coach Serrano doesn't respond. I think, and hope, I've finally worn him out.

We take a 3–1 lead in the top half of the eleventh (Oklahoma State is the home team for this game, and if they beat us and force a second game, then we are the home team), scoring on a suicide squeeze. Now I have three more outs to get.

I retire the first guy, but then Rusty McNamara, the Oklahoma State left fielder and number two hitter, works me for a walk. Not what I am looking to do in that spot—put the tying run at the plate. The next hitter is Peter Prodanov, the shortstop. He's a right-handed hitter and a good stick, so I have to be careful, but the guy I really don't want up is in the on-deck circle: Tal Light, their designated hitter. Tal can tie this game up with one swing, and then

I'll have to have another fight with Coach Serrano to come back out for the twelfth inning. I want to end it here. I want to get Prodanov to hit it on the ground, if possible.

I throw a two-seam fastball away and he goes with it, making pretty good contact, hitting a high-bounding ball to first. Todd Helton snares it just over his head and runs to the bag for the second out, then fires to second to see if we can get McNamara, who beats the throw but overslides the bag. Shortstop Matt Whitley puts the tag on him. Rusty McNamara is out and the game is over, giving Tennessee its first spot in the College World Series in forty-four years. The whole team rushes to the mound, engulfing me. It is one of the greatest thrills of my career. In the pile, Dave Serrano gives me a hug.

You are the most stubborn kid I have ever coached, do you know that? he says. Nobody is even a close second.

I can see the conflict on his face, the pride he feels for one of his pitchers coming through in a big moment, and the regret he has that he allowed a kid to bully him out of a decision. I found out later that I threw 183 pitches.

WITH HELTON departing for pro ball after being selected eighth overall by the Rockies in the June 1995 draft, head coach Rod Delmonico has to replace our best hitter and a dominant closer. I couldn't help any with the hitting, but about a month into my junior year, Delmonico is tired of us blowing late leads and decides to make me a closer.

Whatever you need, Coach, I say.

The bullpen agrees with me from the start. I love the challenge and the stress, the whole hair-on-fire urgency that comes with closing. I love being able to just try to blow the doors off without having to worry about pacing myself over nine, or eleven, innings. In back-to-back outings, I hit 96 miles per hour on the radar gun, my highest reading ever.

Before the year is out, though, I am back in the rotation, because we weren't getting many late-inning leads for me to protect. We just don't have enough to make another run to the College World Series. I finish my career the same way I begin it, with a loss on the road, this time to Clemson in the NCAA regionals, minus the seventh-inning wedding ceremony. In between those two losses, I win a school-record 38 games and pitch a record 434 innings.

I'm sad the year doesn't end on a better note, but it's impossible to stay down for long. The big-league draft is approaching and the Olympics are right after that. There's a lot going on, a big adventure and a big unknown ahead of me. I think of Henry Wadsworth Longfellow and words of his I learned in a nineteenth-century literature course along the way:

> *Go forth to meet the shadowy Future, without fear,*
> *and with a manly heart.*

CHAPTER SIX

COVER STORY

T he summer of 1996 is going to be the best time of my life. I am sure of it. After finishing my junior year at Tennessee, I'm in my third summer pitching for Team USA, preparing for the upcoming Olympic Games in Atlanta. I'm waiting for Major League Baseball to have its June free-agent draft.

I've been thinking about the big leagues since I was a seven-year-old kid who wanted to be the next Nolan Ryan.

Now the time is here. I try to act ballplayer blasé about it, but the truth is this:

It is huge. It is everything.

If the buzz is correct, I will be the first-round draft choice of a big-league organization. By the end of the summer, hopefully after an Olympic gold medal, I will have a big check in the bank. I will buy Anne a beautiful engagement ring and ask her to marry me.

I will be on my way.

Draft day is the first Tuesday in June. I am living in a Navy barracks in Millington, Tennessee, in a Spartan cinder-block room with a bathroom at the end of the hall. A short walk down a lino-leum floor takes me past the rooms of the best collegiate players in the country. Kris Benson of Clemson. Mark Kotsay of Cal State Fullerton. Braden Looper of Wichita State. Travis Lee of San Diego State. Jeff Weaver of Fresno State.

The crème de la crème.

This is my second go-round in the draft, actually. I was taken by the Detroit Tigers in the tenth round out of high school, but I talked with Uncle Ricky and he said that unless they blew me away with money, I should go to college (which is what I really wanted any-way). I wasn't ready for pro ball and figured all along I'd be enroll-ing at the University of Tennessee, so I never seriously considered signing with the Tigers. Now it's three years later and I am draft eligible again. Scouts have followed me the last couple of years, try-ing to gauge how I stack up against the other pitchers available. Start after start, I go out there and audition in front of these guys I've never met, guys who could have a massive impact on my future. They have their notebooks and radar guns and organizational shirts and hats, and their task is to determine if you are worth spending a first-round pick, and a pile of money, on. It's the meat-market part of the business, and you find out about it early. If they like another cut of meat better than you, you are going to stay in the display case awhile longer. It all comes down to what they write up in their reports and how you grade out.

Literally.

Part of the package is a psychological-profile exam, something teams use to assess your makeup and character. I must've taken a dozen of them, forty-five minutes at a shot. You get multiple-choice questions like this:

If you are approaching an intersection and see the traffic light turn yellow, your response is to:

A. Speed up to get through the light before it turns red.

B. Gently but firmly apply the brake so you come to a safe stop.

C. Look around to see if there are any cops, and then gun it.

D. Think about your options, hit the gas, then slam on the brake just before you get to the intersection.

Or:

You take a two-hit shutout into the bottom of the ninth, only to lose when your second baseman boots two consecutive grounders. You deal with the situation by:

A. Taking a bat to the water cooler in the dugout.

B. Telling a reporter—off the record—that the manager screwed up by not putting in the backup second baseman, who has a better glove.

C. Brooding at your locker with a towel over your head, just to make sure everybody knows how heartbreaking the game was for you.

D. Making a point to go over to the second baseman and say, "Hey, you busted your butt out there today. Forget the ninth inning. You can play second base behind me anytime."

I always make sure I give answers that I think will score me character points, not necessarily the truthful answers. In other words, I lie. So, with the first question, I circle B, even though in real life I would've definitely run the light (A). On the second question, I don't have to fib: in good seasons and bad, I try hard to be a good teammate; no way would I bury a guy because he makes an error. In life and on the exam, I go for D:

You can play second base behind me anytime.

I know this probably sounds straight out of Cornball Central, but there's nothing corny about loyalty to me. The day I don't stand by my teammates is the day I don't want to play anymore. The Bible says, "Do not let loyalty and faithfulness forsake you; bind them around your neck, write them on the tablet of your heart."

Besides, I like it when guys stand by me after I screw up.

I WAKE UP anxious in my barracks in Millington on draft day. How could I not be anxious? My life could soon be changing in a momentous way. The Oakland A's seem to have the most interest. They have scouted me the most and have the tenth pick of the first round.

I imagine myself in green and gold, pitching for an organization that has been home to big-time pitchers for years, from Catfish Hunter to Vida Blue to Dave Stewart.

I hear the Bay Area is nice. I decide that this would be a great fit for me.

With the tenth pick in the first round, the A's select a high school third baseman named Eric Chavez.

Oh, well. (The Bay Area is too cold, anyway.)

I wind up going to the Texas Rangers. (Let's hear it for heat.) The

Rangers take me with the eighteenth pick, right after the Cubs take a high school pitcher from Louisiana named Todd Noel. For some reason I find myself wondering about Todd, who he is and what his story is and how he got to be a first-round pick in the major leagues. I wonder how many of the top guys in the draft will wind up being stars and which ones will never be heard from again.

I wonder how I measure up against them. I wonder if I will ever be heard from again.

Every slot you drop in the first round costs you money—a bunch of money, hundreds of thousands of dollars of money—so it's not good that I slip to eighteen. The word I get is that the scouts are concerned that I was overused at Tennessee and that my velocity has dropped from the mid-nineties to the low nineties over the last month or two. When a young pitcher loses velocity, he might as well have a contagious disease; it usually makes teams run in the other direction. In that sense, I am fortunate to still be in the first round.

So how can I be unhappy? The Rangers hardly scouted me because they didn't think I'd still be around when they picked. Now I am in the same organization as Nolan Ryan, not to mention Jonathan Johnson, one of my best friends, whom the Rangers took on the first round a year earlier.

It's all good.

With the draft complete, I dive back into my life as a pitcher for Team USA in the Atlanta Olympics. We have a lineup loaded with big bats, and a starting rotation that consists of five of the top collegiate pitchers in the country: Benson, Billy Koch, Looper, Seth Greisinger, and me. People are calling it one of the best pitching staffs Team USA has ever had. I am the least acclaimed of the five, but that's okay. On July 22, 1996, *Baseball America* puts all of us on the cover before the Games begin. It's a huge deal being showcased on the cover of the bible of amateur baseball. The headline reads, "Armed for Battle." I make sure Anne and my mom save copies for the scrapbook.

This is a press clip I'm never going to forget, I tell myself.

My Olympic coach is J. Stanley "Skip" Bertman, of LSU, one of the best and most inspirational coaches I've ever been around. Skip is always showing us film clips or giving speeches, finding novel ways to fire us up. He calls us together one day in Millington in the locker room during the pre–Olympic tour.

Skip previously had given every one of us a crystal baseball paperweight as a keepsake. He is standing before us holding his own crystal baseball paperweight. He begins to talk, softly. He talks about the Olympics and the opportunity we have before us, and how important it is to put the team above all else. And then suddenly the quiet of the room is shattered, Skip purposely letting his ball drop out of his hand, onto the floor, the crystal shattering on impact, startling everybody.

Skip pauses and then pulls out another crystal ball paperweight. He holds it tightly in his hands.

A team is a very special thing, Skip says. It's something to cherish, to preserve, but it's also fragile, like the crystal ball I just dropped, because once it's broken or fractured—once guys don't stay together and start playing the blame game and splitting up— you can try to glue or patch it and reassemble it, but it's never, ever the same. Never. So be a team. Stay together. If you do that you can do great things.

I love his message.

We believe we are capable of the greatest thing of all in the Olympic baseball orbit: beating Cuba for the gold medal. We played Cuba four times the year before, in 1995, and beat them in all four games. Teams comprising U.S. college kids are not supposed to do that against the Cubans, longtime kings of amateur baseball.

Before we go out to play the Netherlands in our first game in the Olympics, Skip tells us: Remember, you are playing for Your Maker, your family, and the United States of America. He says it before every game.

Our bats are on fire as the round-robin play begins. We hit five home runs in the first inning in a 15–5 blowout of Japan, one of the medal favorites. I start against Italy and we win, 15–3. Not exactly high drama, nor the 1927 Yankees as an opponent, but I feel good about how I perform after a rocky first inning. For the whole tournament we average four homers per game and play a tight preliminary-round game with the Cubans before losing, 10–8— our only loss against six victories as we head into the semifinals against Japan.

We believe we are the team to beat. We've handled Cuba and we've beaten Japan the last nine times we've played them, and I mean thrashed them most of the time.

How can we not be confident?

The Japanese score three in the second inning against Benson, our starter and the number one pick in the entire big-league draft that summer. They score three more in the fifth, and go on to hit five home runs against our pitching. Meanwhile, we somehow turn a pitcher named Masanori Sugiura into the Japanese Greg Maddux. Sugiura's regular team is the Nippon Life Insurance Company, and his policy on this day seems to be to put every pitch just where he wants it.

We fall behind 6–0, then 8–2 and 10–2. I am in the bullpen while all this is going on, and I think I am going to throw up.

I mean it. I am physically nauseous—that's how revolted I am by what is going on, as if I have food poisoning, my system emphatically rejecting the crap that's being stuffed down my throat.

The final score is 11–2. Japan advances to the gold-medal game against the Cubans. Team USA goes for a consolation-game bronze against Nicaragua.

It hurts more than any defeat I've ever been involved in. The nausea takes the whole night to lift.

The next day we play for the bronze. Skip makes sure we are ready to play, tells us that even though this isn't the game we want to be playing, we owe it to our Maker, families, and country to honor the game and play hard. We score four in the top of the first and win going away, 10–3. Cuba beats Japan, 13–9, for the gold. When the bronze medal is placed around my neck, it's the most bittersweet moment of my sporting career. I am one of the top amateur ballplayers in the world. I finish my year with Team USA undefeated (7–0), with a 3.35 earned run average. I am proud to have won a medal in the Olympics for my country.

On the other hand, I am sick that the medal isn't gold and the national anthem that's being played isn't "The Star-Spangled Banner." I pack up my stuff and my swirling emotions and head back to Nashville, and wait for my agent to hammer out a deal with the Rangers so I can start my new life as a professional pitcher.

ACCORDING TO Lloyd's of London, I have a million-dollar arm. That's how much I have it insured for during my sophomore and junior year in college, just in case I get hurt and don't have a pro career. I get the policy at the suggestion of the coaches at Tennessee, where guys like Peyton Manning and Todd Helton and other top athletes were buying themselves protection. The premium is roughly $30,000, but Lloyd's is good about it and lets me defer the payments until some money comes in, which shouldn't be long now. Mark Rodgers, my agent (recommended to me by a friend), and Doug Melvin, the general manager of the Texas Rangers, go back and forth in their negotiation, and Doug finally pushes his signing bonus offer to $810,000. I am not micromanaging this with Mark and don't talk to him six times a day to get the updates. I want to do well, of course, but I never want to break the bank. I just want what is fair. He says it is, and I accept.

I say a prayer of thanks to God and begin planning my first expenditures—Anne's ring, Lloyd's premiums, and something special for my mother and sister, Jane.

The thought of the money is mind-boggling. I'm a guy who started life with cockroaches, my mom's lemon of a Vega, and the Western Sizzlin flatware. Now I am on the verge of being 81 percent of the way to the millionaire club, less commission and expenses. I try to fathom what it's going to be like to sign that contract with my name and that number on it, and I can't, but the bigger thrill, honestly, is what is attached to the money. And what is attached to it is the beginning of my professional baseball career.

Mark and I fly down to Arlington so I can take the obligatory physical and sign the contract. The Rangers want me to meet Nolan Ryan and throw out the first pitch at the game that night. The whole flight down, I am mesmerized by the thought of standing on the mound in the Ballpark, with Ryan in the wings and tens of thousands of people cheering.

It's going to be one of the greatest moments of my life. There is no other way to think about it.

When we get to Texas, I go straight to the office of the team orthopedist, Dr. John Conway. The doctor knows about me already, from the Olympics and Danny Wheat, the Rangers' trainer. In the clubhouse one day, Wheat sees the *Baseball America* where I'm standing, sideways, with the other Team USA starters. Wheat points the photo out to Conway.

His arm kind of looks like it's hanging at a weird angle, doesn't it? Wheat says. This kid is our number one draft choice and he already looks like he's got elbow problems.

The other pitchers' right arms are hanging straighter than mine, which has more of a bend at the elbow.

Conway agrees it looks a bit odd. He files it away.

I am in his office for an hour, contorting my arm in various directions.

This guy's being thorough, but I guess that's what happens when this kind of money is involved.

Everything proceeds fine. As far as I know. The last test Conway administers is called the Valgus stress test. He places my arm in a snug-fitting apparatus, then has me twist my wrist back and forth as an X-ray machine above films what's going on inside. When the test is finished, we go back to the doctor's office. He puts the X-ray on an X-ray illuminator. I am looking at the infrastructure of my right elbow. It looks a lot like an elbow to me.

You have a couple of millimeters of extra laxity in there, Conway says.

What does that mean? I ask.

It means there is a little extra play in there that isn't normal.

That doesn't matter, does it? My arm doesn't hurt. I've never missed a start. I throw the ball in the nineties. I don't see how that could matter if I have no symptoms.

I don't know, Conway says. It's hard to say.

We shake hands and Mark and I head off to see Doug Melvin.

I don't like what he said about the laxity, Mark says. I hope it's not a problem.

It won't be a problem, I say. I'm as healthy as I can be.

This isn't bravado. This is gospel to me; I know my body better than anybody, and my arm feels great.

We get to the Ballpark and take the elevator up to Melvin's office. It overlooks the field in left center and has a balcony adjacent to it. Doug pokes his head out and asks Mark if the two of them can speak for a moment. I walk out on the balcony to check out my future field. It looks spectacular: the richest, most verdant grass I've ever seen.

I want to be on it now. I want to be on that mound, facing a big-league hitter, now.

Right below me, in the bullpen, Roger Pavlik, a Rangers pitcher, is having a side session. He is wearing bright red cleats. They are as cool as anything I've ever seen on a ballplayer. Behind him is Dick Bosman, the Rangers' pitching coach.

It would be awesome to wear red cleats, I think. I look up at the empty seats and take in the size of the place and imagine what it will be like to pitch in a park this big. I am in a place of immense gratitude and I say it out loud, on the balcony:

Thank you, Lord, for all your blessings and for helping me get this far.

My prayer is still in the air when I see Mark walking toward me. His face is whiter than home plate.

You need to come in to Doug's office, he says.

I have no idea what's happening other than that it's not good.

We sit down. Doug is a Canadian with a thick mustache and a

solid middle-aged body, like a guy who might be a Mountie if he weren't running a baseball team. He has a stern, distant look on his face.

We are going to retract our offer, he tells me. We think there's something wrong with your elbow and we want to have further testing done.

Melvin's face is stoical. No emotion whatsoever.

This is business. All business.

I sit there and try to take in those words for a second or two: *We are going to retract our offer.*

I take them in again:

We are going to retract our offer.

I don't feel devastation, or even anger. I feel rage. Complete rage. It feels as if it starts in my toes and blasts upward through my body, like a tsunami, into my guts and right up through the top of my head.

I have an urge as primal as anything I have ever felt.

I want to reach across this desk and strangle this man who, very quietly, very dispassionately, has just taken everything I've worked for, taken my whole life's dream, and crushed it as if it were a bug on the pavement. I want to cuss and tell this man exactly who he is stomping on. Part of me wants to tell him about all the ways my life is screwed up and how this is the one thing, the one thing above all else, that I can do right and that makes me somebody.

I can pitch. I can compete as hard as anybody you've ever seen. That's why you made me the eighteenth pick in the whole stinkin' draft. Don't you remember that? Don't you know how much more important what I have inside me is than a little laxity in the elbow?

I want to make sure he knows how it feels to be me right now, after he's matter-of-factly dropped this atomic bomb on my baseball career. On my life.

But first I want to get on his side of the desk and let him know how it feels to be pummeled worse than he's ever been pummeled in his life.

But I do not lift a finger. I do not leave my chair. It's as if there's a strong hand on my shoulder holding me back, giving me pause. In that instant I have a self-control that wasn't there a moment earlier.

I hear a voice:

Relax, I've got you. Relax, R.A. It's okay. It's going to be okay. I've got you.

The voice is the Holy Spirit. The restraint is the Holy Spirit. I was just talking to God in prayer on the balcony and now He is talking back, bestowing on me a composure that could not have come from anywhere else.

I've got you.

The tsunami passes. I am crushed by Doug Melvin's words but I am not going to do anything stupid. I am not going to lose control.

I've got you.

I get up slowly. I don't say a word. I walk out with Mark and pass the balcony and don't stop to look at the field or Roger Pavlik or his red shoes. I'm in a complete daze, almost as though I don't know who I am or where I am or what just happened, as if my whole life's hard drive has been wiped out.

Mark drives me to the airport. He tries to boost my spirits but it's not going anywhere and we both know it. We pass through security and pass all these people and they're all going places and living their lives and none of them knows or cares what just happened to me, a little laxity leaving me as shattered as Skip Bertman's crystal baseball. I go to the gate, get on my plane, the rage dissipating, replaced by a terrible loneliness. A loneliness that feels terminal. I left Nashville that morning, full of excitement. I come back that afternoon, full of this total, solitary despair.

We are going to retract our offer.

Melvin's words keep running through my head. I look out the window at thirty thousand feet. I search for comfort, any comfort at all, and find it, not in Doug Melvin's seven words, but in the Holy Spirit's three: *I've got you.*

The plane lands. I am home. I am going to be all right.

en route to Orlando

We're on the bus to Walt Disney World, where we'll see Mickey, Donald, and Chipper. Well, Chipper (Jones), at least. We're playing the Braves in my third start of the spring, and I find myself thinking about how much I love spring training. I love it because it comes bundled with hope. Indeed, it is all about hope. This isn't the most original thought I've ever had, I know, but still, optimism abounds when your record is 0–0 and you are starting anew. You see the upside, not the downside. You see possibility, not impossibility. Nobody has yet written what a joke your club is. Sports talk radio has yet to heat up. Nobody has booed or belittled you. In the spring, hope is as palpable as the palm trees, even for clubs coming off a bad year the way we are. Hope is a nice thing to have, however long it lasts.

For me, this spring has another quality for me to savor. For the first time in my life, I have a guaranteed job. I have a two-year deal and I know where I'm going to be pitching. All that does is change everything. I can focus on getting into shape and working on my craft, and not worry about impressing somebody so I can stick around for another week.

Last year, my first with the Mets, I was the first guy cut. The first. I said hello and good-bye in the same sentence.

Against the Braves, I wind up having an ugly line, giving up five runs and four walks in five innings, but I am not concerned at all. The Braves hit only one ball hard. I had a good feel for my knuckleball, and when it missed the zone, it wasn't by much. I thought a bunch of the pitches that were called balls were actually strikes. The plate umpire—a minor leaguer—told me afterward, a bit sheepishly, that he'd never called a game pitched by a knuckleballer before. Honestly, it showed, because he missed a lot of pitches, but I appreciated his candor. Even in spring training, it's the kind of admission you rarely hear from an umpire, and it shows me a whole lot. No names here, because it will seem like I'm trying to work Mr. X for future advantage and I'm not.

CHAPTER SEVEN

THE LONE RANGER

almost forget about the other words Doug Melvin said, about getting additional testing on my elbow done. The Rangers want me to go see Dr. James Andrews in Birmingham, Alabama.

Fine with me. Maybe there's still hope.

The next day, my father (who hasn't been a big part of this whole draft process) decides to come with Anne and me to Birmingham. We ride in my father's maroon Chevy Cavalier, a straight two-hundred-mile shot down Interstate 65. I am sitting in the front passenger seat, still exhausted from the day before. When I am awake, I am praying pretty much nonstop. After we pull into Dr. Andrews's parking lot, my dad turns off the car and the three of us say another prayer.

Please give me the strength to deal with whatever happens today. Please see me through this, God. Please be there for me and make this nightmare go away.

Andrews's office is like a mall on Christmas Eve: crazy busy, people coming and going everywhere. The walls are covered with photos of big-name pitchers he has operated on, from Roger Clemens to John Smoltz. When it's my turn he starts examining me, doing many of the same tests as Conway.

I don't see any real problems with your elbow, Andrews says. The attrition in it is a little worse than most guys your age, but that's understandable because you've thrown a lot more than most guys. Let's go ahead and take an MRI while you're here and make sure we're all good and then we'll be done with you.

I like this doctor. I like him a lot. From what Andrews is telling me, he'll report to Conway that everything checks out and my offer should be back on the table.

I go downstairs and put on a hospital gown. They inject my arm with a dye and I get inside the MRI tube, and the jackhammering sounds begin, harsh and loud and metallic. I have headphones on but they barely help. Finally after forty-five minutes the jackhammering stops. I get changed and go back upstairs. That takes some time. I get off the elevator and turn a corner. The first person I see is Anne.

She is walking toward me. She has tears in her eyes. She hugs me.

I hope the Rangers believe in miracles, she says.

Beyond her, in an alcove at the end of the hallway, I see a cluster of doctors in white jackets in front of an MRI screen, looking at my elbow. There seems to be animated discussion and debate, and lots of pointing at the screen. I walk up to see what's going on.

Andrews gets to me first. We step into his office.

I can't find the existence of an ulnar collateral ligament in your elbow, Andrew says. I've looked at thousands of these. I've seen torn UCLs and frayed UCLs. I've done a million Tommy John surgeries to repair UCLs. I've never in my life seen an elbow with no UCL at all where the patient is completely asymptomatic.

So much for hope. So much for all my prayers. I'm a clinical marvel to Dr. James Andrews, an orthopedic oddity for the ages, a physiological freak. Check it out, check it out . . . See the pitcher with no UCL. I can join the circus, but I can't get my offer back from the Texas Rangers.

Andrews theorizes that I could've been born without the UCL in my right elbow, though he thinks it's more likely that I injured it when I was young and it just withered up and died at some point. He can't believe that I am not in extreme discomfort. Nor can he believe that I can throw the ball pretty much where I want. The UCL—a thick, triangular band of tissue—is the main stabilizing ligament in the elbow. Without it, the infrastructure of the elbow should be about as stable as a car without a steering wheel.

It should hurt you to turn a doorknob, to shake hands, to do the most routine of tasks, he says.

Dr. Andrews's disbelief about what he sees only makes me feel worse. He is so confounded, in fact, that he wants to do another MRI.

I go back downstairs, get back in the gown, back in the tube. I am beside myself. When the jackhammering starts again, I feel as though I might have a full-blown anxiety attack. I distract myself by trying to think of arguments to make to Doug Melvin.

Because I don't have a UCL, that means it can never get torn or hurt. Think of the reassurance that comes with that. Maybe I should be worth even more money!

I'm not so naïve to think the argument will fly. I get through MRI number two and go back upstairs. The new picture shows nothing different. I am still a pitcher without the one indispensable stabilizing ligament that you need to throw a baseball.

After I leave, Andrews calls Conway and tells him the shocking news and of course recommends that the Rangers not sign me.

I am, after all, not whole. Not what I seemed to be. I am damaged goods.

The dream crushing is now complete. It is so unfair; that's the feeling I have above all others. It's just so unfair for this to happen, and in this way. Can you imagine a worse scenario, getting drafted on the first round and offered all this money and then have it yanked away because of a one-in-a-billion medical condition?

I pray to God for understanding, for a way to get through this, but the truth is I have very little understanding. I am angry at God, angry at the Rangers, angry at the world. The whole thing taps into all my old wounds about being different from every other kid, being damaged in a deep way even if the world can't see it. This just confirms it. I am different. I am damaged.

I am the Pitcher Without an Ulnar Collateral Ligament.

Newspaper sports sections report all about this oddity. The tabloid TV shows call to do a segment on me. So does *Strange Universe*. The bizarre tale sweeps through baseball. Did you hear about that kid the Rangers took on the first round? Can you believe there's a pitcher who doesn't have a UCL?

We drive back to Nashville and I hole up in the Bartholomews' house. I don't want to see or hear from anybody. I don't know where I go from here. No team is going to touch me after Dr. Andrews's MRI. I guess my best option is to go back to Tennessee for my senior year. I can finish up my degree. Maybe if I have another strong season, a club will decide to take a chance on me, UCL or no UCL.

The phone rings in the house one afternoon. My future mother-in-law, Vicki, answers it, and a few moments later, from the next room, I hear her voice and anger rising. She sounds as though she's going to start cussing.

Vicki Bartholomew never cusses.

How could you do this to this young man? Do you know how cruel this is, to take his dream and rip it up in his face? Do you have any heart at all?

I walk over to Vicki to try to get her to calm down. I don't know who she's talking to. I appreciate her speaking up for me. I wonder who's getting the earful. She hands me the phone.

It's someone from the Rangers. I think his name is Nolan.

No, it couldn't be. Could it? Don't tell me that Vicki just dressed down a Hall of Famer and my hero. Please don't tell me that.

I take the phone.

Hi, this is R. A. Dickey.

Hey, R.A. It's Nolan Ryan. I can see y'all have some people there who are upset about things, and I don't blame them. I was just calling to tell you I'm sorry the way things happened. I sure hope you stay with it and things work out for the best for you.

Nolan is good friends with Lenny Strelitz, the Rangers' scouting director. I'd gotten to know Lenny pretty well. I'm sure he is the person who asked Nolan to call.

Nolan goes on to tell me that he pitched the last five or six years with a messed-up ulnar collateral ligament. He talks about all the people who doubted him when he was a young pitcher who couldn't throw strikes.

We talk for five minutes and I tell him how much I appreciate him calling, and apologize that he got an earful when he was just trying to do something nice.

Don't worry about it, he says.

A week passes and the semester is beginning at Tennessee. I re-enroll and pick my classes. My senior year begins the next day with a 9:00 a.m. class in nineteenth-century American literature. Melville and Hawthorne await me. Once I step foot in that class-room on the UT campus, then I am committed to school and can't sign with a pro team until the following June. I get my books to-gether and start trying to wrap my head around *Moby-Dick* when my agent calls, telling me he has just spoken with Doug Melvin, my personal Captain Ahab.

Doug has been rethinking my situation. He called his own father and asked for advice. His father tells him: You can't just cut this kid loose and not give him anything. You owe him something—even if it's nowhere near the eight hundred you were going to give him.

Melvin thinks, *My dad's right. I broke this kid's heart. I have to do something.*

My agent tells me: The Rangers want to sign you if you'll take $75,000.

It includes an invitation to big-league training camp. It is a take-it-or-leave-it proposition.

Mark and I don't have to talk long. The UCL, as of this moment, has officially cost me $735,000. Their offer is more like fifteenth-round money than first-round money, but in the Rangers' mind that's about where I am.

I accept the offer, sign the contract, and withdraw from Tennes-see, then hold a press conference at Montgomery Bell Academy so I can go through the whole mess and not have to answer questions for weeks on end. I roll out every platitude I can think of about adversity and about how champions are people who rise above it. I say that I am not sad and not discouraged about my big offer being pulled, both naked lies.

I am sad and I am discouraged. I just don't want to say so publicly.

I use the money to buy Anne's engagement ring, pay off my Lloyd's of London premium, pay the taxes on the bonus, and take care of some of my father's debts. I don't know how he ran them up, but he is in some financial trouble and I have to help him out with it.

I have $7,000 left.

In early October, I borrow a white Dodge Ram and drive fourteen hours to Port Charlotte on the Gulf coast of Florida, where the Rangers have their instructional league team. I pull into the complex and walk into the clubhouse and see a man standing there. I have no idea who he is. Turns out he is Reid Nichols, the former big-league outfielder who is a Rangers minor-league executive.

I don't introduce myself, don't ask him his name, either. I'm being rude, but I don't really care.

Can you tell me where the weight room is? I ask.

Nichols points to his right and I go off and lift for a solid hour. This is how I begin my career in pro baseball—beneath a stack of iron plates. I am defiant. I am going to outwork every human being on the planet.

I am going to do whatever it takes to make it.

This is the face I am putting on for the world, but the truth is different. I'm ready to work my tail off, for sure, but I also am more insecure than I have ever been in my life. For as long as I've been in sports—as a pitcher in baseball or a forward in basketball or a quarterback in football—I've never had anybody tell me I couldn't do something. I've lost games and missed shots and thrown interceptions, of course, but mostly I've succeeded and delivered, again and again, and gotten applauded for it. Now, for the first time, somebody—the Texas Rangers organization—is doubting me.

Doubting whether I can overcome my missing ligament and whether I can ever help them as a pitcher.

I stare at the ceiling in the hotel where all the Rangers' instructional players live and think: *What if I can't do it? I think I can, but what if I can't? What will my life be like if I can't play pro baseball?*

I go back and reread some of my old press clippings from Tennessee, read about big games I pitched and won and being named an All-American. I am trying to convince myself that I am the same guy, capable of the same success.

I look in the mirror. I am the same guy, R. A. Dickey. Six feet two inches, 215 pounds, from Nashville, Tennessee. Throws right, bats right.

You are the same guy, I keep telling myself. You can do this. You can show the whole world that UCLs are way overrated.

It is a tough sell.

CHAPTER EIGHT

MINOR ACHIEVEMENT

Like any prospect, I want my time in the minors to be as short as possible. Succeed, advance, and say good-bye to bus rides forever. That's my career game plan, and after all the emotional tumult of 1996, I try to believe in myself and put it into place. But first there is a little detail to take care of first:

I want to ask Anne Bartholomew to marry me.

From the time I met Anne ten years earlier, I knew in my heart I wanted to be with her. Now that I'm out of college and pitching pro ball, there's no reason to wait. I start by visiting an independent diamond dealer in Arkansas. My agent knows him and tells me I can trust him. I don't trust easily, but as a man who would have a hard time telling the difference between the Hope diamond and dime-store zirconium, what choice do I have? I pick out a rock and the setting, and pray that it's not a fake. When it's all finished, the dealer mails it to me in Tennessee.

It is almost Thanksgiving. The Bartholomews have invited my mother and me to have dinner with them at their home in Belle Meade. My mother has five years of recovery behind her now and is becoming a whole new person, and I'm so happy she's going to be able to share this moment with me.

I start things in motion a few days before, when I ask Sam, Anne's father and a former West Point linebacker, if I might speak with him in his office, an elegantly paneled room with an antique wooden desk and keepsakes from a lifetime. The wood is so rich in Sam's office it seems three feet deep. We're sitting in two plush armchairs in front of his desk. I am very nervous and he knows it.

Sam, I'd like to ask Anne to marry me, and I'd like to ask for your blessings in doing that.

Sam stands up and I follow his lead.

So you're finally ready to get serious, are you? he says. I was wondering when we were going to have this conversation. He gives me a hug and smiles.

I hope you are not expecting a dowry. I've always looked at you as one of my sons and I'm honored that you want to marry my daughter.

Sam's words mean so much because he's someone I've leaned on and sought counsel from, a man who has been a constant paternal presence in my life. I look around at the handsome desk and panels and three-foot deep wood. I am starting to lose it. I do not want to lose it, part of me being afraid that if I start crying I might never stop.

I hold it together.

Thank you, Sam.

The Bartholomews have a Thanksgiving tradition in which each person at the table speaks for a few minutes about what they are thankful for. Sam asks Anne to start and then they go clockwise around, meaning that I will go last. Sam knows just what he's doing. Sam and Vicki give their thanks and so does my mom. Next are Anne's brothers, Bo, Will, and Ben. As they go around I take the engagement ring out of my pocket and put it in my right hand and slightly inch my chair back from the table. My hands are sweating so much I'm afraid the ring might slip out; I keep my grip on it tight. Finally it is my turn. Everybody in the room but Anne knows what is about to happen.

I begin by thanking God for the bountiful provisions and for the chance to be together and then thank Sam and Vicki for having my mom and me to their home. I turn and look at Anne, gazing intensely into her green eyes.

Anne, I am so thankful for you and for our relationship, I begin. I met you one afternoon in this very house ten years ago, and I loved you from the moment I laid eyes on you.

I inch my chair back a little more. My eyes remain locked on hers.

I cannot imagine my life without you, I say, and then I am off the chair and on my knee, with the ring between my thumb and index finger, more slippery than ever, Anne's eyes already glistening.

Will you marry me, Anne?

She brings her hands up to her face, and now she is crying and nodding, not even able to speak. I slip the ring on her finger; with all the moisture, it slides on as if I'd coated it in WD-40. Anne pulls me closer to her and holds me, my head near her waist.

I love you so much, she says. All around the table there are hugs and handshakes and an abundance of gratitude. Nobody has more of it than me. I am engaged to Anne Bartholomew.

MY FIRST full year as a professional ballplayer doesn't follow my script. It ends after eight appearances, six starts, and thirty-five innings in the Florida State League, cut short by bone chips in my right elbow. They're painful but not particularly serious, and after I get an arthroscopic cleanup—totally unrelated to the absence of a UCL—I am ready to rock.

ANNE AND I GET MARRIED on December 13, 1997, in Nashville before an intimate gathering of five hundred people, including Winfield Dunn, the former governor of Tennessee, and Lamar Alexander, another former governor and a 1996 Republican presidential candidate—the type of men who my new father-in-law, a prominent Nashville lawyer, moves with. Two months later we're off to Port Charlotte for our first spring training. Late in camp, a Rangers player-development executive pulls me aside and tells me the organization has an experiment in mind.

We want to give you a look as a closer, he says.

This is just a couple of days before the season starts. I say nothing and report to the bullpen, same as I did at Tennessee. If that's where they think I can help, that's where I'll pitch.

I take to it well and save thirty-eight games and make the all-star team, moving up to Double-A ball in Tulsa in 1999. I learn a valuable lesson along the way:

If you want to get by on a minor-league salary, you need to watch every penny and look for any way you can to supplement your income. Anne and I get by with one car and start our married life by sharing an apartment with another couple so we can split the $650 rent. Anne gets a job at The Limited and is teaching aerobics too. Sam and Vicki help us from time to time, but we want to make it on our own. I aim to further boost our cash flow with a business

My dad and me, age **four**, building a snowman.

...rgarten picture from
...entary School, Nashville.

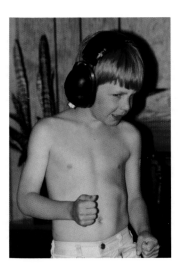

Me at age seven.

venture that I start with my friend Jonathan Johnson, another Rangers pitcher and the best man at our wedding.

Our apartment in Port Charlotte is a short distance from three golf courses, all of which have ponds and lagoons all over the place. Jonathan and I play the courses whenever we get a chance, and after I lose my third ball of the day in a lagoon on a par-five hole on one of the courses, I say to Jonathan, Can you imagine how many golf balls there must be at the bottom of this thing?

Hundreds, maybe thousands, Jonathan says.

Don't you think that if we could somehow fish the balls out of there, we could sell them and get a pretty good business going?

You may be onto something, Jonathan says.

I briefly ponder if this is how Apple or Starbucks got started, with an innocuous, spur-of-the-moment brainstorm. I don't take the argument too far, turning my energy instead to the challenge of getting the golf balls up from the bottom—and doing it discreetly, as there are houses lining every inch of the course. We invest in fifty feet of rope and two golf ball rakes with little baskets at the end that allow us to scoop up about sixteen balls at a time. We buy waders, buckets, a couple of gallons of bleach, and a scrub brush for the cleaning operation, and lift a few dozen bundles of sanitary socks from the clubhouse.

Our overhead is low, our start-up costs only about sixty dollars, key factors in any new venture.

We are almost ready to plunge the rakes in the water when we realize we haven't accounted for one factor:

Alligators.

They are all over the place on this golf course. Look on the banks of the lagoons and you see them sunning themselves in the reeds.

Look in the water and you see them skimming along the surface, possibly trolling for Titleists.

The gator factor, I decide, is not going to foil our plan.

We'll be fine, I say. We'll just be on the lookout for them. It's not like we're going swimming.

At 10:45 on a moonlit night, we set out with our rope and rakes and buckets, wade into the shallows, and extend our rakes and haul them back in, dragging them along the bottom, hoping for dimpled white pay dirt. We attach ropes to the rakes, then throw them out there as far as we can and drag them back in toward the shore. After the first half hour, business is booming. We already must have a hundred balls. No stopping us now. We keep flinging the ropes and raking the balls in, but on one throw my rake gets snagged on the bottom, on a stump or rock, I don't know what. But it's really stuck. I pull on the rope every way I can think of but can't shake the rake loose. I put more muscle into it. I start to feel a burn in my shoulders and don't want to overdo it, thanks to a horrible headline premonition:

RANGERS PROSPECT WRECKS ROTATOR CUFF
FISHING FOR GOLF BALLS IN LAGOON

This would be right up there with the most ridiculous baseball injuries of all time, alongside Cardinals outfielder Vince Coleman getting his leg mashed by a mechanical tarp and Braves reliever Cecil Upshaw suffering a career-ending finger injury supposedly while practicing imaginary dunks on an awning. No, this is not a club I want to join, so I ease up a bit.

What are we going to do? I say to Jonathan.

Mom and me, age eight months,
at David Lipscomb University in 1974.
It was my first baseball game.

Mom, Dad, and me, age three.
My parents got divorced when I was

My kind
Glencliff Ele

Me at age seven, playing in the instructional
(coach-pitch) league for the YMCA.
(Note the nice socks).

Anne's brother, Bo, and me in 1988.

Trying to steal a kiss from my future bride in seventh grade.

Mom and me, age eight months,
at David Lipscomb University in 1974.
It was my first baseball game.

Me at age one, in 1975.

Mom, Dad, and me, age three.
My parents got divorced when I was eight.

My dad and me, age four, building a snowman.

My kindergarten picture from
Glencliff Elementary School, Nashville.

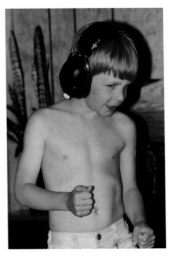

Me at age seven.

Playing quarterback for Montgomery Bell Academy, Nashville, 1992.

LEFT: A picture from my senior year in high school, pitching for Montgomery Bell Academy.

BELOW: After the Tennessee state championship. *Left to right:* my stepmother, Susan; Dad; Grandma Dickey; my dad's cousin Dustin; me; my dad's cousin Randy; and Mom.

Anne and me when we started dating in 1993.

ABOVE: Anne and me after a University
of Tennessee game in 1995.

RIGHT: Grandaddy and me after a University of
Tennessee baseball game in the spring of 1996.

MAJOR LEAGUE,
MINOR LEAGUE
MIDSEASON
UPDATES

ON SALE THROUGH AUGUST 4, 1996

ARMED FOR BATTLE
Our Gala Olympic Preview

Kris Benson, R.A. Dickey, Braden Looper,
Seth Greisinger & Billy Koch (from left)
lead Team USA into Atlanta
BONUS SUMMER SHOPPER SECTION

$3.95 ($5.50 CANADA)
PRINTED IN USA

I was thrilled to appear on the cover of *Baseball America* before the 1996 Olympic Games, with the four other U.S. starters. (*Left to right:* Kris Benson, me, Braden Looper, Seth Greisinger, and Billy Koch). I was less thrilled when the photo—check out the bend in my elbow compared with the other guys'— prompted the Rangers to put me through tests that revealed the lack of an ulnar collateral ligament in my right elbow, costing me almost my entire $810,000 bonus.

(*Photo courtesy of Robert Gurganus,* Baseball America)

Second baseman Warren Morris and me after the U.S. men's baseball team received a bronze medal at the 1996 summer Olympics in Atlanta.

Anne Bartholomew and I were married in Nashville on December 13, 1997, before an intimate gathering of five hundred family and friends. *Left to right:* Anne's father, Sam Bartholomew; Anne's younger brother Will; Anne; me; Anne's youngest brother, Ben; Anne's mother, Vicki; and Bo.

With Anne's family.
Left to right: Will; Will's wife, Shelly; Sam; Vicki; Ben; me; Anne; and Bo.

My mom and her brothers and sisters. *Left to right:* Lynn Caldwell, Mandy Bowers, Bob Bowers, Mom, Ricky Bowers, Helen Bowers, and Debbie Bowers. They all cared for me in some way.

My good friend and fellow pitcher
Jonathan Johnson and me in the Rangers
bullpen during my first call-up in 2001.

My sister, Jane, and me with my daughter
Gabriel, age one and a half, and Jane's
daughter Abby, age nine.

At my first big-league game. *Left to right:* YMCA organizer Darlene Wilkes; Dad; my step-mom, Susan; Jennifer Binkley (Trig and Darlene's daughter); YMCA organizer Trigg Wilkes (Darlene's husband); Mom; Anne; Rob Merriman; Rob's wife, Denise; and my high school friend David Fitzgerald.

Anne and our son Eli in Seattle, in July 2008. I was playing for the Mariners then.

Phil Niekro and me
in the winter of 2009.
I drove to Atlanta to
work with Phil on
my knuckleball.

Mom and me
at the beach in 2010.

Going underground:
Eli, Lila, and Gabriel join me
for our first family outing
on the New York City subway
system, not long after
I joined the Mets in 2010.

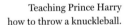

Teaching Prince Harry
how to throw a knuckleball.

I haven't always made it easy on Anne,
but it's nothing but marital bliss as
we celebrate our fourteenth anniversary
on December 13, 2011.

Introducing Van Allen Dickey.

Cuddling with my girls: Gabriel is on my left and Lila on my right.

Darth Vader Senior (me)
and Darth Vader Junior (Eli)
get primed for Halloween.

Eli and I figure it's time to start
teaching Van the wonder of words.

Van's probably not sure what
to make of me or my
Darth Vader costume.

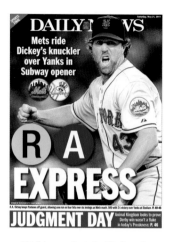

Pitching against the Yankees in
New York is always a special event.

(*Photo courtesy of* New York Daily News)

Battling the Marlins at Citi Field.

(*Photo courtesy of* New York Daily News/*Robert Sabo*)

LEFT: Me, in the dugout
after losing my no-hit bid
against the Phillies.

(*Photo courtesy of* New York Daily News/
Howard Simmons)

BELOW: A nightmarish moment:
a tendon injury took me down
during the third inning
against the Chicago Cubs,
May 26, 2011, in Chicago.

(*Photo courtesy of AP Photo/Jim Prisching*)

Eli and me at the beach, fall 2010.

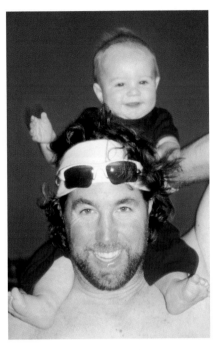

Van and me at the beach in 2011.

Cheek to cheek with Van midway
through his first season, 2011.

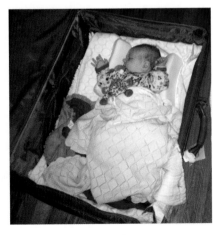

Already a traveling man,
Van catches a nap inside a suitcase.

Closer to home, at the Dekalb County Fairgrounds, Alexandria, Tennessee, June 2011.
Left to right: Eli, me, Van, Gabriel, Anne, and Lila.

(Photo courtesy of Mark Tucker)

I don't know, but if we don't get the rake unsnagged, our business may be closing its doors after one hour.

Well, I think we may just have to dive in there and free it up by hand. What do you think?

I think you're right, Jonathan says. Neither of us even mentions the wildlife factor.

It's dark, it's late, and we're in alligator-infested waters, but what can I tell you? Jonathan and I are bent on freeing up our rake so we can keep collecting golf balls and become moguls. I wade in up to my waist and then follow the rope, which Jonathan is holding taut, into the middle of the lagoon. When I get there, I take a big breath and dive down, into about eight feet of water. I yank and yank at the rake, but it's really stuck. I come back up for air.

I go back down. Yank some more. No luck.

I come back up, make another descent, and—with hands on either side of the rake basket—rock it back and forth and finally get it free, then swim back up to the surface.

I hold it up like a trophy and get back to shore.

We return to the lagoon the next night, and for many nights thereafter we make the rounds of the three golf courses, searching for water hazards and doing our dragging thing.

The rakes work well, but they do get stuck now and again. Which means we swim now and again. Jonathan makes me look cautious. He's all over the diving and rake-freeing part of the enterprise. I put the alligators out of my mind, but I don't think they are even on his radar.

Back at the apartment, we scrub the balls with bleach and get them as white as we can, then put a dozen of them in a sock, separated by brand. We have Titleists and Maxflis and Nikes—a sock for every budget. On a good night we will collect three or four hundred golf balls. Over the spring we collect thousands. Our best customer is probably Kenny Rogers, the pitcher and a Titleist man, who gets a dozen for ten dollars. Will Clark is a regular customer too. Other guys buy lesser balls for six or eight dollars per dozen. I keep track of all of the transactions in a little notebook, with entries such as this:

3/1 Will Clark 2 socks of Pinnacles $18 paid

By the time the spring is over, we have $3,000 or so that we didn't have before. Jonathan, who got a $1.1 million signing bonus, insists that I keep everything, even though he worked as hard or harder than me, diving to the bottoms of all those lagoons.

I don't think that's fair. You were in the water with those gators more than I was, I tell him.

Nobody's keeping score, he says.

AFTER SPLITTING 1999 between Double-A Tulsa and Triple-A Oklahoma City, I am in Oklahoma City from the start in 2000. The major leagues are just one step away. I begin the year in the bullpen and get knocked around a little, then move into the rotation at the end of April and proceed to lose my first four starts. I finally start getting guys out with some consistency in late May and June, but by then I have other issues crowding my plate.

It never makes the papers, or the evening news, or Deadspin, but I test positive for a banned substance in 2000. It is the only positive drug test of my life. And it is not just any positive drug test.

It is a positive drug test for opiates, the class of narcotics that derives from opium—the substance used to produce heroin. I may only be a Triple-A ballplayer, but I am now in the crosshairs of a major-league drug problem.

I find out about the mess when the Texas Rangers' employee-assistance program (EAP) sends me a letter. They leave it on the stool in front of my locker. No envelope. No manila folder. Just a letter in plain view for the entire world to see that R. A. Dickey is apparently not the straight arrow he pretends to be. It informs me about the positive test and says I will be hearing from John Lombardo, one of the executives in the Rangers' minor-league department.

It is so ridiculous that I laugh out loud and take the letter into the trainer's room to show Greg Harrell, our trainer and a friend of mine.

Look at this, Greg. I've tested positive for an opiate. I bet you didn't know that about me, did you?

Greg laughs too.

How on earth did this happen? he asks. You doing heroin on your off days?

I don't know how it happened, but I do know I've never had any heroin products in my life.

Lombardo calls and asks me a few questions, seeking information about the situation and telling me that an employee-assistance counselor would be calling me to follow up.

John, all I can tell you is that there must be some mistake. I don't know whose mistake it is, but I promise you I am not on opiates.

The EAP guy calls and wants to know the whole story. Let me put this as simply as I can, I say. I have never had as much as a sip of alcohol. I take Advil occasionally and that is a big deal to me. I have never had any narcotic or mood-altering, mind-altering drug, ever.

You can test me and retest me. You can come to my house and I will meet with you and talk to whoever you want, but I do not have any sort of drug problem and I am not going somewhere for treatment or to talk to an expert in the field to help me with my supposed problem.

The guy probably thinks I'm just another drug addict who is either in complete denial or lying because he can't live without his fix.

Nothing I can do is going to change his mind.

The whole thing began two weeks before, when I attended our regular Thursday afternoon lunch and Bible study at the home of Mark Brown, our team chaplain. I go straight to the ballpark from there, and when I arrive in the clubhouse, Greg comes up to me.

It's your turn to pee in the cup, he says. Baseball has random testing, and every so often when you get to the park the trainer will tell you you've been selected.

I go get my driver's license and give it to the drug tester, then head off to the bathroom to fill the cup. I've always prided myself on my ability to pee on demand, dating back to my days at Tennessee and in the Olympics. I don't need to run water or drink a gallon of liquid or use any other bladder-enhancing techniques. I'm on top of my game again this time. I fill 'er up and go back to my locker, and don't think about it again until the letter comes.

The mystery finally gets unraveled well after I speak to the EAP officer, and the culprit is outed. It is the chaplain's wife who did it, who is to blame for everything. I would hold it against her, but in good conscience I can't. She fixed us a sumptuous lunch for our

Bible study, and I freely admit that I pigged out on it. I had seconds and then thirds, then took a doggie bag to the clubhouse so I could have fourths later. It was the best poppy-seed chicken casserole I ever tasted. Poppy seeds are from the poppy flower, and the poppy flower is where opiates come from. I have no idea how many poppy seeds I devoured, but it was a very large number. I happen to mention my predicament to an Oklahoma City cop who works at the ballpark, and he tells me that he has heard that poppy seeds, taken in copious amounts, can indeed trigger a positive test for opiates.

Who knew?

I never hear from the EAP counselor again. The Rangers never bring up the matter again. I have no idea if my sample was run a second time or if they just believe my story, as far-fetched as it sounds: that the entire thing is set off by me pounding on chicken casserole. The next time we go to Chaplain Brown's home for lunch, I ask his wife for grilled cheese.

LIFE IN THE MINORS for Anne and me is all about saving money and hoping I pitch well enough to get a shot at the big leagues. In 2000 we move into a Tudor-style apartment complex in Oklahoma City called Warwick West, where we have a small, one-bedroom place next to a Dumpster with a rented bed and couch and a coffee table that consists of a cardboard box with a bedsheet thrown over it. Lifestyles of the broke and anonymous.

In our second year in Warwick West, I begin the season with a strong start against Salt Lake City, but the much bigger news is that Anne is feeling funny in the morning and thinks she might be pregnant. We do the home pregnancy test and when the little stick changes color, she immediately books an appointment with an obstetrician. I have to go the ballpark, so Anne goes to the doctor alone and calls me when she is finished.

How do you feel about being a father? I hope you give the right answer because I am eight weeks pregnant, she says.

Oh, Anne, that is the greatest news. God is blessing us in so many ways, I say.

We get a copy of the baby bible—*What to Expect When You're Expecting*—which becomes the second most important book we own, after *the* Bible. We share the news with family and friends, and even though there are thirty-one weeks to go, it feels as though we need to start getting ready now.

Shortly after we get the news, Anne comes to the ballpark with friends for my first start as a father-to-be. It's a surreal, and joyful, feeling to see Anne in the family section. Midway through the game, she has to go to the bathroom. She doesn't feel quite right and is a little concerned. She passes a trace of something, and her instincts tell her that she should be home. She drives back to Warwick West and I meet her there later. By the time I get home, she is that much more alarmed. I see a look on her face that I have never seen before, and that raises my own alarm. Her maternal instincts have already fired up and they are telling her that our unborn child is in distress.

I do my best to reassure her. We put a call into the doctor. We pray together.

God has a plan for us, Anne. We have to remember that, I tell her. I don't know what is happening or why, but I do know that God loves you, loves us, and He will never, ever forsake us.

Anne goes to the bathroom again and hopes and prays that everything will be okay. She feels helpless, because more than anything in her life she wants to save her baby. In a few minutes she calls for me, her voice trembling and halting. I hear her crying. She opens the door and the moment I see her all I want to do is hold her and protect her. Anne is sobbing in my arms, and she can barely speak. She doesn't need to. She really doesn't need to.

Our baby is gone, she says finally. The baby is gone. Anne doesn't need confirmation from a doctor or nurse or anybody else. She knows.

You want to ask God why in a moment such as this. As much as you keep faith as the centerpiece of your life, you still want answers to unanswerable questions. You want to know how and why this is His plan for you, what the possible good could be in this. You want to rage and feel victimized and scream to the heavens, How could You let this happen, Father? What did this unborn child do to deserve this? What did we do to deserve this?

The questions don't take you anywhere, of course. Pain and tragedy exist in our world, side by side with God's boundless love and grace. It is impossible to reconcile in so many ways, but ultimately Anne and I are able to surrender to our belief that God has a perfect plan for us. That comes later, though. For now we are in grief.

I take Anne's hand and we go to the sofa, and we weep.

Nationals Park, Washington, D.C.

With two outs in the top of the first, David Wright crushes a ball off of Livan Hernandez to the deepest part of the park. The Nationals' center fielder turns and races back for it, his graceful strides making it seem as though he's not even exerting himself. Rick Ankiel chases it down and makes the catch, and I marvel at how natural he looks out there, and at the career he's made for himself.

Still, for me, Rick Ankiel will always be a pitcher—probably the greatest pitching prodigy I have ever seen.

I first saw him pitch on a sultry summer day in Memphis in 1999. I was in my first full year with the Oklahoma City Red-Hawks. Ankiel was a twenty-year-old left-hander with this easy, flowing windup and a fastball that just exploded out of his hand. I watched him and thought, How can someone look so effortless and throw the ball that hard? *His curveball didn't just fall off the proverbial table; it looked as if it might fall off the earth.*

He gave up one hit and struck out seven in seven innings, a low total for him. He made our hitters look so bad, they might as well have gone up to the plate with a noodle. His command was ridiculous. On the best day of my life, I couldn't throw the ball like Rick Ankiel.

Ankiel was in the majors at the end of that season, and in 2000 went 11-7 for the Cardinals and averaged almost ten strikeouts per game, and was on his way, until Tony La Russa named him the game one starter in the National League Divisional Series against the Braves. Ankiel pitched two scoreless innings, and then walked four guys and threw five wild pitches in the third inning. A complete meltdown. In game two of the National League Championship Series against the Mets, he lasted twenty pitches, each seemingly wilder than the next. The next year he was back in the minors, throwing balls everywhere but over the plate.

I saw Ankiel again in Triple-A in May 2001, when Memphis was in town to play us in Oklahoma City. He threw a half dozen pitches up on the screen. My heart ached for him: a lost soul at age twenty-one, trying desperately to recapture the gift that once came so naturally.

Ankiel spent several years trying to find his command, the plate, but he was never close to the same pitcher again, a victim of the dreaded Steve Blass disease, named after the Pirates' all-star pitcher and World Series star who mysteriously lost his command and within two years found himself out of baseball. (In 1972, Blass won 19 and had a 2.49 ERA; the next year he was 3–9 with a 9.85 ERA.) Watching Rick Ankiel's decline was one of the saddest and most inexplicable falls I've ever seen in baseball.

As a pitcher who once gave up 6 homers in $3\frac{1}{3}$ innings, I know how it feels to be on the mound with no place to hide. This game can humble you in a heartbeat, or faster.

Rick Ankiel went on to reinvent himself as an outfielder, a conversion that makes my switch from conventional pitcher to a knuckleballer seem puny by comparison. He has been one of *the great defensive center fielders in the National League for a number of years. I've seen him throw guys out at third base from the warning track. He doesn't need anybody's sympathy, and I'm sure he doesn't want it, but whenever I see him, I can't help harkening back to his days as a teenage wunderkind who seemed destined to be one of the greatest pitchers in baseball.*

CHAPTER NINE

SHOWTIME

The timing is terrible, but right after the miscarriage I have to go on the road to Salt Lake City and Colorado Springs. I hate to leave Anne alone in the apartment where we lost our baby, but I don't have much choice. We pray together before I leave and I ask God to keep my wife safe and to be faithful in my trust in His plan for us.

On our first day in Colorado Springs, I am at my locker getting changed when a familiar voice calls out, "Dewclaw Dickey."

The speaker is Lee Tunnell, the RedHawks' pitching coach and the originator of the nickname. Lee, one of the best pitchers ever to come out of Tyler, Texas, has been calling me Dewclaw since the latter stages of 2000. He promotes his creation at every opportunity:

Way to battle tonight, Dewclaw.

Go up the ladder, Dewclaw.

Don't give him anything too good to hit, Dewclaw.

How I came to be Dewclaw Dickey is a story that promises to be told, and retold, for generations. Or not. The RedHawks play in the Pacific Coast League (PCL), where one of the most popular fan promotions is called Dog Day, or Bark in the Park, depending on where it is. Fans are allowed to bring their dogs to the game, and get treated to an exhibition of dogs that can catch Frisbees, send text messages, and perform other stunning tricks. I heard that in one ballpark, Dog Day included chef pooches whipping up frittatas, but I have never been able to confirm that. Anyway, in the 2000 season, there were a bunch of Dog Days at various parks around the PCL, and I seemed to be the pitcher for every one.

If dogs were in the house, Dickey was on the mound.

Lee could've called me Dog Day Dickey, or 3-D, but for some reason he latches onto Dewclaw, the term used to describe the claw on a dog's vestigial thumb. I show up at a park to pitch at that week's Bark in the Park event, and Lee says, Go get 'em today, Dewclaw. And that's how it begins.

As tragically as the season starts for Anne and me as a couple, my pitching life is going okay. I win my first two games and we head to Colorado Springs to play the Sky Sox in a ballpark that makes Coors Field seem like a pitcher's paradise. Balls don't just fly out of the thin air of Colorado Springs. They get launched. From a pitcher's perspective, it's the worst place on the planet to start a baseball game.

I get to the park early to do my running and long tossing.

Hey, Dewclaw, come on over here for a second, Lee says.

I walk over to Lee's locker.

They're calling you up, he says.

No they're not.

Yeah they are. They want you there ASAP, so you better get your collar and your chew toys and get your tail to Texas. He reaches out and shakes my hand.

You deserve it, Dewclaw. Now, don't come back.

I have no idea what to say. I've never been called up to the major leagues before. I'm twenty-six years old. In dog years, I'm ancient. In baseball, I'm getting there.

I let Lee's news sink in for a minute.

Thank you, Lee. I appreciate all you've done for me, friend. I have a smile on my face and it won't leave and I think that I must look like some caricature of a minor leaguer after he gets the call. The first thing I do is call Anne.

Guess what, honey? I'm going to the big leagues.

Oh, my God. You're kidding? Anne says.

I am not kidding.

I would never say to Anne, or even think, that a call-up to the big leagues can make up for the loss of a child, but isn't God's timing remarkable? Isn't it nice to have wonderful news even as we continue to grieve for our baby?

I've got to catch a flight to Texas. I hope you can be there.

I'll be there. I am not missing this.

Good, I say, because this is happening. I don't know how long it will last, but your husband is going to be a big-league ballplayer.

I reach my parents and Anne's parents, and Uncle Ricky, and start gathering up my gear, and by now word has spread through the shoe box of a clubhouse that I'm going to the big club. Right away I sense a dichotomy as big as Pike's Peak in my teammates' reactions. Some guys, most of them, are genuinely happy for me and wish me well. A few, though, can barely conceal their bitterness that they are not the ones going to the majors. You can tell by their insincere congratulations or evasive glances. I don't blame them. I've been in this position, watching other guys get the call. It's no fun being left behind. It's the dream we all share, but there are only so many spots in the big leagues, so it's a zero-sum game we are playing: If you get called up, it means that I'm not. If I get called up, it means you're not. I get that, totally.

I'm not letting somebody's dour expression rob me of one of the best days of my life.

I hustle back to the hotel, check out, and hop the first shuttle to the airport. At the airline counter, the ticket agent says, "You will be traveling first-class, Mr. Dickey." I've never flown first-class before.

Real glassware, here we come.

When I get to the ballpark, the guard directs me to the Rangers clubhouse. At the door I stop and remind myself not to act like some doofus from Dixie on his first trip to the big city.

Cool, that's what I'm going to be, I tell myself. It's only a room in a ballpark. A place where guys pull on their jerseys and jock-straps, not some mythical lair populated by supermen. I'm going to act as though I've been in big-league clubhouses a thousand times before, even though I've never spent one second in a big-league clubhouse.

Yes sir. I'm going to take coolness to new heights.

I walk in.

I am there about two seconds when goose bumps start popping and my jaw starts dropping. I am spellbound. I am deep in Doofus City.

How bad an actor am I?

I am a very bad actor.

The sheer size and wood-grain splendor of the clubhouse—at least, compared to the frayed carpets and cubbyhole lockers I'm used to—is mind-blowing. The trainer's room looks like a high-end health club. The lounge is the size of a small house. The clubhouse guy directs me to my locker. I pass lockers that belong to Alex Rodriguez and Pudge Rodríguez and Ken Caminiti. I walk a little farther and pass Rafael Palmeiro and Rusty Greer territory, and see the locker of a promising shortstop, Michael Young, who is just twenty-four years old. I look around for my fellow golf-ball retriever, Jonathan Johnson.

I finally get to my locker. It says DICKEY on the nameplate up top already, as if I'd been around as long as any of them. A white number 51 jersey hangs in my locker with my name on the back. Not iron-on. Stitched. It looks almost too perfect to get sweaty in.

Manager Johnny Oates comes out of his office.

Happy to have you, R.A., he says. Pitching coach Dick Bosman shakes my hand and asks when I last threw.

A nameplate tells me my next-door neighbor in the clubhouse is a veteran right-handed pitcher. He hasn't arrived for the game yet. I am curious about what sort of guy he is. Getting settled in, I put my stuff in the locker and start to get changed. I take off my shoes and put them on the floor where my space adjoins his. I'm sitting on the little stool pulling on my socks when my neighbor arrives. He looks down, looks at my shoes, and then kicks them to the center of the room. I guess my shoes were trespassing on his territory by a few inches. I look at him, stunned. His face is angry and hard, about what you'd expect.

He doesn't say, Hello, welcome to the big leagues, or remark on the supple brown leather of my shoes. He says absolutely nothing. I go and retrieve my shoes and don't say anything, either. I don't know if anybody else sees his kick, but if they did, they don't say anything.

I am a rookie, but I've been around the game long enough to know about baseball's caste system, where the time-honored custom is for rookies to keep quiet unless spoken to and to be as invisible as cellophane. I don't get this, and never have. Why do you need to have a certain amount of big-league time or a particular set of credentials to be treated like a human being? How is that to anybody's benefit? Why not make a young guy comfortable? Apart from being the nice thing to do, don't you think he might even play better if he has a sense of belonging?

Some baseball customs are just plain absurd. And downright dumb.

Respect is earned over time; I understand that. It doesn't mean that the people like this veteran have the right to degrade somebody just because he is getting his first shot. The pitcher would get released—and his career would end—a short time after he kicked my shoes. My schadenfreude is brief. Really. I don't think about him ever again, until now.

The Oakland A's are in town for a four-game series. I get dressed and walk up the dugout steps out onto the field, and can't comprehend where I am. Before the game I head to the bullpen and suddenly I stop. I am nearing the exact spot where I saw red-shoed Roger Pavlik throwing a bullpen session five years earlier, before Doug Melvin retracted my offer.

I feel powerful and exhilarated. I feel profoundly grateful. Nobody thought I'd ever be heard of again. I was, after all, damaged goods, *Baseball America* cover boy turned nonprospect.

The Pitcher Without a UCL.

And now here I am. A major leaguer. For at least a day.

A big day. I want to believe it might last a lot longer than that, but optimism doesn't come naturally to me.

Anne, my mom, and a dozen or so other family and friends make the seven-hundred-mile drive from Nashville for the series; Susan and my father drive down too. I don't get in the first three games, and now it's Sunday. I'm dying to get on the mound, but it's not as though I can ask Johnny to put me in because my wife and family are in town. I'm in the bullpen, keeping to myself, noting what a horrible view of the field you have from the lower tier of the Rangers' bullpen. We score four in the third and four in the seventh and go up, 11–2. Pudge and Palmeiro homer and ARod goes three for four. In the top of the eighth, the bullpen phone rings.

Bobby Cuellar, the bullpen coach, answers it. The conversation lasts about five seconds.

Cuellar looks at me.

You got the ninth, kid, he says.

I get off the bench and stretch a little and get on the mound. I start throwing easily and gradually increase velocity. I feel good. I feel strong. The bottom of the eighth ends and now it is time. No fooling.

It is time.

When I first met Anne in seventh grade, I told her three things were going to happen:

She and I would get married.

U2 would play at our wedding.

I would one day become a big-league ballplayer.

I am about to increase my batting average to .667.

I RUN IN from the pen and try not to look up at the crowd or the size of the stadium around me. I steal a quick look at the family section, where Anne and my parents and everybody are sitting, but I don't want to get caught up in it. On my first warm-up pitch to Pudge, my left leg, my front leg, is quivering, shaking like a bowl of jelly. It won't stop. I throw several more pitches and it's still quivering. I'm getting worried.

What if it doesn't stop? What if I have to pitch from the stretch? I'm going to balk on every pitch. I wonder if any pitcher in history has ever had to bail out of a game because of leg tremors.

The first batter is Mark Bellhorn, the A's third baseman. I look in and get Pudge's sign. Fastball.

The quivering continues.

I wind up and fire and it's over the plate, the inner half. Bellhorn swings and lifts a fly ball to left. One out.

Whoa. I feel better now, more relaxed. The quivering, mercifully, has subsided.

Sal Fasano, the A's catcher, steps in. I throw two more fastballs. He pops up a 1–0 pitch behind the plate. Two out.

The next hitter is Mario Valdez, who has replaced Jason Giambi at first in the blowout. I miss with two fastballs and then throw another on 2–0. Valdez swings and pops it up behind third. Alex Rodriguez gets a good break from shortstop and races into foul territory and makes the catch not too far from the seats. The ball game is over.

As I watch the third out of my first inning in the big leagues, a perfect inning, settle into ARod's glove, I feel a pure, sweet surge of elation. It's one inning, a mop-up inning at that, but I've just set down three big-league hitters. It's a good way to get it all started. I keep my eyes fixed on ARod and can't wait to get the ball from him and hold it and smell it and give it to Anne.

It's the only first ball I will ever have.

With my eyes still riveted on the scene by the third-base railing, I watch Alex Rodriguez take the ball out of his glove. I watch him put it in his right hand. Then I watch him flip the ball—my ball—

into the stands. It all unfolds in agonizingly slow motion, the giving away of my precious keepsake, from glove to palm to a fan I will never see again. ARod trots off the field.

Did I really see this happen? Did he just throw the ball from my first big-league game into the stands?

I am in disbelief. I am deflated beyond measure. I watch the fan head up the aisle, and as I stand in the infield, accepting congratulations, I am half-numb. I feel great about what I'd done, but what about my ball?

I want my ball.

The handshakes are done. I walk to the dugout and go to the bucket where the batboy keeps game balls to give to the ump. I reach in and fish a ball out of the bucket. I put it into my glove.

I'll pretend this is the game ball. *Nobody will ever know,* I tell myself.

I NEVER TALK to ARod about what happened. He's one of the greatest players ever and I am three days removed from Oklahoma City, so what am I going to do, cop an attitude with him? No. I'm sure he just got caught up in the moment and didn't even realize it was my first big-league appearance.

But I have bigger items on the agenda, such as staying in the big leagues, and for a fringe prospect, that is by no means certain. We head out to Toronto for my first road trip. Jeff Brantley, veteran reliever and fellow Southeastern Conference guy—he went to Mississippi State—invites me to join him for lunch at a nearby mall.

That would be great. I need to get some clothes, anyway, since I didn't get home before I was called up.

Okay, no problem, Jeff says. I'll tag along with you.

At the store, I pick out a pair of slacks and a couple of collared shirts and a blazer. Jeff is with me as I comb the aisles, not saying much. I try a few things on and go back to the dressing room to change before I pay for the four items I want. After I get dressed and emerge from the changing room, I see Jeff standing at the register, signing a credit card receipt. Next to him are two large bags stuffed with clothes, shoes, belts—the works.

I glance at the receipt. What?!! The total is more than $1,200.

What are you doing? I ask him.

Don't worry about it.

No, Jeff, what are you doing? I want to pay for the things I picked out.

You needed a few clothes, so we got you a few clothes. I'm happy to help you out.

I don't know what to say, Jeff. This has got to be the most generous thing anybody has ever done for me. How can I ever thank you?

You know how you can thank me? Someday you do it for a rookie, he says.

We go to lunch and have a great talk about pitching in the big leagues and he won't let me pay there, either. His unsolicited kindness just blows me away. The grouchy pitcher kicks my shoes, then Jeff Brantley buys me shoes, and a whole lot more. It's a 180-degree turnabout in four days, and I'll take it.

I make two more appearances over the next ten days or so, one good, one not so good. I'm throwing the ball pretty well, starting to believe that I can get big-league hitters out, slowly settling into the daily rhythms of life in the big leagues.

In the bathroom one day before a game, I turn to get a towel after washing my hands and notice something underneath one of the stall partitions. I take a step closer.

It is a syringe.

The sight of it makes me cringe, the shiny thin needle lying randomly on the tile floor. My mind races with thoughts about how and why it got there. I know as much about needles as I do about jewelry, but I'm pretty sure this isn't a sewing needle. I don't know if this syringe injected a Texas Ranger with insulin or cortisone or B_{12} or anabolic steroids, though you can hazard a guess when you run through the roster of my muscle-laden teammates. I'd never seen a syringe in a baseball clubhouse before. I've not seen one since. It may have been used for the most benign of purposes, but the mere sight of it makes me feel as though I am looking straight at Evil—like seeing a weapon somebody left behind at a crime scene.

I walk out of the bathroom and never tell anybody about what I saw. I want to think the best, try hard to think the best, but whatever chemical residue is in that particular syringe, there's no denying the scope of the wreckage caused by needles around baseball, by the so-called steroid era, and by all the artificially fueled feats that came with them. I know two things about performance-enhancing drugs: they are pervasive, and I hate them, because they have hurt the game, and hurt me too. How many long balls hit by juicers would've died on the track and gotten me out of an inning if not for the extra muscle? How many balls muscled over the infield would've wound up in guys' gloves? Of course, I will never know. Nobody will know. I don't stay up nights thinking about it. I don't forget the sight of the syringe on the bathroom floor, either.

The bottom line for me on performance-enhancing drugs is simple: guys who used them cheated. Cheated their opponents, their fans, the game. But it's more personal than that: they cheated me too. Cheated all of us who didn't succumb to the temptation.

So, yeah, I don't stay up thinking about it. But when I do think about it, I get angry, because cheating is cheating. The guys who did it robbed me of the opportunity for fair play and fair competition.

WE'RE ABOUT TO START a weekend series with the White Sox at home when I find out that Johnny Oates has resigned as manager with an 11–17 record. His replacement is Jerry Narron. I'm sorry to see Johnny go. He's not just a nice man who has been more than fair with me in my short time with the club; he's a devout believer who balances his faith and the rigors of his job masterfully. Johnny used to joke that he had no idea how he made it to the majors as a catcher, because he couldn't really hit and couldn't throw a lick. He's a man who was always willing to give an underdog a chance. The news gets much sorrier still six months later, when word comes that Johnny has brain cancer.

As for Jerry Narron, another ex-catcher, I don't know him well— I haven't had the chance to talk to him much—but I just hope he sees something he likes in me. That can be as important as anything. Baseball, I am learning, is a maddeningly capricious game. Sometimes whether a ballplayer gets a chance hinges on a coach or manager looking his way when he rips a home run in spring training or throws a nasty cut fastball on the black, or on a manager just liking the action on a pitcher's ball or the liveliness of a player's bat. I've seen fates be kind, and cruel. You can't dwell on it, either way.

I believe Johnny saw something in me. Jerry, I have no clue about.

On the final day of the series, Darren Oliver is our starter. The first batter in the bottom of the first is Tony Graffanino, the Sox second baseman, who drills a ball up the middle that rockets into Oliver's left hand, his pitching hand. It swells up immediately and Oliver can't continue. Narron scans the relief corps and selects me to come in to take over. I get all the time I need to warm up, and proceed to get lit up like a gas can. Carlos Lee and Chris Singleton hit two-run doubles, and Lee and Paul Konerko hit back-to-back homers. My line is hideous—four and two-thirds, seven hits, six runs. I wind up with my first major-league defeat. My mood doesn't improve much when I hear White Sox manager Jerry Manuel in a postgame interview saying that the Sox knew they had a good chance after Oliver got hurt because teams usually bring in one of their worst relievers in such a situation.

I file it away. You never know when you might need some extra motivation.

After the game, Doug Melvin asks me to come into Jerry Narron's office. Dick Bosman is there too. It's the Texas trinity, but they have not gathered to bless me.

We need another arm for tomorrow, since we had to use you for so long today, Doug says. We're sending you back down.

The words send a chill through me, but I can't say I'm shocked. I didn't think I was a lock to stay up for the year. I don't have a real high opinion of myself as a pitcher right now. Maybe they even picked up on that. After four appearances, twelve innings, and eighteen days, my first trip to the big leagues is over. I'm sad, but I'm not borderline homicidal, the way I was on the day of The Retraction.

Okay, I understand you need to do what you think is best for the club, I say. I thank them for the opportunity and shake their hands and walk out. I guess my gut feeling that Jerry may not be sold on me is not far wrong. He doesn't owe me an explanation, and neither does Doug. It's up to me to change their opinion.

I go back to Oklahoma City, to the apartment by the Dumpster, and Anne and I find out the best news: she is pregnant again. We thank God for this gift and make a decision not to tell anyone for at least three months; with the child we lost, we told everybody and that made it much harder when Anne had the miscarriage.

I wind up having one of my best years, going 11–7 with a 3.75 ERA in a notorious hitters' league, using a fastball, a cutter, a changeup, and an occasional knuckleball—a pitch I've messed around with for years, ever since Granddaddy told me that he threw it. I wait for the call up to the Rangers when the rosters expand to forty players, but it never comes. This is a much bigger blow than being sent down in May. In September, clubs usually call up everybody who is remotely on the radar.

The Rangers not only don't call. When I'm back in Nashville at the end of the year, playing for the RedHawks against the Sounds, Lee Tunnell calls me over in the outfield—I'm R.A. in this conversation, not Dewclaw—and tells me they have taken me off the forty-man roster, leaving me completely unprotected, free to get picked up by anybody. Lee breaks it to me as gently as he can. But he knows what it means.

We both know.

It means the Rangers think I'm worth about as much as a used resin bag. It means, one month from my twenty-seventh birthday, I am looking at an extremely murky future.

Or none at all.

Money is tight and getting tighter, so I take a job in the offseason working for a place called STAR Physical Therapy, doing ultrasound treatments. I work on middle-aged businessmen with balky hamstrings and eighty-year-old women with frozen shoulders, trying to convince myself I am something other than a 4A player. It is not an easy argument to win. By the time I start 2002 in Oklahoma City—and don't even get a look at big-league camp—I am six years beyond the draft and doing a lot of wheel spinning. I look at the big picture of my career and it's hard to see anything that resembles progress. When other RedHawks get a call-up that year, I find myself turning into one of those jealous types who thinks he should be the one getting the call.

I don't like where my career is going—or not going. I do a lot of praying about it. I decide that I really need to start thinking ahead—and outside the baseball box. The fact is that at my age, with my track record, the end could be imminent.

I have to make plans for that contingency. In the middle of the season, I call my friends Trigg and Darlene Wilkes. I went to Trigg's YMCA camps in Nashville for years as a kid, and he's always been kind to me, a good-hearted soul who you could always count on. Now he's based in Jacksonville, overseeing operations of some eight YMCAs along the east coast of Florida.

I think I'd have something to offer the YMCA, I tell Trigg. I grew up in the Y. I know the difference it can make in kids' lives. Can we talk about any job possibilities there might be in case baseball doesn't go anywhere?

Sure, Trigg says. But I hope you aren't ready to pull the plug on baseball. You are still a young guy with a lot of potential.

I'm not sure if Trigg fully believes what he's saying, I'm not sure if I do, either.

You know me, Trigg. I don't give up. I want to be tenacious but I also don't want to be stupid if this doesn't go anywhere.

I finish 2002 with an 8–7 record and a 4.09 ERA. I give up 176 hits in 154 innings, which, if not pitiful, is pretty darn lousy.

Another off-season arrives and I return to Nashville, wanting to be hopeful but mostly feeling discouraged. I've spent my whole life hearing country singers warbling about guys with dead-end jobs and hard-luck lives. I don't want to be one of them. The more I think about it, the YMCA might be a pretty good option.

I DECIDE to play winter ball after the 2002 season, for a familiar reason: we need the money. I get a deal worth about $10,000 and become a member of the Zulia Eagles in northwest Venezuela, a region that is home to Lake Maracaibo, one of the largest lakes in South America, and massive oil and gas reserves as well.

Venezuela is far from the most stable place in the world; President Hugo Chávez was ousted by a military coup earlier in the year, only to force his way back into power forty-eight hours later. By the time I get there, the country is still in plenty of turmoil. At the U.S. State Department's urging, I check in with the U.S. embassy upon my arrival, and the consul general or whoever I talk to doesn't sugarcoat it: This is a dangerous place and you need to be careful at all times.

It's not an outright military coup that is going on that winter, but it's close, brigades of protesters and marchers taking to the streets, and machine guns as ubiquitous as the street-corner carts selling *cachapas* (corn pancakes). I hear gunshots all the time. Two U.S. pilots who stay in the same hotel as me tell about having to dodge bullets on their way from the airport.

Because I am a person who swims in lagoons with alligators, I walk around the streets a couple of times to observe the commotion firsthand. I go to a bullfight and sample the local cuisine, and try to assimilate into Zulia life as best I can. But people are angry and there's no getting away from them.

The protesters want to try to force a new election. They don't succeed, but midway through the schedule they do succeed in shutting down the baseball season, the spasms of violence just making the whole thing untenable. A day later, after the season officially gets called, I get a letter from the U.S. embassy telling me to stay in the hotel until further notice. For once I heed the warning. I stay confined and eat pizza with pork and pesto, the only available food option, for the next five days, reading and watching TV and looking out at the platforms and oil derricks in the distance.

The flights back to the States are full, so they are trying to free up some seats to get the Americans out of the country as soon as possible. Finally I get word that I've got a seat on an American Airlines flight. My team arranges a two-car escort to the airport, vehicles on either side of the one I am in. I get to the airport with no bullets buzzing around me, no problem at all. On the flight back home, I decide that as much as I like extra income, I am going to do my best to have a coup-free career from this moment forward.

SHORTLY BEFORE THE 2003 season, I'm at home, getting ready for spring training, when my phone rings. I have our baby daughter, Gabriel, in my arms. The caller is the Texas Rangers' new manager, Buck Showalter. I've never gotten a call from a manager in January before. My first thought is that something bad must've happened. Buck asks me how the off-season has been and I say fine and decide not to tell him about the near coup and dodging bullets in Zulia.

I just wanted to let you know we're going to give you a good long look in camp this spring, Buck says. I know you've kind of been swept under the rug and that you may not have always gotten a fair shot to show what you can do. But you bring a lot to the table and I think you have a lot to offer this organization, and you are going to get a chance to prove it.

I can't tell you how much I appreciate your calling, Buck. All I want to do is help the club and I believe I can do that too.

When we hang up, I tell Anne what Buck said and I'm so fired up for the spring that I wish I could report that afternoon. I have to wait a month. I spend it going on long nighttime runs through the quiet streets of Green Hills, visualizing myself on the mound as I go, getting big-league hitters out. I am in as good a shape as I've ever been when I arrive in Port Charlotte in mid-February. I am going to get a fair shot and you can't ask for more than that.

CHAPTER TEN

REQUIEM FOR MY FASTBALL

I am in a small space, surrounded by concerned faces, an inquisition without the bright lights. The topic of the day is my lifelong run as a conventional pitcher. It is not being decided on a mound.

It is being decided on a sofa in Buck Showalter's office. The sofa is comfortable but I am not.

I wonder why they've called me in here. Have I run out of road? Could they finally be giving up on me?

Across from me are Buck, pitching coach Orel Hershiser, and bullpen coach Mark "Goose" Connor. It is mid-April 2005, a full nine years after the Rangers drafted me. I've been a member of Buck's staff for the last two seasons, a spot starter and long reliever, my first extended time in the big leagues. I hate to say those Baseball Prospectus writers were right, but the truth is that I am probably not even as good as marginal. My ERA is 5.09 in 2003 and 5.61 in 2004, and I give up a bunch more hits than innings pitched. I have enough promising moments to convince the front office to keep me around—I throw a complete-game, six-hit shutout against the Tigers in late '03—but as hard as I compete, I just can't seem to sustain any success against major-league hitters.

And now Buck and Orel and Goose want to talk to me about it.

Two days earlier, pitching in relief against the Angels, I'd thrown a sinker to Garret Anderson and felt as if I'd been stabbed in the right shoulder. The pain landed me on the disabled list and now on Buck's couch. My senses are on high alert, noticing everything from the tight weave of the carpet to the reddish, round contour of Buck's face. His desk is obsessively neat, with a tidy stack of papers and game notes, a well-ordered lineup of framed photos, and a row of books about warfare and leadership. Behind him is a whiteboard with the names of the Rangers' top minor-league prospects. Buck likes being a general, on top of everything, no detail escaping his ever-darting eyes. But this time he lets his lieutenant, Orel, do most of the talking.

I like it when Orel talks. He knows a lot about pitching. He is a man with a good heart, a man I trust. He gets right to the point.

After you finish rehabbing your shoulder, what would you think about going back to Oklahoma City to learn how to become a full-time knuckleball pitcher? Orel asks. I'm sure you don't want to go back to the minors, but we think it's your best chance for success. You have a good knuckleball already. You have the perfect makeup to make it work, because you know how to compete and we know how hard you'll go after it. We think it can be a great thing for you and for the ball club, but we want to know what you think.

I squirm on the sofa and make eye contact with all three of them, one after another. It doesn't feel as I'm being ganged up on. It feels as though they are all on my side.

Orel and I have had some general conversations about this, but nothing concrete. I've done bullpen sessions for him in which I've thrown nothing but the knuckleball, a pitch I throw once or twice a game, if that. He's always been positive and supportive of me. So have Buck and Goose Connor. Positive is exactly what I need right now, because I'm full of doubts and short on hope, a thirty-year-old journeyman whose career is hanging by a glove string. I've never been a guy to obsess about stats, and I believe the game has gone berserk with all its number crunching and slicing and dicing of statistical metrics. But I cannot run from my numbers. Over parts of four big-league seasons, I have pitched in seventy-two games. My record is 15–17, my earned-run average 5.48. I've given up 293 hits in 239⅔ innings. Those are some ugly numbers.

Fringe big-leaguer numbers.

Later, Goose confirms for me just how precarious the situation is.

They aren't going to bring you back to the big leagues as a conventional pitcher, R.A. You're going to come back as a knuckleball pitcher or you are not going to come back at all.

I fidget on Buck's sofa and contemplate the end of one career and the beginning of a new one. It's hard to wrap my mind around it. Okay, so not many people have ever confused me with Nolan Ryan. I get that. But still, I've always been able to throw a hard sinking fastball, at 92 or 93 miles per hour. I became an All-American and an Olympian and a first-round draft choice because I had stuff—a big-league fastball and a big-league changeup to play off it.

Now I am supposed to say good-bye to all that and join the lineage of Hoyt Wilhelm and the Niekro brothers and Charlie Hough?

That's exactly what I am supposed to do. And it is what I have to do, because radar guns don't lie, and this whole spring, my fastball has been topping out at 85 or 86. My arm feels fine and I cut the ball loose, and what?

Nothing.

Your fastball isn't coming in the way it used to. How's your arm feeling? Goose would ask.

It feels fine, Goose. Really. I don't know what's going on.

Throw it again, Goose would say.

I'd throw it again and again, waiting for the gun reading to change or for someone to tell me the gun was busted and it was all a big mistake. The reading never budges. The gun isn't the problem. I try to rationalize the predicament any way I can. I'd hurt my arm at the end of 2004; maybe it's just taking longer than usual to get my strength back. Maybe I'd fallen into some bad mechanical habits that Orel and Goose and I can sort out. Lots of pitchers go through little dead-arm periods.

Don't they?

It could be a lot of different things, I keep telling myself.

I want to run from the truth. I want to escape, the same way I did when I slept in empty houses. But in my heart I know what is going on. Know I am feeling good and throwing freely, and throwing slop.

I know my arm is spent.

As we break camp and the season starts, my fastball remains AWOL. Bleakness sweeps over me. Anne and I now have two little girls and I have no backup plan if the Rangers let me go. No family business. No standing job offer. Nothing. Worse still, I have lost all belief in my ability to get big-league hitters out. Every time Buck calls for me, I feel as if I'm showing up for battle without a single weapon, using a peashooter against guys carrying bazookas.

Baseball isn't fun anymore, I think. I feel overmatched. I don't even want to come to the ballpark. I imagine a future making widgets on an assembly line.

So I look at Buck and Orel and Goose from the sofa, and I tell them:

I'll do it. I'll go to Oklahoma City. I'll become a full-time knuckleball pitcher and I promise you I'll give it everything I've got.

I stand up and shake hands with all three of them, a life-changing, seven-minute meeting complete. I feel as if a weight has been lifted, as if they're throwing a lifeline to me. Lightness doesn't come easily to me, but I walk out of there feeling almost buoyant, reminded of a quote from Romans 5:3–4 in the New Testament: "We rejoice in our sufferings, knowing that suffering produces endurance, and endurance produces character, and character produces hope…"

Hope is good. Long-term hope is even better. Packing up for my trip to Surprise, Arizona, the Rangers' winter home, to rehab my shoulder, I pause to Google every knuckleballer I can think of. I'm not looking for tips. I am looking to find out how many games they won after turning thirty years old. A few clicks yield the astounding truth:

Phil Niekro won 287 games after the age of thirty. Charlie Hough won 182. Phil's brother, Joe, won 163. Tom Candiotti won 122 and Wilbur Wood 105. Tim Wakefield has 156 and he is still going.

Add them all up, and the best knuckleballers of the last three or so decades have won over one thousand games in their thirties and beyond. Phil and Charlie weren't far from pitching with AARP cards in their pockets. It is one of the best perks about life in the knuckle world: because you don't throw it hard and you do no twisting or contorting, the knuckleball puts almost no strain on your arm. It enables you to not only eat innings but inhale them.

The same week that Buck and Orel and Goose sit down with me to redirect my future, Tim Wakefield dominates the Yankees twice in five days. Not that I need any more convincing, but it's good to know. I leave behind my career as a conventional pitcher with the paltry fifteen victories and the farcical 5.48 ERA, the precise reasons why the knuckleball is my only option.

I tell myself:

Who cares about throwing 90 miles per hour? I'm tired of being average, or worse. Tired of being lost, hiding on the margins of life and the Texas Rangers' roster.

Tired of pretending that I am something that I am not. I have no idea how this experiment is going to go, but I can't wait to find out.

Tonight I am pitching against the world-champion Giants. I am eager to get my season on a better track after a 1–3 start. This turns out to be unlike any night of pitching I've ever had.

Anne and the kids have just arrived from Tennessee. We are settling into our rented house in Manhasset, a Long Island community about a half hour east of Citi Field, doing it on about two hours of sleep, because our six-week-old baby, Van, isn't much interested in sleeping. Our oldest daughter, nine-year-old Gabriel, quickly makes friends with our neighbors, and in the late morning she is playing on one of those zip lines—where you hang on to a wheel as it slides along a clothesline-type wire—in their backyard. Gabriel is in mid-slide when she loses her grip. She falls hard. She braces herself with her right arm . . . and winds up fracturing it in two places.

I quickly put in a call to our trainer, Ray Ramirez, who recommends a hand specialist in Huntington, about twenty miles farther out on Long Island. Anne and the baby and Gabriel and I get in two separate cars and drive to the doctor's office. It's about 3:30 p.m.—about the time I usually get to the ballpark. The doctor sets Gabriel's arm and she is in fierce pain and very scared, and crying a lot. I hold her hand, wipe her tears, and try to comfort her. She gets a cast that goes all the way up her arm, wrapped in Mets colors.

"Daddy, I know you have to be at the field. I am keeping you from practice," Gabriel says to me. "You should go and get ready to pitch."

"You are way more important than the field," I tell her.

By the time we're done at the doctor, it's past 5 p.m. I walk Anne and Gabriel and baby Van out to the car. I kiss them good-bye. Gabriel is still in tears. As I drive to the ballpark, I am sad for Gabriel, sad I have to leave, but I also feel a strange sense of peace and God's mercy. I am ridiculously late for the game, but I am not frantic. Even when I get stuck in traffic on the Long Island Expressway, I am not frantic. I am grateful that I got to show—not just tell—my daughter how important she is to me. I got to show her how much I love her. I take my job very seriously, but when it comes down to it, being on time for a start or being there for my daughter when she has her first traumatic injury… well, it's not a tough call.

I get to the park about 6:10, an hour before game time. Nobody but Ray Ramirez knows what has gone on at this point. My routine is compressed, but I get into it, and get mentally ready to pitch. I set down six Giants in a row in the first two innings. I am off to a great start. I come off the mound thinking about how much I want to win the game for Gabriel. I fantasize about giving her the game ball, leaving it next to her bed when I get home. It is so sweet to think about it.

Alas, and ouch, the game doesn't unfold that way. The Giants knock me around for four hits and four runs in the third inning and I am gone after six innings. I wind up with a no-decision and we lose, 7–6. It is not remotely the ending I want, and I am certainly not happy about it, but as I drive back home, the sting is not so sharp as it usually is after a defeat. I am filled with thanks that I had been able to be there for my daughter. Earlier in my career, I am sure I would've just gone to the ballpark and let Anne handle it. I would've been completely consumed with my start. This is a big switch for me. It doesn't mean I care less about doing well as a big-league pitcher. It just means that I am able to have my priorities straight and be there for my daughter. When I walked in the door of our house after the game, I realized that this day was a special sort of gift from God—a day that centered much more on the importance of being a father than being a pitcher. It was a day when I was able to tell my daughter, "I'm going to be there for you, because you are more important than anything," and know that it wasn't a lie.

It was a day when I showed up. It was a day when I took a big step to break the dysfunctional cycle of my own experience as a kid. This is how families become healthier, how lives can change and children can be nourished. Moments such as this.

CHAPTER ELEVEN

REDHAWK REDUX

t's hard to throw the ball slow. It doesn't take long in my latest stint as an Oklahoma City RedHawk to learn that. After throwing thousands of pitches at 90 miles per hour or faster in my life, I am now floating some of them up there in the low sixties. It's as if I've traded in a sports car for a tricycle. My arm and my psyche are not wired for this. I have nobody coaching me, nobody holding my hand. On my own again, except now I yearn for help and it's not there. My pitching coach, Lee Tunnell, is as nice a man as you could ever meet. He'll talk pitching with me all day and half the night and would give me his own arm to help me if he could.

But he's like most everybody else in baseball: he doesn't know anything about the knuckleball.

I do some on-the-fly research. I go up and down the bench and ask the hitters: Have you ever faced a knuckleball pitcher? What was hard about it? What was easy about it? I start with Adrian Gonzalez, a kid first baseman and future superstar.

I hate hitting against knuckleball pitchers, he says. It messes up your balance, timing, everything.

Next up is Ian Kinsler, another star in waiting.

It's no fun because every knuckleball is different, he says.

I am heartened by the responses, because everyone who had ever faced a knuckleball thought they were a pain in the butt to hit.

I can do this, I tell myself. I can make this pitch work for me. I do a quick checkup of my new reality:

I am a knuckleball pitcher. I am committed to being a knuckleball pitcher. This is my last chance. I don't want to screw up my last chance.

My first start as a full-time knuckleballer is against the Iowa Cubs in Bricktown, the home ballpark of the RedHawks. This is my sixth year in Oklahoma City. I know the names of the vendors and the cleanup crew, am good friends with the cops, and have logged more miles up and down Mickey Mantle Drive, the main road outside the park, than any other RedHawk. I own more official team records, too, none of which I am in a rush to add to, because I don't want to be here very long.

An hour before first pitch, I duck into a little room wedged between the players' lounge and the kitchen.

I fall to my knees.

I clasp my hands.

I begin to pray. I don't pray for a no-hitter or a shutout, or for the best knuckleball since Phil Niekro no-hit the Padres in 1973. That would be tantamount to me playing God, choosing the outcome I want and asking God to rubber-stamp it.

I just pray with what I am feeling.

Please give me the strength and courage to stay the course and do my best, and to trust in Your will for me, no matter what the outcome.

The night turns out to be an excellent test of my trust, because I am horrible. The game resembles one long BP session for the Iowa Cubs. Line drives rain all around me. Our outfielders look as if they are in the Olympic trials, running wind sprints to the wall in pursuit of my swatted knuckleballs. I am behind hitters all night, can't throw a strike when I need it. Just before the Cubs' run total hits double figures, I pause on the mound in the midst of the carnage.

I rub up the ball. I look off to the horizon. I feel wretched. So wretched, I think I might vomit right there on the mound—the same disgust I felt in the Olympic bullpen when we were getting clubbed by Japan in 1996. I am not just embarrassed. I feel naked, exposed, a retread getting strafed without mercy. I knew there would be a learning curve, but did I ever expect this?

No, I did not.

A heated debate commences in my head, with my old pals, the voices:

VOICE ONE: *You need to go back to pitching conventionally. This is a disaster. You know it. The Cubs know it. Everybody in the park knows it.*

VOICE TWO: *You need to stick with the knuckleball. How can you even think about quitting on it so soon? What happened to being strong and staying the course? You need to stay with it.*

VOICE ONE: *You want to give up twenty runs? You want to be a complete laughingstock? This isn't working. Can't you see that? Go conventional.*

VOICE TWO: *You prayed for courage and I'm giving it to you.*
You have to think long-term, not about one outing. Stay with
the knuckleball.

When my manager, Bobby Jones, finally comes and gets me in
the sixth inning, my final pitching line is five and two-thirds innings, fourteen hits, twelve earned runs, five walks, no strikeouts.
I depart to a hearty chorus of boos, all of them richly deserved.
When Bobby gets back to the dugout, he finds me on the bench.

You are getting the ball again in five days, he says.

Okay, thanks. I'll be ready. After a fierce battle, Voice Two wins.
I am staying with the knuckleball.

I go out to the movies after the game to forget what happened.
Fat chance. I eat popcorn in the dark by myself—I don't even remember the movie—and tell myself again that I have to give everything I have to embrace this experiment. I am still not being honest
with myself, or Anne, or anyone, really. I am still trying to hide
from all of my shame. But I am not a kid. I am completely honest
with myself about one thing:

I am fighting for my professional baseball life. I need to turn the
page, and turn it fast. I need to learn what I can from this disaster
and make dang sure I am better next time. This is what athletes do:
process information and use it to get better.

I still have no knuckleball coach and no clue, but I do get better.
The next start, I give up six hits and four runs. I wind up winning
seven of my last eight decisions. I am not very good, but I am a lot
better than I was against the Iowa Cubs. The Rangers call me up
to rejoin them in September. Buck tells me I am going to start
against the Orioles. It is a hot Tuesday night.

I am petrified.

I am about to face major-league hitters for the first time throwing 60 or 70 miles per hour. I am thinking about survival, nothing more. I scan through the Orioles roster and look at their most dangerous hitters, guys like Miguel Tejada and Jay Gibbons. I go into the film room with Orel and study a video of Tim Wakefield pitching against the Orioles. I say a prayer, but I don't know what to expect.

The Orioles' leadoff hitter, Bernie Castro, hits a line-drive single to start the first. Melvin Mora, the number two hitter, follows with another lined single.

Two batters. Two hits.

Too much stress.

Then I walk Tejada. The game is three minutes old and I am in a bases-loaded, none-out jam.

Is this going to be the Iowa Cubs all over again? Can I handle it if it is?

Jay Gibbons steps up. All I can do is battle. That's it. I fall behind two and one, but I don't give in and get Gibbons to ground into a double play. I wind up giving up two runs, which is a lot better than where I thought the inning was going.

I settle down well enough to pitch seven innings of five-hit ball, giving up three runs. At this stage of my knuckleballing career, I will sign up for that every time. I am the most relieved man in Texas as I depart the mound.

Great job. Way to battle, Orel says. He waits a day or two to give me a more thorough review.

We want you to approach this more like Tim Wakefield, he says. We want you to throw more knuckleballs, and throw them slower.

About 65 percent of my pitches against the Orioles were knuckleballs. Orel wants that number at 80 percent or higher.

Your future is with the knuckleball. You've got to throw it more, he says.

The Rangers organization has been good to me. Orel has been good to me. I want to please them, so I do as they ask, even though I feel lost. I have no real feel or command for the pitch I'm throwing. I can't rely on my sinker or changeup if I get in a jam, because they want me to be Tim. I am going to do my best.

I go against the Mariners in my second start. I am committed to following Orel's instructions, throwing many more knuckleballs. I am full of fear. I try not to be, but my head isn't budging. I am in a throw-the-ball-and-hope-for-the-best place. I hate that place. I have always been a fighter. I take pride in being a fighter. From the time scouts started looking at me when I was in high school, I always got high marks for being a competitor who would go at the opposition with all I had, even if it wasn't much. I could grind out victories even when I didn't have my best stuff.

Now?

Now I am ashamed because I'm standing on the mound thinking that I am not good enough.

I try to convince myself that I am the same guy I was at Tennessee—the exact conversation I had with myself when I reported to the Rangers' minor-league camp after I signed and met Reid Nichols.

Remember the pitcher who threw 183 pitches to get the team into the College World Series and who threatened to fight the coach when he tried to take him out? That is who you are still, I tell myself.

I am having a hard time believing that. Because I feel like a pale imitation of that guy.

Somehow I get the victory against the Mariners, even though I give up six hits and six runs in five-plus innings. I struggle through the rest of the year. I have little idea of where the ball is going. I put up very shaky numbers. It all seems very precarious—until I meet the man who will change my knuckleballing life.

CHAPTER TWELVE

THE WORLD
ACCORDING TO CHARLIE

An old knuckleball pitcher named Charlie Hough is standing at my locker in the visitors' clubhouse in Anaheim, and truth be told, you wouldn't take him for a former ballplayer. He has the leathery look of a character from an old Western, a guy who has smoked too many cigarettes and used too little sunblock. He looks as if he'd spent most of his life squinting and the rest of it in a saloon. His shoulders are sloped, his hands weathered, his crow's-feet all but carved into the corners of his eyes. I'd heard the stories about his bullpen sessions; how he'd drag on a cigarette, put it down at the end of the rubber, and throw a pitch. Then he'd pick the butt up and take another puff, and keep the pitch/puff routine up until his work was done or his pack was empty.

That would be funny to watch, I think.

No, Charlie Hough isn't going to turn up on the cover of *Men's Journal* or put George Clooney out of work, but then, a leading man is not what I am after. Expertise is what I am after, and Charlie Hough has that in abundance. He pitched twenty-five seasons in the big leagues and won 162 games after the age of thirty-four. He'd been an all-star, a workhorse, an indefatigable pitching force who once threw 285 innings and became an eighteen-game winner for the Rangers.

Meeting Charlie Hough, for me, is akin to meeting Cy Young himself.

Like a hyped-up schoolkid, I start peppering Charlie with questions within minutes of shaking his hand, the subject, of course, being baseball's most mysterious, most misnamed, and most unappreciated pitch.

It is a pitch, I am learning, that is as hard to predict as it is to catch.

Or as Charlie once said: "Butterflies aren't bullets. You can't aim 'em. You just let 'em go."

The Rangers want Charlie to take a look at me and assess my prospects for succeeding as a knuckleball pitcher. I want him to teach me everything he knows. We have a lot to get done. I look at his squinty face and think: *This is probably how it feels to talk about the Bible with the pope, or about social networking with Mark Zuckerberg.*

Let's see you throw, Charlie says to me.

We make our way down the tunnel to the dugout, across the field, to the bullpen, shoulder to shoulder, the sensei and the student. I am nervous.

What if Charlie tells the Rangers he thinks my knuckleball stinks? What if he tells them it is his considered opinion that this four-month-old experiment—reinventing R. A. Dickey, a long-ago phenom and ninety-three-mile-per-hour sinkerballer, into a flutterballer—is going nowhere?

I hate my insecurities. I do my best to ignore them.

Why did you start throwing your knuckleball? I ask him.

I hurt my arm in the minor leagues, he says. I started throwing it for the same reason almost all of us do: because it was my only chance of getting to the big leagues.

How long did it take you to learn it?

I learned how to throw it in a day, but it took me most of a career to be able to throw it for strikes. And that's the key to everything. You can have the best knuckleball in the world and it ain't worth a darn thing if you can't get it over the plate.

How do you learn to control it? What can I do to speed up my learning curve?

You throw it and you keep throwing it. You throw it every day. You find guys to catch you. You throw it against outfield walls. You throw it against alley walls. You keep at it. It takes time and it takes patience to get the feel for it and to master it, and even after you think you have, you better have a real thick skin if you are going to be a knuckleball pitcher.

Why is that?

Because you are going to have games when you throw five wild pitches or give up four home runs—games when you just don't have it. Every pitcher is going to have games when he doesn't have it, even Hall of Fame pitchers. The difference is that when you have an ugly game as a knuckleball pitcher, it's really ugly. It's going to happen, I promise you. You have to keep faith in yourself and your pitch, even if everybody else loses faith.

In the bullpen, I anxiously throw a dozen or so knuckleballs for Charlie. He asks me to show him my grip, and I hold the ball up with the fingernails of my index and middle fingers biting into the runway, the part of the ball where the seams come closest together. He suggests I move my nails to just underneath the horseshoe, a small change but actually a completely different grip.

I think you'll find it's a better way to kill the spin and control the pitch, Charlie says.

I do as he says, throwing a pitch with his grip. It feels weird. I keep throwing. The weirdness never lifts—not that day, not for days and weeks afterwards—but I stay with it.

I never throw a ball with my old grip again.

And from that day forward, I never fail to take the mound without thinking about staying inside the doorframe, either.

Charlie is big on visuals, and the doorframe is the best of them. After watching my delivery, with an overhead windup and arms and legs extending in various directions, Charlie stops me and tells me to imagine a doorway. Imagine throwing the pitch in such a way that all of your movements, and your limbs, are confined to that opening.

If you are flying all over—if your hand is hitting the side of the imaginary doorframe—what's going to happen? he asks. The ball will be more likely to spin. Spin is the enemy, especially backward spin. You want to simplify things. You want fewer moving pieces and to have all those pieces moving forward toward the plate.

Why is spin so bad?

Because the knuckleballs that spin are the ones you don't get back, Charlie says. Maybe you can get away with a little forward spin, but backward spin? Forget it. Those are the ones that sit up. Those are the ones that wind up way back in the seats.

I nod, and start trying to control my limbs, to stay inside the doorway. My mind is tumbling, trying to process all the new information. I throw for Charlie on successive days. After about a hundred pitches on the second day, Charlie tells me to stop. We head back across the field. I am drenched in sweat and doubt. I don't have any feel for how I've done. Charlie is a jolly, affable man, but he's also totally old-school, not one to go overboard with compliments. Finally I get up my courage and ask him straight-out.

Do you think I can do this?

He squints at me and gives me a tight little smile.

I think you have a chance, he says.

THE KNUCKLEBALL is the only pitch in baseball that works by doing nothing. Curveballs curve. Cutters cut. Sinkers sink. The knuckleball? You want it to float to the plate, rotation-free, and let the laws of entropy or aerodynamics or whatever else is in play take over from there, the air rushing around it, the seams creating a drag, the ball wobbling and wiggling and shimmying and shaking. Or not. Sometimes the knuckleball will be unhittable and sometimes it will be uncatchable, but rarely is it predictable. You can throw two knuckleballs with the identical release, the identical motion, in the identical place, and one might go one way and the second might go another way. It's one of the first things you have to accept as a knuckleballer: the pitch has a mind of its own. You either embrace it for what it is—a pitch that is reliant on an amalgam of forces both seen and unseen—or you allow it to drive you half out of your mind.

I embrace it.

If you like order and logic to your baseball world, you better find another pitch to throw. If you like your manager to fully understand what you are doing, you better change pitches too. Midway through my year with the Mariners in 2008, manager Jim Riggleman walked up to me one day and basically said he had no idea how to manage me or help me. Terry Collins said pretty much the same thing when he took over the Mets in 2011. I didn't take it as an insult. I took it as honesty.

Baseball people are loath to trust the knuckleball and quick to judge it. If there were a caste system of baseball pitches, the knuckleball would be the untouchables. This isn't idle knuckleballer's paranoia. It's the truth. What happens when a conventional pitcher gets lit up and is knocked out in the fourth inning? What do you hear?

"He couldn't command his breaking stuff."

"He didn't have his good fastball."

"He was working from behind in the count."

There are umpteen reasons why the guy's getting hit. When Tim Wakefield or I get roughed up, it's that weirdo pitch we throw. You never know what you are going to get with it. You just can't trust it.

Because it's a dadgum knuckleball.

The knuckleball's lowly status, I'm convinced, has everything to do with velocity. Or lack of it. Baseball is completely obsessed with speed, with the readings on the ubiquitous radar guns—devices that have done more to screw up the evaluation of pitchers than probably anything else in the history of the game. Pitchers want to know what they hit on the things. People go nuts if somebody registers triple digits . . . and go into a full panic if the numbers slip. I'm not saying the radar gun can't be a useful measuring stick at times, but to reduce pitching to little red digits on a machine is absurd. Ray Miller, the venerable pitching coach, once described pitching as the art of missing bats. You miss bats with location and deception and by messing up a hitter's timing. You don't just miss them with a 99-mile-per-hour heater. Greg Maddux is lucky he isn't coming up now: he might have a hard time getting out of Double-A ball.

Is it any wonder that knuckleballers stick together? We may not have anybody else, but we have each other. We are part of the game's tightest fraternity. You don't often see guys who throw splitters or circle changeups trading tips or techniques, but knuckleballers do it all the time. When I was in the American League and we were facing the Red Sox and Tim Wakefield was on the mound, I always rooted the same way: for Wake to pitch a great game, and for us to win. Knuckleballers may be a freak show at sixty feet six inches, but the freaks stick together.

My first throwing session with Charlie convinces me that I need to spend more time with him. Twice in that offseason I go out to see him at his home in California. We head out to a ball field at Cypress College. I throw and throw some more, and because I'm not stressing my arm by maxing out the velocity, I can keep on throwing.

Pitch count should never be an issue for you again, Charlie says.

With every pitch, I stick with Charlie's grip, staying inside Charlie's doorframe. I am starting to get it, though I am still confused.

How do I know when I've thrown a good one? I ask.

You'll know by how it comes out of your hand. You'll know in that instant. You won't need to see it cross the plate or see a batter swing.

If the knuckleball is so effective, how come so few people throw it? I ask.

Because it's really hard and it takes a lot of patience. More patience than most people have, he says.

Ten thousand? Twenty thousand? Fifty thousand? I don't know how many knuckleballs I throw that winter, but it's a lot. A whole lot. I throw the bulk of them against a white cinder-block wall in the gym of the Ensworth School in Nashville. My uncle Ricky is the athletic director at Ensworth. He lets me come in and borrow the wall. I don't want a catcher. I just want to be with the wall and my bucket of balls. I start at forty feet from the wall, then back up to fifty feet, then sixty. I am there most every day, throwing for up to an hour. Some days are better than others. On the bad days, the ball feels as foreign as a hunk of volcanic rock. On the bad days, the sound of me screaming bounces off the gym walls.

I still can't get the feel for this pitch, I tell myself. *I still don't have any consistency with it.*

I keep throwing, and keep thinking of Larry Bird in his number 33 Boston Celtics uniform as I throw. Bird did an interview once where he talked about never letting himself be outworked, about being haunted by a fear that somebody, somewhere, was taking shots while he was resting.

I don't want anybody to outwork *me*, either. I may not make it as a big-league knuckleballer, but it won't be from lack of effort. So I keep throwing against the cinder blocks, picking out a particular block to hit with every pitch, knowing that whatever happens, I will never regret not putting in more time. Even when I'm not in Uncle Ricky's gym, I am working. I keep a baseball in my car and drive around Nashville with only my left hand on the wheel so I can practice my knuckleball grip with my right hand.

When I drive our daughter Gabriel to nursery school, the ball is in my right hand.

When I run out to get diapers or go to the bank, the ball is in my right hand.

It's another one of Charlie's suggestions. There's no substitute for having the ball in your hand. I still keep a baseball in my car. You never stop working on your grip.

I go back to Charlie's for a one-week refresher in early February, right before I head to Surprise, Arizona, for spring training. I am beginning to feel what he's talking about, feel when I've got it right. I can tell by the friction of the ball as it leaves my fingernails, by the way it slides out of my hand. It feels almost as though the ball has an agreement with you: Okay, you throw me right, and I'm going to dance like no ball you've ever seen.

You're coming along, Charlie says. You're starting to get it.

I have no idea if I can make the Rangers in 2006 and make a living getting big-league hitters out with my knuckleball, but I know I'm better than I was at the end of 2005. I show up early in Surprise, a journeyman in search of a no-spin zone. I ride my bike to the park and have most of my meals at Arby's to save money. Every day I fill up a five-gallon bucket with baseballs and go to the batting cage and throw knuckleballs into the net. Then, right before lunch, I corral Andy Hawkins, the former big-league pitcher and our Triple-A pitching coach, and throw another three or four dozen knucklers to him. Andy wasn't a knuckleball pitcher, but he gives me helpful information about my motion, my arm angle, and the spin.

After a few weeks, I notice he's not catching the ball as often. I am hitting him in the knee, the groin, the stomach.

I'm going to have to start wearing armor, he says.

I've never been happier about hurting someone.

I start a game against the Japanese national team, which is getting ready for the World Baseball Classic. I pitch well and strike out Ichiro Suzuki twice. In another start I shut down the Cubs for five innings. When I started throwing the knuckleball, I threw maybe two good ones out of ten. Now I am throwing five or six good ones out of ten.

One afternoon, after throwing on a back field at the Rangers complex, I ride back to the clubhouse with Goose Connor, who has replaced Orel Hershiser as pitching coach. Goose is behind the wheel of a golf cart, with me riding shotgun. Like Charlie, he is not inclined to gush or give you a football-style pep talk. His encouragement is much more measured. He's like a background vocalist: never flashy, but you sure like listening, because he's always solid and steady.

Keep doing what you're doing, Goose says.

It's getting to be the end of camp. The Rangers of that era are not known for pitching. They're known for having a completely stacked lineup that tries to outscore the opposition. When one of the projected starters, Adam Eaton, gets hurt in spring training, it looks as though there are at least one or two starting spots that Buck and Goose are looking to fill.

Am I ready to be a starting pitcher as a knuckleballer? Can I help the Rangers win? My anxiety about making the club builds by the day. In my heart, I know I'm not yet where I want to be with the pitch. I also know I am getting close. The thought of going back to the RedHawks for a seventh season and hearing more chatter about running for mayor is not anything I want to dwell on. I pray for calmness and for the strength to keep working on my craft. Whatever the Rangers decide, I know God will not present me with anything I cannot handle.

On a late March afternoon, a clubhouse guy comes over to my locker.

Buck wants to see you in his office, he says.

Okay, thanks. I swallow hard. The moment of truth has arrived.

Have I shown them enough? Am I big leaguer again?

I'm not sure what to expect.

I walk across the clubhouse into Buck's little office in the back of the room. Goose is there with him. I try to read their faces as I walk in the room, but they're giving nothing away. I think again about Bird and how I have nothing to be ashamed of even if the news isn't good.

Buck's blue eyes fix on me. He wastes no time with preambles.

Congratulations, R.A., he says. You've worked your tail off and you've made the club. You are going to be in the rotation.

I pause a minute and let it sink in. I'm not stunned, but it's still a life-changing thing to hear.

Thanks, Buck, I say. I really appreciate your faith in me and all the ways the club has supported me. I shake his hand and Goose's hand and walk/float back across the clubhouse. I call Anne and my new agent, Bo McKinnis, and then I call the man who made it all possible.

Charlie Hough.

Hey, Charlie, this is R.A. I made the club. I just wanted to thank you again for all your help.

Woo-hoo, Charlie says. This is Charlie's all-purpose exclamation. Whenever I throw a good knuckleball in front of him, that's what he always says: Woo-hoo. It's as good as it gets from Charlie. Woo-hoo.

We open the season against the Red Sox, at home. I am starting the fourth game of the year, against the Detroit Tigers. It is not only a new season. It is a fresh start, a whole new career.

I say a prayer of thanks. I can't wait to get on the mound.

Minute Maid Park, Houston

Thank you, Aaron Harang, wherever you are. I don't mean this flippantly, or obnoxiously. I mean it sincerely. I've never met Aaron Harang, a pitcher for the Padres, but he gives me a lift today and doesn't even know it. Whenever I have a rough outing—and I had a brutal one here today—I have a strange custom: I go on my laptop and surf baseball websites until I find somebody who had an even worse day than me. It's not that I delight in other people's misfortune; it's just that misery does like company, and after my eighth start of the year I am definitely looking for somebody to point to and say, "Hey, this guy's a respectable pitcher and he got lit up too." Harang gave up nine hits and seven runs in four and a third innings against the Rockies. Today he supplies the comfort.

I feel less miserable for knowing this.

Against the last-place Astros, I give up six hits in the first inning, get myself into a four-run hole, and wind up seeing my record fall to 1–5 and my ERA climb to 5.08. Man, is that a stink bomb of an ERA. A complete embarrassment. I settle down after the first and use a lot of fastballs and changeups for a few innings to get back into the game, but then in the sixth I get taken out of the park by Bill Hall and a pinch hitter named Matt Downs on an 0–2 pitch. My final line is 6 innings, 11 hits, 6 runs. My worst start of the year, by far.

If there is good news, it's what I feel now, in my hotel room. Though I feel lonely and almost grief-stricken about the start, I can tell the feelings don't consume me the way they once did. That is a big switch for me. It used to be that after a bad outing I'd take it out on everybody: I'd be a bad father and a bad husband and not a very good teammate, either. Now, thanks to the grace of God, I am able to keep my gaze fixed on things above. I do not get all worked up over critical media reports or bad statistics or lost games the way I once did. I passionately want to turn this season around and do well, but I truly believe that if this year doesn't go as I'd hoped, it only means that God has something even better in store for me. What a peace of mind that knowledge gives me. I don't know how Aaron Harang is holding up after his debacle, but after mine I am doing okay. I really am. I am already thinking about how I can't wait for my next start. I remain unshaken in my conviction that I am better than this—much better.

I know some people in the organization who are getting mighty nervous—and maybe even panicking—thinking I am reverting back to the pitcher I was before I came to the Mets. But I honestly don't feel too far away from where I was last year. I truly feel like I just need to stay the course and continue to work as hard as I normally do and this poor beginning will turn. The problem is that, like most folks, I am not judged in my occupation based on my feelings but rather my output, and my performance thus far—let's be honest—has been shoddy. The dichotomy between what you believe you can do and what you actually are doing can wreak all sorts of havoc on your confidence. Being able to walk that tightrope well is something that separates good from great. To lament a bad outing is *healthy, but to let it take you to a place of despair is competitive death. I am thankful that my frustration is motivating me to work harder, and trust that the hard work will pay off and that my knuckleball can—and will—get big-league hitters out consistently.*

I have to believe that. If I don't, why am I even here?

CHAPTER THIRTEEN

KNUCKLEBALLER NON GRATA

I am pedaling a ten-speed bicycle through the darkness, getting out of Dodge before any more baseballs fly over the fence. Baseball has records for everything. There's probably a record for most doubles by a second baseman on an overcast Tuesday. Now I am two-wheeling on a back road toward a T.G.I. Friday's, about the last place I want to be, thinking about my newest historical claim to fame:

Shortest-lived euphoria to start a season.

How could it get any shorter, really? One minute I am heady with the news that I am in the Rangers' rotation, starting what I am thinking will be my thriving second career, as a knuckleballer. The next I am joining my fellow knuckleballer, Tim Wakefield, in long-ball lore, giving up six home runs to the Detroit Tigers.

One minute my wife is in town with my father-in-law to celebrate my new beginning and to look for a nice rental home to live in for the season. The next I am thinking that I may not need a house in Texas after all.

I park the bike outside the restaurant and find Anne and her father, Sam, at a table in the back. The back always suits me fine. I really want no part of dinner or the ersatz T.G.I.F. nostalgia, but I had told Anne I would join them after the game, never imagining that I would be doing so after making one of the worst starts in the last hundred years.

So I honor the commitment. I sit down and order my usual beverage: sweet tea. Anne comes from a long line of problem solvers, successful people who bore into troubles like miners drilling into bedrock. And so it begins again, she and her father launching their fact-finding mission before I've even chosen an appetizer: What was wrong with your knuckleball tonight? What can you do to correct it? Should you be throwing more of your conventional pitches?

The questions are well-meaning. They don't know what to say, so I think they figure they'll help me analyze things and find a solution. I do not want to analyze anything in that moment—not the game, not my career.

Nothing.

I just want to get through my Jack Daniel's chicken and bike back to the Hyatt. A few times I shoot Anne a vaguely dirty look, a Do-we-really-need-to-do-this-now? look. I am terrible company. I give them terse, disinterested answers and mope and pick at my chicken. I am still half in shock, and that's how I behave.

Back in the hotel later that night, Anne and I pray together before we go to bed, holding hands, asking God for comfort, peace, and another opportunity. I have a crappy night of sleep. I just hope that tomorrow is better. Early the next morning, I open the curtains to a perfect Texas morning, the sky deep blue. I say out loud, for Anne and myself, "Let's remember, God's mercies are new every morning."

I barely finish saying "Amen" when I look down and see a white

Hummer pull up to the hotel. A strapping young man gets out of the car. When he turns around I get a look at his face.

It is Rick Bauer.

I had met him in spring training. He is a former Orioles draft pick whom the Rangers signed after the 2005 season. He was slated to start the season in Oklahoma City. Now he's checking into the Hyatt. You don't have to be a sabermetrician to connect the dots. Bauer, a six-foot-six-inch right-hander, is here to join the big club, which means that somebody will be leaving the big club.

That somebody is going to me, I am pretty sure.

A shiny new Hummer delivering my shiny new replacement. Not exactly the answer to my prayer I was looking for.

When I get to the clubhouse that afternoon, Buck calls me into his office right away. It's the same office where my knuckleballing career began almost a year earlier. Buck closes the door. General manager Jon Daniels and Goose Connor are in the office too. Buck has always been a big supporter of mine. He played the game, had some good years, but never got out of the minors. I know he doesn't want to be doing this.

I am positive of it. But business is business.

We need a fresh arm for the bullpen. We had to use a lot of arms last night and we're short. We're going to send you out to Oklahoma City, he says.

I look at him and don't say anything for a minute, for a good reason. I am crushed.

This will be my seventh season as an Oklahoma City RedHawk. It's a town I've grown very fond of, but nonetheless a place that I associate totally with my mediocrity as a pitcher. I already own all the RedHawk pitching records. Is this going to be the top line of my baseball résumé: a RedHawk immortal? Is this how it's going to end for me: another sad-eyed prospect playing out the string on the prairie in front of a thousand fans and a mascot?

It's not quite how I envisioned it as a little kid.

Of course, I was brutal the night before. Nobody needs to tell me that. I just never thought I'd get only one start to prove myself.

One start? Are you kidding me? I've been with the Rangers my whole career. It's the only team I ever wanted to play for.

Now I'm thinking I may have worn a Rangers uniform for the last time.

Jon and Buck and Goose are quiet and are almost ghost-like in their pallor. I take a moment to collect myself.

Don't lose it, hang on, I tell myself. *Keep it together.*

When I think I've collected myself, I stand up and look squarely at each of them in succession. My voice starts to crack.

I understand why you are doing this, but I just want to tell you one thing: that outing last night will not define me as a big-league pitcher. It won't. I can promise you that.

I shake their hands and go to my locker and throw my stuff in a bag. I scan the room and wonder if I'll ever be in a big-league clubhouse again.

When I walk out this door, will that be it?

I pack up the hotel room. I wonder how Rick Bauer is going to do. Anne flies home with her dad so I can drive the car to Oklahoma City. She wants to come to Oklahoma with me, but I want to be alone. I want to brood. I head north on Interstate 35, out of Texas and the big leagues, a stretch of road I know all too well. It is hot and quiet and the red earth just goes on and on. I cross into Oklahoma and pass through towns named Lone Grove and Springer and Joy. I pass a sign for Crazy Horse Municipal Airport and a place called Slaughterville.

Slaughterville. How perfect. It's where I spent the night before, getting butchered by the Detroit Tigers.

It's a place I never want to go back to again.

TWO DAYS after I arrive back in Oklahoma City, Jon Daniels calls me. I am in the office of RedHawks manager Mike Boulanger, alone. Jon tells me that the club is taking me off the forty-man roster again, or designating me for assignment, as they say in base-ballspeak. (I had been put back on the forty-man when I made the big club.) So I am a used resin bag again, completely expendable.

The Rangers figure there is no risk of losing me, because—let's face it—what's the market for a thirty-one-year-old knuckleballer who has just given up six home runs?

The Rangers are right. Not a single club in the major leagues claims me. So I stay a RedHawk, go right into the rotation, and perform miserably. In one twenty-three-inning stretch, I give up eight home runs. Through my first eight starts, my record is 2–5 and my ERA is over 7.00. My shoulder's barking and we decide to give it a rest and I spend a few weeks on the disabled list. I am marginally better when I come back. I try to keep in mind that I am still a knuckleballing novice, but how can I not wonder where this is going—where my life is going?

This switch to knuckleballing was supposed to make things better, not worse. I have so many questions, so many worries. Baseball is the least of them.

ANNE IS PREGNANT with our third child that summer. It should be a joyful time, with our two healthy girls and a baby boy on the way, but it's not. I am worried sick about money, for one thing. We've just bought a house in Nashville. Anne and the kids stay there so we can save on the cost of a rental house in Oklahoma City. I go back to my nomadic days, staying with a pastor friend, at a Red Roof Inn, or at an Econo Lodge for $70 a night. When we go on the road, I check out of the hotel and haul my stuff to the clubhouse, then haul it back to the hotel when we return. I spend hours poring over our bank accounts and credit card bills and mortgage payments, trying to make the numbers work. We may not be going under, but I have a hard time seeing beyond my financial fears. I didn't grow up with money, and when you are not used to having it, you want to hold on to every penny. I will troll around the Internet for hours trying to save fifty bucks on an air conditioner. If you give me the choice between a label and a bargain, I'm going for the bargain. Anne grew up in a notable Nashville family, with money.

Guess what one of our biggest marital issues is?

Hint: it's not my pitch selection.

One day that summer Anne goes to a flea market, looking for something to put on the front porch of our new house. She finds these beautiful decorative urns. In a typical store they would probably be $300 each. In the flea market they are $100 for the pair. She knows how concerned about money I am and does a great job finding a bargain for something that she wants for our home. She calls me to talk about it. I immediately step into the hallway of a hotel somewhere in Middle America; you never want to have an argument with your wife in front of your roommate.

What do we need decorative urns for? What's the point of it, other than to clutter up the porch? I say.

I really like them, R.A. They will look so nice. They fit perfectly and they really don't cost much when you compare it to getting them from a store.

I don't give a crap what they cost in a store. A hundred bucks is a hundred bucks. Our resources are not infinite. We can live without decorative urns for now, don't you think?

I keep badgering her. I am being totally controlling. A complete jerk. It's not as if Anne is being reckless. On the contrary, she is being careful. She wants our home to look nice. I keep trying to beat her down, with my harshness and criticism.

Go ahead and get your urns, I say. But don't complain to me when the next check you write bounces. Anne gets the urns. They're lovely, I hear. They get stolen off the porch a month later.

It's one more thing to argue about, one more marital sparring session.

Between mounting financial pressure on one side and mounting baseball pressure on the other, I feel like Luke Skywalker, Chewbacca, Han Solo, and Princess Leia from *Star Wars*: Episode IV when they fall into a trash compactor and the walls start closing in on them. It feels as if the trash is getting squeezed right up in my face. That seems about right.

Because I feel like trash. I feel like trash for lots of reasons, one much bigger than the rest.

I have strayed.

I have broken a vow I made to Anne and to God. I have become what I promised to myself I would never become: a caricature of a lustful ballplayer. I am not a serial offender, and do not sleep all over town, but the scope of it doesn't matter. What matters is the breach of trust.

I look in the mirror and I hate what I see, what I have evolved into. I feel distant from Anne, distant from myself. Even more, I feel like a fraud, in that the R.A. the world knows is so different from the R.A. who *I* know. I feel scared and burdened, and those feelings are overpowering my wobbly faith. So I resort to my time-worn strategy: I run. I escape. I get lost in books and go to movies, sitting in the back and eating popcorn. I play baseball for a living, which is an escape in itself. It is a life that can make you a perennial adolescent, where your needs and whims are catered to, and narcissism is as prevalent as sunflower seeds, a life that is about as un-family-friendly as you can imagine. People see the glamour and the big money of being a ballplayer, but they may not see the dysfunction and profound stresses it puts on wives and children. You are away for six weeks in spring training, and then you flit in and out of your family's life for the next six months. You say "good-bye" more than any other word in the English language, and even if you try to be a dedicated family man, you invariably miss things. Hugely important things.

You know where I was when our daughter, Lila, was born? In a Chick-fil-A in the Dallas/Fort Worth International Airport, trying to get a connection flight home.

You know where I was when our son, Elijah, was born? In the visitor's clubhouse in Round Rock, Texas, right before a start, my mother-in-law holding up the phone as Anne Dickey was giving birth. (There was no such thing as paternity leave in the minor leagues in 2006.)

When you are away so much, almost every conversation back home seems to be conducted in a pressure cooker, where you talk about new tires for the car, kids' ear infections, and the swelling cell phone bill, all in rapid order.

If you have any self-awareness at all, you realize how uneven the distribution of responsibilities is. Your wife is going to the pediatrician and calling the plumber and meeting with the teacher, and you are working on your knuckleball grip in a bullpen session.

Your wife is reading bedtime stories and checking for monsters in the closet and then getting up first thing for school, while you are hanging with the guys after a game and sleeping until eleven in the morning. Don't get me wrong: I work hard at what I do. I want to make the most out of every appearance on a big-league mound. And I love my work, and feel blessed to be doing it. But at the top level, let's face it, it's an otherworldly existence in which there's all this adulation and fanfare and you travel by charter jet and stay in $350-per-night hotels, and it's as if the whole world is telling you, not very subtly: You are very, very special.

I know in my heart I am no more special than any other of God's children. I know that the kid in the clubhouse and the attendant in the parking lot are just as important in the universe as I am, and maybe more so. Maybe they are doing more to make a difference and to help people. Maybe they are more faithful to their beliefs. I'm just a flawed human being with an unreliable knuckleball, and in the summer of 2006 those flaws feel as if they are overwhelming everything else in my life.

I feel inadequate in every way possible: in my walk with God and especially in my role as husband and life partner to the former Anne Bartholomew. I am not giving her what she needs—and what she deserves. I have a picture of what a good husband should be. He is loving and kind and patient and loyal and makes his wife feel as if she is the only woman in the world. He knows how to tend to her heart.

I have no idea how to tend to her heart. That is not close to who I am. I am aloof and not often physically affectionate. I don't routinely grab her hand or tell her how much I love her or surprise her with flowers.

I retreat from intimacy. Intimacy terrifies me. I know, more unconsciously than consciously, that it has everything to do with my past and the horror of my sexual abuse. My experiences have obviously shaped me, but I don't live in the past anymore. I live in the present. When am I going to have the courage to face the demons I've been hiding and fleeing from my whole life? I can't help but feel that if Anne had to do it again, she would want no part of marrying me. I feel alone. So does she.

Sometimes I wonder if you even love me. *Do* you love me? she asks.

Of course I love you.

Then why don't you show it? Why are you always getting angry at me and tearing me down? Why are you tender and loving with the kids and not with me?

Well, it's different with the kids. They need that affection. They need to feel loved and secure.

Don't you understand that I need it too? Why am I the last one on line?

You aren't last. I don't know. It's just easier with the kids.

Why is it easier? Why can't you show me that you love me too? Why is that so hard?

Anne is 100 percent right, of course. But I can't admit it. I am too walled off, too defensive. I find excuses. I blame it on her and her spending habits. I blame it on my bad ERA. I blame it on anything but myself. I go into rages and I am ashamed of that, and even more ashamed that I have lied to Anne and deceived her.

Before we got married I told her I was a virgin, and I was not. I never told her that I was sexually abused and never told her that I was exposed to pornography at a young age, the same summer that the abuse happened. I never told her how physical touch had become something I associated with being violated and bullied and taken advantage of. She had a right to know all of that and I didn't tell her because I was afraid I would lose her.

Or was the guilt and shame so powerful, there was no way to begin to even speak about it?

So I clammed up. Made stuff up. That was unfair and manipulative, and now she finds herself in a marriage with a guy who may be well-meaning but is doing everything possible to push her away. A guy who is damaged.

A guy who, like so many other sexually abused children, is tormented and shamed.

I am having a difficult year on the mound, and an even worse one in my marriage. Every time Anne and I talk, I hold out hope that it will be amiable, but most of the time we argue.

One afternoon in early August, eight and a half months pregnant, Anne calls me. In the clubhouse. She has never done that before. She never would.

I think the worst. Has something happened to one of the kids?

We need to talk. You need to come home now, Anne says. She's hysterical.

What's wrong?

Come home now, she says. If you want any chance at having this marriage work, you need to come home now.

I can barely swallow. My throat feels constricted. All around me, guys are getting ready for the game. I have an idea what I am getting ready for, and I deserve it.

I tell Mike Boulanger that I have to take a three-day personal leave. He sees the look on my face and says, Go. I get a six a.m. flight

to Nashville. As the plane descends, I look out at the Nashville sky-
line, terrified about what is going to unfold with Anne.

Carter Crenshaw, our pastor, meets me at the airport.

I am praying for you and Anne, but the one thing I can tell you
is that you have to be completely honest with her, Carter says.

Anne is at her parents' house. When I see her for the first time,
her eyes are red. She looks as if she's been crying for days. I want to
dissolve into the rug in her father's office. The wood still looks three
feet thick and I feel about three inches tall.

Jen, a family friend and therapist, is there to offer support and
help us through the process.

I want you to tell me everything, Anne says.

I don't know what to say, where to begin. I'm responsible for her
pain. My guilt is overwhelming. The next two hours are excruciating. I leave the house not knowing if our marriage will survive. I
leave wondering if I'll be one of those fathers who can see his kids
only on Tuesdays, Thursdays, and every other weekend.

My heart isn't in baseball, but I have a job I have to hold on to,
a paycheck we need. I finish the season with the RedHawks with a
9–8 record and a 4.92 ERA, the sort of numbers that get you released. I have no clue where I am going. I have no clue if I'm going
to get home after the season and be a single dad. I pack up my stuff
at the end of the year, my eleventh in pro baseball. I drive back to
Nashville and get off Interstate 40 East at Exit 204 and go straight
to West End Community Church, where I am meeting Anne and
Carter. I pull into the parking lot. I pray for God's mercy. I know I
do not deserve it.

CHAPTER FOURTEEN

THE BOTTOM

B ad things go through your head when you spend too much time alone with your shame. Horrible things. This is where I am at the end of September. When the season is over, I return to Nashville and move into our old house (we still haven't sold it), while Anne and the kids are in the new one. This is how Anne wants it for now.

I'm not sure if I can trust you, she says. I'm afraid that you are a different person from the person I thought you were.

I don't try to talk her out of it. There's no point in that. This isn't about winning an argument. It's about regaining her trust.

It's about rebuilding what has been broken.

That is not an easy thing to do after you have been unfaithful.

It is not easy at all.

How could you do this? How could you lie to me and deceive me? Anne asks.

She deserves to have answers. She deserves that and a lot more. There is nothing I can say to convey how sorry I am. Nothing.

I don't blame you for feeling angry and betrayed, because I did betray you. All I can do is come to you humbly and admit my wrong and ask for your forgiveness.

Maybe in time I can forgive you, she says. But I don't know when that will be. I am just so scared. I trusted you so completely. Do you know how much I trusted that you were an honorable man?

What can I tell her?

Nothing. That is what I can tell her.

I don't even know how it happens. It's not planned, and there's little emotional attachment to the person. There's just a sense of escape, a no-strings-attached simplicity to it. The affair just happens, and then it's over, except for my guilt and shame over committing a sin and shattering a marital vow. Those things do not go away, ever. They are things I live with every day.

Every morning for an hour I meet with Carter. I tell him everything, share every last failing of mine. Carter is compassionate towards me but he doesn't baby me, and I don't want him to baby me.

You have to stay in the ring and take Anne's punches and not fight back, he says. You have to own everything you did.

I stay in the ring, and I stay in the old house too. I walk in the yellow front door and look at a mostly empty living room. I sleep, or try to sleep, on a white couch with red flowers. I see Anne and the kids during the day and go back to the house at night. It is dark and lonely. *I* am dark and lonely, so it's a good fit. Things are so bad, Anne is thinking of changing the locks on the house, fearful that I might drive over and pick up the kids and take off. I stare out the window and take an inventory of my sorry life.

I am a minor-league lifer whose career has been one prolonged disappointment.

I am a man who was sexually abused as a child, with no equipment to deal with that trauma.

I am a man who desperately wants to bury the truth of his past, but there's no hole deep enough to do it. I am a hypocrite, a man who masquerades as a devout Christian who has betrayed his wife and God.

My self-esteem is so low, it doesn't even have a reading. God has blessed me with health and intelligence and a beautiful family, and look at where I've led them. I've turned my life into a hopeless tangle of problems.

I lie in the darkness and pray for God's help, but I am fighting it.

Why would God want to help someone like me? I think.

Because He's infinite and compassionate and He forgives you, I remind myself.

One morning I wake up on the couch and feel a bleakness I've never experienced before. I don't know what triggers it. It doesn't matter.

Maybe I should just end it now. Maybe it's time for me to stop all this pain once and for all.

I think about options. Carbon monoxide? That's a possibility. We just built a new garage; the old carport would've had too much fresh air.

A knife or a gun? Not in a million years. I don't like blades or bullets.

What about going out and enlisting in the Army and going to Iraq, or having a high-speed car wreck without a seat belt? That should get the job done.

My mind is spinning fast, way off-center. The options blur together. In my heart I doubt that I will follow through on these thoughts. I'm much too afraid to do that, and there's too much I want to reconcile. I want to win back Anne's trust and her family's trust and be a loving father to our children. I want to make amends and humbly ask God for mercy, and I want to be in a healthy marriage where I can be myself, scars and all. The problem is that I am beating up on myself so hard that the toxic voice inside me won't go away:

You've screwed up everything you've ever loved or cared about. You've done the worst thing a man can do to his wife. You are not even close to being the man you pretend to be.

The voice is convincing because it is using the awful truth against me.

So, what's the point? Why continue the charade? Isn't it easier to be done with it?

I fight back. I'm not listening to this devil's diatribe. I hear the Holy Spirit: *You are no quitter. You have too much to live for. You've made horrible mistakes and you've hurt people, but you have the Lord in your heart and you are loved.*

You can't take the easy way out, I tell myself. *Is that what you want to teach your children: when the going gets tough, the tough take their own life?*

The suicidal thoughts continue to infest my psyche as fall turns to winter. One day I'm strong. The next day I come up with a new, pain-free way to check out, two massively conflicting forces dueling for my life. The more I think of leaving my children fatherless, the more abhorrent the thought becomes.

Slowly, mercifully, I regain my resolve.

Choose hope. Don't choose despair. Choose hope. Fight harder than you ever have on the mound or anywhere else. You need to give that to God and Anne and the kids and yourself—to be a man and put your life back together. The voices continue to rage at each other. My torment runs deep. I choose hope.

I PULL UP into the parking lot of a little run-down office building in the Green Hills section of Nashville, next door to a beauty salon and art gallery. It's a Friday afternoon. I am here to see a man named Stephen James. He is a counselor and therapist. He has been recommended to me by a friend. I take a creaky elevator up to the third floor. I am afraid and wary when I walk into his office. For years I have had preconceptions about counseling: that it's for the weak-minded, for people who are lost and don't know how to find their way, and that it's a bunch of touchy-feely fluff. Now that I am the lost one, my preconceptions are about to change. I am in a place of secret surrender, yearning for help but still terribly reluctant to open myself up to get it.

Stephen's office has two chairs and a couch, and a window overlooking a Ruby Tuesday. I am face-to-face with this man, Stephen. It's too late to skip out and order potato skins. We shake hands and I sit down. I eye him warily. He is about my age, with sandy-colored hair and blue eyes and a warm demeanor, but it's not going to work with me. I am good at stiff-arming people, keeping them a safe distance away. I've been doing it my whole life. Stephen looks me over. I can tell he's looking me over. I am wearing sweatpants and a ratty T-shirt. Maybe I brushed my hair. Probably not.

I look disheveled and I'm sure he notices—how could he not?—but he doesn't remark on it.

Stephen says: Tell me what brings you here.

I've been going through a little bit of a tough stretch and some people thought it would be a good idea for me to talk about it.

Do you think it's a good idea?

You are highly recommended and I have an open mind, and I thought it would behoove me to give this a chance.

Stephen nods. He looks directly into my eyes. He lets silence fill the room. He and I both know that I didn't really answer his question, and I suspect he knows I am mostly full of crap. It makes me very uncomfortable. Whenever I talk, I can tell how carefully he is listening. How present he is with me.

That makes me uncomfortable too.

What's up with all the pauses? Can't we just talk? I feel like saying.

Stephen asks a lot of questions.

Are you willing to be completely honest with yourself and with me?

Can you tell me about what's going on with you right now, and how you are feeling in this moment?

If we do work together, are you willing to be committed to the process, even though it will be painful at times, probing into issues that are hiding behind walls you've probably spent years building?

I tell Stephen I understand it will be painful, but of course I really don't understand. I don't know what issues I have or what walls he's talking about. Mostly in that first meeting I bob and weave and give him inauthentic boilerplate and platitudes, answering questions as if I were being interviewed on *SportsCenter*.

I have spent years honing the ability to be genial to the world, but letting almost nobody into my private, fractured piece of it. I allow myself to be as vulnerable as a boulder. Stephen knows exactly what I am up to.

This guy has perfected the art of practiced sincerity, Stephen says to himself.

For the whole hour I am with Stephen James, I am asking questions of my own, to myself. Is this someone I can trust? Someone who I can share the deepest, darkest secrets of my life with—secrets I haven't shared with anybody else on earth?

Is this someone who won't leave me?

Even as I sit in a chair across from Stephen, I feel enormously conflicted. Part of me wants nothing to do with therapy or delving into the past and all the pain that's going to come with it. The other part is tired of hiding and telling half-truths and wants to be free.

What's it going to be? I ask myself. *You want to keep going down the same grim track, or do you desire the rich, joyful life God wants for you?*

I shake hands with Stephen.

I will see you next week, I tell him.

ALL WINTER LONG, I take the creaky elevator to the third floor and do the work I promised Stephen I would do. I give him the *SportsCenter* answers at first, but Stephen calls me on it. It's the hardest thing I have ever done in my life. I tell Stephen about the babysitter. I tell him about the fights in school, and the reckless risk taking, and the nights spent in abandoned houses, and the secrets I kept from Anne, and about how certain I was that if I kept moving and kept starring in sports that I could outrun all of it.

I tell him all about the guilt and shame I've lived with, sure that if people knew the real R. A. Dickey, they would want nothing to do with him.

I tell Stephen that now that he knows all this, I am terrified that he will leave me, too, the way so many others have.

Isn't that how it always goes? People abandoning you? People using you and then going on their way?

I will not leave you, R.A. I promise you that I will never leave you, Stephen says. The room is still. He looks me in the eye. I don't want to look back at him. Stephen says, Look at me and listen to me, R.A.: I will never leave you.

I believe him. I do. I want to cry, and I do a little. But mostly I hold myself back.

I'm so sorry. I'm so sorry. I know how painful this must be, Stephen says.

As the weeks turn into months, the scabs gradually get peeled off all the old wounds. I am raw and vulnerable. It's as if somebody backed up a garbage truck to the house and dumped every last thing on the front lawn.

Where do you start picking things up, and where do you put them?

I don't know. I have no clue. But I do know Stephen will be there to help me find out how. He is the first human being I have ever unconditionally trusted—the first person I can share everything with, a skilled and steadfast guide who is leading me on the scariest and most important journey of my life.

Even in my pain I know what a blessing that is.

I spend the whole winter searching for my true self and being okay with what I find. I spend it trying to reconcile with Anne and throwing my knuckleball against the gym wall and baring my soul with Stephen. Gord Ash of the Milwaukee Brewers calls and invites me to minor-league training camp. It is the only offer I get. Gord is the assistant GM to Doug Melvin, who moved on to the Brewers after the Rangers let him go. Even if I don't make the Brewers, their top farm team is right in Nashville, meaning that I could continue the work with Stephen.

What are the odds of that—getting your one and only offer from an organization with a top farm team in your hometown? Exactly the place I need to be while I am fighting for my soul.

Thank you, God, for this miracle, and for the miracle of providing me with the perfect person to help me turn around my life.

I have a ton more work to do on myself. I am learning that the truth-telling process—taking stock of who you are—isn't tidy or predictable. But as I head off for Arizona and spring training, I hold more hope than I have in a long time. I have let almost everything out, told Stephen almost every secret.

I am becoming a free man.

It's 2:02 on the scoreboard clock and I am in the visitors' dugout, being flooded with a Texas-size torrent of memories. The field is peaceful and exquisitely manicured, the quiet before batting practice almost surreal. But inside I have so much going on, being back in a place where I have some of my greatest memories—and some of my worst. I look out at the office suites beyond center field and think of Doug Melvin's face the day he retracted my $810,000 contract offer in the summer of 1996. I look on the mound and see the place where I gave up six home runs to the Detroit Tigers and tied a modern-day record for gopher balling as a neophyte knuckleball pitcher.

But on that mound I also see the place where I also made my big-league debut in 2001, and where I won my first game, in relief, two years later. I see a club that Anne and I were a part of when we had our first three children, Gabriel, Lila and Eli, and where I became friends with quality people like Mark Teixeira, Michael Young, Jeff Brantley, Rusty Greer, and Jay Powell, among others.

I see the place where I underwent a complete metamorphosis—from conventional pitcher to knuckleballer—and dealt with a wild ride of emotions and results in the process.

Through my time in Texas, I played briefly for Johnny Oates and Jerry Narron, and then for Buck Showalter, who was the first manager to really give me a chance. I had fantastic coaches in Orel Hershiser, Mark Connor, Rudy Jaramillo, Bucky Dent, Lee Tunnell, and Andy Hawkins.

Being here reminds me of one of the enduring challenges of living on this side of eternity: how to live fully in the pain of a moment as well as the joy of a moment. Learning to walk through this world holding both has been one of the real gifts my God has given me.

My life here was not always easy, but it was rich, and I have much to be thankful for about it.

CHAPTER FIFTEEN

INTO THE MISSOURI

How many times have I been here, at this window, in this exact place? Ten? Twenty? How many times have I told myself that one day I will stop with the excuse making and take the plunge?

That one day I will prove to everybody and myself that I mean it—that this isn't just the usual testosterone-fueled ballplayer bravado?

I don't know why—or maybe I do—but as I look out the window again at this moment on June 9, 2007, I decide.

It is time.

It is finally time.

The window I'm looking out of is in the Ameristar Casino Hotel in Council Bluffs, Iowa. It is about as nice a hotel as you will ever stay at in minor-league baseball, spacious and well-appointed and even equipped with a gift shop. You know you are in the big time when you've got a hotel gift shop. Even though I dislike everything about casinos, from the recycled oxygen, to the sad sound track of the slots and the craps tables, to the desperate-looking people who don't know when to stop, I actually like staying in the Ameristar, mostly because it has a good bakery, with killer chocolate cake. I make the rounds on the casino floor, trying not to gag on the cigarette smoke and the stale smell of alcohol, and playing the role of elder statesman, making sure my younger teammates are not being foolhardy with their twenty-dollar per diem. I always root for my guys to win, and not just because I'm a good teammate: when somebody hits the jackpot, it often means a big upgrade on the postgame spread, maybe barbecue and cornbread instead of the Sam's Club chicken and Van Camp's baked beans that have been on simmer since the second inning. Call me an altruist in progress.

When you take the elevator to your room in the Ameristar, you get an unimpeded view of the Missouri River. It is big and brown, probably 250 yards across, swift of current and sludgy of texture. The first time I saw the Missouri from this elevator was in 2002 as an Oklahoma City RedHawk coming into town to play the Omaha Royals. Now I am a member of the Nashville Sounds, still in town to play the Royals. The uniform changes, but not the fixation with the Missouri.

The absolute first thought I had when I saw the mighty Missouri? *Boy, would it be cool to swim across that.* The second thought I had was: *One day I'm going to do it. One day I'm going to swim across this river.*

I'm not sure why the Missouri has this pull on me, but it calls to me every time I stay in the Ameristar, almost taunting me to take it on. Washington crossing the Delaware, Joshua crossing the Jordan, Perseus crossing the river Styx—I think of all these epic feats as I look at the river. I am no general and I'm certainly no figure from Greek mythology. I'm a knuckleballer in desperate straits, a bad outing or two away from being finished with professional base-ball. I'm a husband and father who feels terribly inadequate, a dam-aged person who is trying to convince the world—and myself—that I'm fine.

Maybe if I can get across the Missouri it will say something about me and my courage.

Maybe it will prove my worth somehow—be a metaphorical baptism, a renewal, a chance to start fresh.

Maybe if I somehow get across, swim like a madman through the turbidity, God will help me close the prodigious gap between the man I am and the man I want to be.

Or maybe I'm just a reckless fool, the way I was when I once jumped eighty feet off Foster Falls, near Sequatchie, Tennessee, or went swimming in the Atlantic Ocean during a hurricane. You could say—and some have—that I have a death wish. Not sure. I believe it's more accurate to say I have a risk wish, somehow cling-ing to the notion that achieving these audacious feats will somehow make me worthy, make me special, as if I'd taken some magical, esteem-enhancing drug.

The reasoning of a child? I can't really argue with you there.

In the elevator, I float my plan by Chris Barnwell, my roommate.

Are you out of your mind? Chris says. Do you know how big that river is and how strong the currents are? That is one of the most idiotic ideas I have ever heard. It's completely idiotic. You can't do this. You can't.

Chris, of course, is 100 percent right. I must've been wild-eyed enough that Chris knew he wasn't getting through. So he calls Anne to let her know what is going on with his badly deluded teammate and see if she can drive sense into me.

He's a grown man. He knows his limitations, Anne tells him.

Thank you for calling, but I know R.A. wouldn't do anything that he wasn't sure he could handle.

Anne is, in some ways, a traditional southern woman, a woman who will stand by her man, and looking back I think her response to Chris's call was almost autonomic. One of the things I love most about my wife is that she respects me as a man even though I'm still a boy in so many ways.

Word about my impending swim spreads through the team like a rash. Outfielder Laynce Nix, one of my best friends on the team, asks me if I'm serious and I assure him that I am. He emphatically joins Chris in the incredulity chorus.

Get off it, man. That's a crazy, stupid idea, he says.

Other teammates aren't so worried. They're more interested in doing some wagering on my proposed feat, because if there's anything ballplayers love more than a spectacle, it's action. Some people pick me to make it, others don't. I quietly do some half-baked reconnaissance, asking the bellhop and the front desk people if the river is okay to swim in.

Oh, God, no, you don't want to swim in the Missouri. It's dirty and the currents are strong, a half-alarmed, half-amused bellhop says.

If I had any common sense, this would give me pause. But I have no sense. My idea of precaution is buying a pair of flip-flops in the gift shop so my feet don't get cut up on the rocky, steeply sloping banks.

At eleven-thirty in the morning the next day, I get into the elevator and stare at the Missouri the whole ride down. I follow the course of a big log as it flows along and note how fast it is moving. In a room adjacent to the lobby, people are finishing up their continental breakfasts. I pass on the powdered donuts, and get down on the floor and start stretching my back, my hamstrings, my shoulders. Chris is by my side. He's given up trying to talk me out of it. Now he's my cornerman, pumping me up and trying to make sure I've got everything I need.

Warmed and stretched out, donut-less, I head out to the river. I'm wearing white shorts and a tank top and have the flip-flops taped to my feet, and a gaggle of teammates, probably fifteen, is traipsing along behind me. I've studied the river and have a good plan in place. (I actually believe this.) I am going to start upstream about a hundred yards or so. This way, when I get across, I should be directly opposite the hotel, ready to wave triumphantly to my adoring fans. There are small orange buoys bobbing in the middle of the river, about a hundred yards from shore. The current is much more placid near the banks. My plan is to swim furiously to the buoys, then throttle it back for the second half, when I'll be more tired. I'm a strong swimmer. I used to swim the two-hundred-meter freestyle for the Seven Hills Swim and Tennis Club swim team.

I have no doubt that I can do this.

We walk around the back of the hotel. Inside the casino it's not even lunchtime, and people are already busy gambling their day away. It doesn't occur to me that I am walking down to the river to do my own gambling. I climb over a chain-link fence and snake through a few backyards. I descend the rocky bank to the water's edge and peel off my tank top and shorts. I stand alone at the river's edge in all my glory—a thirty-two-year-old minor-league pitcher, husband, and father of three, in his boxer briefs and taped-on flip-flops. Most of my teammates are on the bank, some of them hooting; the guys who aren't there are up in the hotel, faces pressed against the windows. Laynce has the video camera, recording it all for posterity. My own lens shifts to the water, which, up close, doesn't just look brown but almost inky, with the viscosity of motor oil.

It also looks a lot wider and a lot faster than it does from the eighth floor of the Ameristar. For an instant I wish Anne had bailed me out by joining Chris Barnwell's vigorous protests. I take a hard look at the river. I see a few branches go by in front of me and they are *flying*. I'm struck by how loud the rushing sound of the water is. It's getting noisy in my head too. I say a silent prayer.

I can't back out now. Well, I guess I can, but I am not going to, and who knows why? Ego? Pride? Mulish, juvenile stubbornness? Probably all of the above. Whatever. I'm not backing out. Something else for Stephen James and me to talk about.

I take my first tentative steps into the water, up to my knees, just to get acclimated to the temperature. It's tepid, with a cool edge to it. I don't turn around, don't wave, don't say anything more to my teammates on the bank and in the windows. It's game time. I push off hard and dive in. The adrenaline surge is so strong, it's as if it's rushing into me intravenously. My strokes are powerful as I cut through the first twenty or thirty yards or so.

It's a long way but it's not going to be all that hard, I'm thinking. *Just keep wheeling those arms.*

I keep wheeling, and wheeling. I start to feel the current intensify. I can feel it beating against the right side of my body. I concentrate on my cadence... one, two, three, breathe... one, two, three, breathe. I am moving along at a good clip, but it's getting harder.

Sixty yards in, I have new respect for the river. I'm pretty sure I can get across, but I am not thinking this is going to be easy anymore. I dig harder.

Just keep going forward, I tell myself. *Keep powering through the water and you'll get there.*

I can feel my strokes starting to lose power and efficiency. I'm not moving through the water the way I was even ten or twenty seconds earlier. With each weakening stroke, it becomes clearer that I have greatly underestimated the power of the rushing water.

As I approach the buoys and the midway point, I begin to feel an undertow tugging me downward. The current is stronger still. I am starting to get seriously fatigued. I pause and pick my head up for a second, treading water, and can't believe where I am: a quarter mile downriver. The buoys in the middle are bobbing ahead of me, an orange tease. The other side seems hopelessly far away. A wave of panic overtakes me. It feels as real as the waves in the water.

You are in trouble. It's too far to go. You need to turn around, I tell myself.

I put my head back down. I keep going.

I'm not quitting.

I swim as hard as I ever have in my life for the next two minutes. I am not in the Seven Hills pool anymore. If I get to the buoys, beyond the halfway point, I know I can get across. I also know I can't last much longer. The undertow is getting stronger and the force of it begins to pull the flip-flops off my feet. I stop and wrestle with the things, trying to pull them off. All it does is waste some of my rapidly dwindling energy.

Meanwhile, the undertow is making it hard to keep my head above water. I am not brave or cocksure anymore. My fantasies about a heroic crossing are as spent as I am.

I do a quick athlete-systems check and assess my plight. My

lactic acid is building up fast, my muscles shutting down at the same rate. Later I learn that Laynce Nix puts down the camcorder to say a quiet prayer, fearing he has seen the last of me.

I have one more push in me. But which direction should I go in?

Do I keep going forward, hoping it's enough to get across? Or do I turn around and try to make it back to the bank I started from? Either way, I know there is a good chance I won't be getting out of the Missouri River alive. I am positive of that. In a microsecond I feel a deep hopelessness, and brokenness, sweep over me, a man completely humbled by his vast limitations, flailing about in a polluted river, adrift and alone again, this time entirely because of his own flawed character.

I decide to swim back toward my teammates, who are now hundreds of yards upriver from me. I power out fifteen strokes and have to stop because I'm so exhausted. When I stop, the undertow pulls me down. I crank out another set of strokes, but don't make it to fifteen this time before I lock up, the painful, wrenching cycle getting me not far enough, not fast enough.

From somewhere, I have no idea where, I get the idea to swim underwater. I think of Michael Phelps in the Olympic pool in Athens in 2004, the way he'd push off the wall and swim underwater as long as possible before surfacing. Maybe it'll work for me, too, and get me there faster, because Lord knows the current at the top is as choppy as all get out.

I last for twenty seconds and come up for air. When I go back down for another swim, I open my eyes and can see absolutely nothing. It's as if I am swimming in a black hole. I come back up and look toward the bank. I am about fifty or sixty yards away.

I can't believe it's still that far. I start to see gigantic spots everywhere. I am getting delirious.

I can't swim anymore, my stroke reduced to a pathetic dog paddle. My muscles have completely shut down. My lungs are burning and my throat feels as if I've swallowed a thousand lit matches. I feel tears start welling behind my eyes. I am sinking. I accept that I am not going to get out of this river. I am underwater and I begin to cry. It's a very odd sensation, weeping in water. I am filled with contrition. I know I'm not getting to the surface again.

It is time to say good-bye and to make amends.

Anne, I am so sorry that I am leaving you and the kids alone. I am so sorry about my stupidity and recklessness, that I'd allow an asinine attempt to prove something—I don't even know what—to take me away. I am so, so sorry.

God, please forgive me. Forgive all my trespasses and all the ways I've fallen short. Please give me peace. Please, when You take me, make it not so painful.

It occurs to me that if I just open my mouth underwater, I can apologize to God in person.

I am sinking fast now, well below the surface. I am ready to die, and as I spend the final moments of my life engulfed in sorrow and regret, I feel solid ground beneath my flip-flops.

I have hit bottom. Literally. Normally the bottom isn't good when you are drowning, but it does give me something to push off from. I haven't felt any spurt of adrenaline for what seems like hours. Now, suddenly, I have one. I use it to coil my legs and push hard off the riverbed floor and power up, power up with strength I had no idea I still had, through probably eight feet of water.

I break through the surface, my head finally out of the river. I can't remember when my last breath was. The air is delicious. I'm only the distance from home to first away now. I don't really know how I got so close. I don't care. I swim with utter fury, with my last bit of energy, I'm sure.

One more stroke. One more stroke, I keep telling myself.

I am completely done. I don't have another stroke in me. I stroke again. I lift up my head and see Grant Balfour, a friend and teammate, lying on his stomach on a little platform jutting out into the river. Grant is from Brisbane, Australia, the guy who I have cut my hair to save a few bucks. "Give me the Brisbane," I always say, and he gets out his scissors and has at it. He gives a pretty good haircut. He's also good at scrambling over fences and navigating riverbanks, which is how he gets to the platform.

Grant is a reliever, and this is definitely a save situation.

He extends his right arm to me as far as it will stretch.

C'mon, R.A. You are almost there. Grab my hand, he says.

His hand is maybe eight feet away. I make a few more floundering strokes and reach out. I dog-paddle and flail. Five feet now. I keep looking at Grant's hand. Grant's hand is the most important thing in my world now. I am two feet away and I paddle a little more and reach and finally I feel Grant's hand, feel it clasping mine, good and strong. He hauls me in toward the bank as if he were a tugboat. At river's edge, he wraps his arm around me and guides me toward a small clearing, where I collapse and stay on the ground, sprawled on my back.

You okay? Grant asks.

I nod. I stay sprawled out for a few minutes. Eventually I clamber onto all fours. Grant helps me to my feet. I turn and look at the Missouri. I half expect to see a flying fish emerge, giving some biblical meaning to the ordeal I've just been through.

No fish emerges.

Finally I trudge up the bank toward the hotel, Grant guiding me the whole way. When we get to where the rest of the team is, they make sure I'm still breathing, and then the razzing begins about my oil-colored boxers, my bravado, my failed crossing.

Today's score: Missouri 1, Dickey 0.

Hey, R.A., you do a heck of a dog paddle. You ever think about the Olympics?

If you were going to soil yourself, you should've worn a Depends.

They are ballplayers. I expect nothing less.

A few of my closer friends—Chris and Laynce—make sure I'm okay and quietly ask me questions and are quick to appreciate how close a call I'd just had. Back in the hotel, utterly exhausted, I throw out the boxers and tank top and take a scalding hot shower for about forty-five minutes, hoping to rinse off the contaminants before I sprout a third arm.

I lie on the bed and don't have anything to say—not a common occurrence. I fall asleep for an hour. Chris makes sure I'm up so I get to the ballpark on time. We have a game against the Omaha Royals that night. I am not pitching, of course.

For the rest of the day and night, I reflect on my swim and thank God not just for sparing me but for teaching me. I began this crossing looking to be a hero, to use my strength and my will to forge some sort of epic transformation. I ended it as humbled as a man can be, nearly crushed in body and spirit on the banks of the mighty Missouri, left on all fours, in a posture where God could do His most significant work with me.

I jumped in the water thinking I was in charge. I found out He was in charge.

As I throw in the outfield before the game that night, swells of gratitude and humility keep washing over me. I don't have a grand epiphany in Johnny Rosenblatt Stadium on June 9, 2007.

It's more subtle than that. God has already given me a second chance as a husband and father. He's already given me a second chance as a pitcher. Now He has given me a second chance as a human being. When I was weeping underwater in the big brown currents of the longest river in North America, I was sure my time was over. God, it turned out, had other ideas, giving me a chance to see if a man who had spent a lifetime running away from the present could possibly find a way to embrace it.

It is late at night. I am sitting in my hotel room, surrounded by slumbering Dickeys (Anne and the four kids came up from Nashville to visit). I feel as if I am writing an obituary. Nobody died, so I guess I'm being a tad melodramatic, but today my friend and teammate, Carlos Beltrán, was traded to the San Francisco Giants. I'm not happy about it. In fact, I'm pretty angry about it. Mostly, I'm feeling an acute sense of loss.

You'd think, with all my stops in pro baseball, that saying good-bye to a teammate wouldn't be a big deal. But with where I am in my life—trying to be fully present with all of my feelings—it does feel like a big deal.

I've known Carlos for more than a decade, going back to our time as teammates in winter ball in Puerto Rico. We became closer still as Mets teammates the last two years. Anybody who has followed Carlos's career knows how gifted a player he is, but what I appreciate is his generosity of spirit, his constant willingness to help young players like Jason Pridie and Lucas Duda—to help everybody. It is a side of Carlos that I think is completely unknown to fans.

Ask José Reyes which teammate was always there for him whenever he was going through a rough patch, and José will tell you it was Carlos. Late after one game earlier this year, I was in the sauna with Carlos and Duda and was fascinated to listen to Carlos share with twenty-four-year-old Lucas his thoughts about hitting—not so much the mechanics of it as the psychology of hitting and the thought process he brings with him to the plate. Carlos has never been one to cultivate the media—it's just not on his list of things he regards as important—so this side of him is not widely known, but this is a good man and a good leader, a man who cares about other people.

When Pridie got called up from the minors, Carlos set him up with his tailor and bought him a couple of suits so he'd have something to wear on road trips. I know he's done it for other guys too—not because Carlos told me, but because the players with the new threads did. Last night, when it became clear that a deal was close, Carlos took the whole team to a fancy Cincinnati steak house. I wished I could've gone, but I stayed back with Anne and the kids. You might find it odd that I didn't honor Carlos by being there, but if I've learned anything in my itinerant ball-playing life, is that any family time you have, you better seize it, because your next good-bye is never far away. I heard later that Carlos spent $8,000 on the baseball version of a last supper.

As for the trade itself, I am trying to be fair and see all aspects of it. I understand the front office has a vision for the future and think they are getting a good deal in receiving young Zack Wheeler, a promising pitcher, from the Giants. I also understand that, as a free-agent-to-be, Carlos was just about ten weeks away from heading out the door anyway. But what sort of message does this send when you deal one of your best players when you are fighting for the playoffs? Doesn't it say that Sandy Alderson and the front office don't really believe in us? As I write this, we are two games over .500. Okay, we're not catching the Phillies, but there isn't a player in the clubhouse who doesn't think we can make a run at the wild card. I look around the league and see teams with similar records to us adding players, not subtracting them. So in this moment the competitor in me is perturbed that we seem to be getting written off by our own organization.

Of course, Sandy and his lieutenants—John Ricco, J. P. Ricciardi, and Paul DePodesta—have to think long-term and sometimes tough decisions have to be made. Maybe Zack Wheeler will turn out to be as good as his scouting reports and the trade will ultimately be seen as a steal. I believe in Sandy. Is my reaction to the trade one of emotion more than a dispassionate assessment? No doubt about it. I am a ballplayer, an emotional one, a guy in the midst of a six-month grind. Dispassion isn't in the mix for me right now. Either way, it doesn't make writing this baseball obit any easier.

I know that for a lot of Mets fans the enduring image of Carlos will be taking that strike-three, game seven curveball against the Cardinals' Adam Wainwright to end the 2006 National League Championship Series. I know, too, that there is a perception of him as a passionless player, a guy who has one and only one gear. No, Carlos doesn't throw stuff and burn hot, but just because he isn't demonstrative doesn't mean he doesn't care. He is one of the best players the New York Mets have ever had. You'd be hard-pressed to find a more even-keeled player—a guy you can count on to be the same person and the same competitor every day, whether he went 0 for 4 or 4 for 4 the day before. That's huge in baseball, the ultimate get-up-and-do-it-again sport. I'm not making excuses for him; I'm just saying that Carlos is a pro's pro, a man who makes a hard game look easy. He is somebody I'd want to have on my side any day.

I found out about the trade just before batting practice today. The clubhouse was stirring with the usual activity, guys getting treated and dressed, picking up their bats and balls, heading toward the field. I spotted Carlos at his locker. He was packing up his stuff, number 15 of the New York Mets no more.

"I appreciate you as a player and as a teammate. I am really going to miss you," I said. Then I hugged him and said good-bye and went out to the field to do my work.

· ·

CHAPTER SIXTEEN

SOUNDS OF THE MOMENT

Before I ever dip a toe in the river, here is my biggest problem: I can't get anybody out. In my second start of the season I give up eleven hits and ten runs in five innings. After that, I get raked for seven hits and five runs, including three homers.

Start after start, I pitch glorified batting practice, doing wonderful things to opponents' batting averages. When I emerge from the dugout in Nashville's Herschel Greer Stadium, or run wind sprints in front of the big guitar-shaped scoreboard in center field, people do not say, "There goes R. A. Dickey, our stopper."

A once-promising career has turned into a big Music City mess. I have no clue how close I am to being released, but I can't be far.

On June 1, my record is 3–4 and my ERA is 6.24, earning me a demotion from the starting rotation. Pitching in my hometown, in the place where I became the state prep player of the year, I feel like I'm letting everybody down, a colossal failure. I reach out to Charlie Hough in the hope that he can help me find an answer. Charlie is as encouraging as ever, and reminds me of all the basics we've worked on, but even he can't sprinkle me with flutterball fairy dust.

How bad is it?

Bad enough that I go online, make out a résumé, and talk to a guy about a job for the first time since I called about the YMCA job five years earlier. Bad enough that I am trying to pretend I know all about the construction supply business. The man's name is Bruce McClure and his business is called Seven Products Plus, based in Anderson, South Carolina. I don't know what the seven products are and know even less about Anderson, other than that they call it the Electric City because it was at the forefront of hydroelectric power during the Industrial Revolution. Chris Barnwell is a close friend of the family and Bruce knew about me from my days in the Southeastern Conference at Tennessee and from the 1996 Olympics.

I speak to Bruce about a position in sales. My job would be to get people to buy insulation products.

We have a couple of nice conversations. It seems to be a prosperous business and Bruce is a good guy. I am making $12,500 a month for the five-month minor-league season. We have a new mortgage and a growing family and I need to start formulating a back-up plan in case the Brewers decide they have seen enough.

Let me talk to my wife about it. I'll stay in touch, I tell Bruce. I think about what it would be like to do this work and not to be a pitcher and an athlete anymore. I think about what it would be like to live in the Electric City after my career goes dark, and to call Charlie Hough with the news that I've given up the knuckleball for foam and caulk.

It is a call I can't imagine making. Not yet, anyway.

Much as I believe in energy conservation, I decide that the first thing I need to save is my career. Bruce actually pushes me in the same direction.

We'll still be here if and when you decide to call it quits, he says.

But the biggest baseball backer of all is Anne. After eleven years of mostly minor-league life, of picking up and moving more than thirty times—of difficulties in our relationship and dealing with my deceit and emotional remoteness and having to carry so much of the family load—Anne says, "You can't give up on your dream. You don't want to regret not giving yourself every chance to succeed. You owe it to yourself to give it everything you've got."

How amazing is that?

It is the ultimate in selflessness, the ultimate act of love. I'd like to think I would do the same if the roles were reversed. I am not so sure I would.

Three days after my swim, Sounds manager Frank Kremblas calls on me to pitch in relief against the Memphis Redbirds at home. I pitch a scoreless inning and strike out two. It's an absurdly small sample, admittedly. But something feels different.

Something feels very different.

A couple of games later, Frank says he wants to start me again. I take the ball against the Omaha Royals at home. It's ninety-three degrees and as humid as a steambath. I strike out Mitch Maier and Ángel Berroa to start the game. I feel better than I have all year, have a better feel for the knuckleball. In the third, I get the Royals' first baseman, Billy Butler, on a knuckleball, and as I am coming through Charlie's doorframe and concentrating on my release, I can't help being struck at how much in command I feel. It's only three innings, but I walk back to the dugout feeling strangely empowered.

I give up four hits and one earned run over seven innings. Grant Balfour comes in and gets the save—a more conventional one this time—and I get the victory.

At second base, Chris Barnwell is struck at the baseball rejuvenation going on before his eyes.

The guy almost dies in the river and comes out of it a whole different person, Barnwell says to himself.

I am not a whole different person, but I am surely a changed person. I am not obsessing about how good I have to be to get back to the big leagues, or what numbers I have to put up, or about the time pressure because of my age. I am focusing not on the next month or year or uniform but on the next pitch, putting all my energy into the process of pitching.

Trite but true: my life is about the daily journey, not the final destination.

I don't mean to make this sound like magic: jump in a big river, cure all your problems. But the difference I see in myself is pretty profound.

In the clubhouse after the game, I say a prayer of thanks and own the fact that I have been a derelict Christian in so many ways. As a Christian, you are supposed to seek God's will, not follow your own. You are supposed to be a believer all the time, not just when it's convenient. I fall short in so many ways. I have a hard time surrendering control. I want to be in charge, want to be the director of the show. I have a hard time trusting anybody, even God, to be the guiding force of my life.

I have come to see how hypocritical this is. How can I call myself a true follower of Christ if I subconsciously believe that I should be the one calling the shots?

Since Grant hauled me out of the Missouri, I am beginning to understand that I've been bearing a burden almost all of my life, alone and afraid.

Now I am starting to let God carry more of the burden, to trust in His plan for me. If that includes a call-up to the big leagues, great. If it doesn't, everything will be okay. I used to say that.

Now I'm beginning to truly take it in.

Now, for the first time in my life, I am fully immersed in each moment. Maybe it's because my moments were very nearly taken away from me; I don't know. The reasons for the shift are not important. What is important is that I feel so grateful and so present.

What is important is that I am not living on the edge of a self-created abyss anymore, clinging to every stump or branch I can find as the river of life flows by, because I'm terrified of where it's going.

Without even being conscious of it, I am not trying to take on a river. I am flowing with it.

Or as Lao Tzu, the Chinese philosopher, said, "By letting it go, it all gets done. The world is won by those who let it go. But when you try and try, the world is beyond the winning."

One of the supreme paradoxes of baseball, and all sports, is that the harder you try to throw a pitch or hit a ball or accomplish something, the smaller your chances are for success. You get the best results not when you apply superhuman effort but when you just are—when you let the game flow organically and allow yourself to be fully present. You'll often hear scouts say of a great prospect, "The game comes slow to him." It means the prospect is skilled and poised enough to let the game unfold in its own time, paying no attention to angst or urgency or doubt, funneling all awareness to the athletic task at hand.

This is what is happening to me, post-Missouri. Without conscious thought or concentrated effort, I am completely present with my knuckleball. I am not stewing over it or rushing it. I am just throwing it and reveling in the chance to do so, the grace of God in full glory at sixty feet six inches.

And, better still, I am throwing it my way, with my own imprint. As much as I am grateful to the Rangers for giving me a chance to become a knuckleballer, I never really warmed to the idea of becoming a clone of Charlie or Tim Wakefield, which is what they continually emphasized.

We want you to be like Wake, the club kept telling me.

I want to be like me, I kept thinking.

Be like Wake, they insisted.

What's wrong with being like me? I insisted.

I am a different pitcher than Tim Wakefield, with different strengths. Why not play to those strengths? The idea of throwing virtually every knuckler in the 60-mile-an-hour range just because that's what Tim does never made any sense to me. I like to throw 80-mile-an-hour knucklers. I like to throw them at all different speeds, and I like to mix in an occasional fastball and cutter, because I know they can be effective weapons in disrupting a hitter's timing.

As 2007 goes on, more and more God helps me see and believe that it is time for me to stake out my own knuckleballing turf.

What's the worst that can happen? I think. *That I stay in the minors?*

If I'm serious about getting back to the big leagues, the only way it's going to work is if I pitch *my* way. I become more committed than ever to throwing my own knuckleball—and throwing it more than I ever have, not just 60 percent of the time. Once I had resistance about turning my pitching life over to the knuckleball, but that has been obliterated by my uneven results.

I'm going to throw 80 or 85 percent knuckleballs now. I'm going to throw a lot of them fast, and let's see what "they" can do with them.

After the strong start against Omaha, Frank Kremblas puts me back in the rotation for good, it turns out. Five days after shutting down the Royals, I do the same to the Iowa Cubs, pitching into the seventh inning and giving up three hits, striking out eight. I win ten out of my next eleven decisions, the best run of my entire professional career. Chris Barnwell and Grant Balfour and Laynce Nix—they were all there when I almost drowned, and they are all there when I stop taking on water on the mound.

How can you explain what's going on, this change in you? Laynce, a fellow believer, asks me.

I'm just pitching knuckleball by knuckleball and surrendering to the results. I'm not sure if I shrug when I say this, but Laynce does.

In the last week of July, I am at my locker in the clubhouse when Frank comes over.

Gord Ash is on the phone and wants to talk to you, Frank tells me.

I don't think I've spoken to Gord since he invited me to spring training. I pick up the phone in Frank's office. The Brewers are in first place and have a big four-game weekend series in St. Louis. Gord asks me if I'd be willing to meet the team in St. Louis and be on standby in case the club needs me to start one of the games.

Sure, I'll be happy to meet you in St. Louis, I tell him.

I'll crawl to St. Louis to meet you, I think.

I get to town on a Friday and meet Gord in the hotel. He fills me in on the situation. Because they aren't yet sure if they'll need me, they're not ready to officially call me up and send somebody else down. Gord doesn't want any of the pitchers getting worked up if they see me in the lobby or at the coffee bar, so he instructs me to stay in my room. I'm in Westin house confinement, complete with meal money slipped under the door. I'm not allowed to leave lockup until the club leaves for the ballpark. Then I can have the run of the place.

In a strange way, I feel as if I am the Brewers' secret weapon, ready to be rolled into Busch Stadium when the Cardinals least expect it. Mostly, though, all I am tunneled in on is my hope. Hope, after all, is what keeps me going.

My biggest hope, of course, is that I will get back to the big leagues.

The Brewers win big on Friday night. I never get the call.

Maybe Saturday will be different, I tell myself. *There's a double-header, so obviously we're going to need two starters.* I wake up early, praying to hear from Gord Ash.

No call. The Cardinals sweep. Toward the end of the second game, I go out for a walk, so close to Busch Stadium that I hear the roar of the crowd and see the lights, a billion bulbs bathing the night sky in warm, welcoming whiteness. I haven't been this close to a big-league park since the six-home-run game about six-teen months before.

I keep looking up at the white lights over the dark city; it's almost as if they are summoning me, like the Missouri. The lights look breathtakingly beautiful.

Will I ever make it back? Is this as close as I'm going to get? I keep walking. Albert Pujols or somebody must've hit a double or homer, because a gigantic roar goes up. It's almost more than I can stand.

I have to get back there, I tell myself. *I know I have the ability. I just have to make them take notice.* Hearing the sounds of the game

I love, standing alone in the darkness, close enough almost to touch the action but still so far away, feels like an out-of-body experience.

The series wraps up on Sunday. Gord never calls. The Cardinals take their third in a row. My weekend in St. Louis consists of a lot of quality room service... and three days of crushed hopes. What a colossal waste. I never get inside Busch Stadium. I miss a start for the Sounds. I pack up and head back to Nashville.

The three-hundred-mile drive home is long and lonely. *Just keep doing what you are doing. Keep making good starts. That's the only thing you can control,* I tell myself.

But would that be enough? What if I keep it up and nobody notices or cares? Then what? I've been sent back to the minors four times now. Whenever this happens—I don't care who you are—you fear disappearing forever. You fear that once you are out of sight, you will be completely out of mind. I've seen it happen so often. People think that big-league ballplayers are at an entirely different level from Triple-A players. Some of them are, but the truth is that in many cases the line of demarcation is no bigger than the splinter of a bat. Joe Dillon is a Sounds teammate, a corner infielder with big muscles and a lunch-pail work ethic. Joe is a positive guy, a team-first fellow to the core. He hits .317 with 20 home runs and 75 RBIs in two-thirds of a season in 2007, following up other Triple-A years in which he hit .360 with 34 homers and .329 with 39 homers and 117 RBIs.

Joe Dillon's big-league career consisted of 246 big-league at-bats with three different clubs—or about 200 more at-bats than Chris Barnwell got, even though Chris had a tremendous glove and could play anywhere and would do all the little things it takes to win games. Chris and Joe got typecast as journeymen who were good but not good enough. The label stuck.

All it did was cost them big-league careers, which I don't doubt either one of them would've had.

I have a journeyman label of my own, and I hate it. I finish the year 13–6 and am voted the Pacific Coast League pitcher of the year, and still, the Brewers do not call me up to join the big club in September.

What more do they want me to do? How else can I prove my worth to them, beyond winning ten of my last eleven and being named the best pitcher in the league?

The Brewers say that they don't have a roster spot for me but tell me to stay ready in case they need me for the pennant race in September. They are fighting for a divisional title and I am their top minor-league pitcher and they don't want me. You try not to take it personally, but how can you not?

Is it age discrimination? Knuckleball discrimination? I don't know. I don't think it's fair. I am sick about it.

So I stay home in Nashville but, for a switch, I let myself have my lousy feelings. All of them. Anne is one of the first to see the difference. She tells me about an upcoming dinner party, one that I am not at all keen on attending. Here's how I would've reacted, pre–Stephen James:

I'm sick and tired of you roping me into these stupid outings with your friends when you know darn well I don't want any part of going and having all these people I don't know asking me a million questions about my baseball career. When are you going to stop trying to run my life?

Then I exit, slamming the door after me.

Here's how I react this time:

I'm having a lot of anger about not being called up. It's not about you, it's about me. I don't want to take it out on you, so forgive me if I'm short- or ill-tempered. I just really don't feel like going to this party. I know it means a lot to you and that you just want to have fun. I'm just not into it.

"The unexamined life is not worth living," Socrates said. I'm not that much into ancient Greek philosophy, but I do know I'm a heck of a lot better human being for my ongoing self-examination. I'm baby stepping, but I am getting places.

Every day of my life, I repeat the mantra I've picked up from my work with Stephen: Don't repress your feelings. Be honest with your feelings. If you are present with them now, they aren't going to come back later in much more pernicious form.

It's one of the hardest things I've ever had to do. I've spent years locking sadness and anger away, toughing it out alone, taking flight from fear and frustration and everything. I never wanted to look inside me because I was afraid of what I'd find. Then, inevitably, the pent-up emotions come up in an unhealthy and inappropriate way, like being impatient with the kids or verbally brutalizing Anne.

I don't want to be that person anymore. I don't want to hurt the people who I love the most anymore.

And I don't want to take flight anymore. I want to start taking risks, letting people know how I feel.

Being authentic.

I've learned that when I hide or brood and play the role of victim, the first victim is always me.

The Brewers finish in second place, behind the Cardinals. I tell Anne: As angry as I am about not getting back to the big leagues this year—as much as I don't think it's fair—I am not going to let somebody else define who I am as a pitcher or what I'm capable of as a pitcher. I didn't let it define me when I found out I had no ulnar collateral ligament. I didn't let it define me when I gave up the six home runs.

Why start now?

After a short break, I go right back to Uncle Ricky's gym wall and, for added convenience, to the walls at Lipscomb University, near our home in Nashville. I get my five-gallon pail and fill it up with baseballs and throw knuckleballs by the thousands, from my meticulously manicured nails into a long white wall of cement. I am a thirty-three-year-old free agent and I know more than ever that God has a plan for me. I am not worried about being an underdog. I love *Rocky* and *Rudy* and *The Rookie* and every overcoming-the-odds movie ever made.

Wouldn't it be nice to join *that* club?

It doesn't take long to get over the Brewers' snub. Day after day I throw my knuckleballs, full of faith that something will open up; full of optimism that my success with the Nashville Sounds was not a fluke; full of conviction that my misadventure in the Missouri River has changed the narrative of my life.

I entered the Missouri with a 3–4 record and a 5.87 ERA. I came out of it with a 10–2 record and a 2.42 ERA. The Missouri may not be holy water and people may not go there to be baptized and seek absolution of their sins, but nobody can tell me that God didn't use it to humble me and help me and recharge my faith and reset my focus. I jumped in to prove my worth and failed spectacularly, but wound up with one of the greatest gifts of my life. What a deal. What a day—the day God's grace showed me how to stop clinging . . . and start living.

....

BEFORE I CAN get any clarity on where I'll be playing ball in 2008, I need to get more clarity about myself. I need it in the worst way. I have been holding back from Stephen James. I am hanging on, desperately, to my last secret, the most painful boxed-away item of all. We are out in the country at the Bartholomews' family farm, a half hour outside of Nashville, sitting in the living room of a rustic farmhouse, rich with wooden beams and plank floors and the comforting smell of God's earth.

We came here for an intensive day of therapy—to get to the bottom of the story. But I'm still unsure if I'm ready to tell all. It's a brisk autumn day, and the house is quiet and warm and safe. We set up in the living room. Baseball and my future are the furthest thing from my mind.

I look into Stephen's eyes, and think: *Do I tell him? Am I ready to tell him? Is he ready to hear it? What if what I need to say is as repulsive to him as it is to me? What if he decides he's finally had it with me and all my crap and just bolts out the door and runs back to Nashville? What if he hates my story as much as I do?*

That could happen, couldn't it?

I am terribly afraid. I thought I was beyond this point. Stephen knows everything else about me, knows every failing and sinful thought and act and source of shame. If your secret is safe with anyone in this world, it is Stephen James.

I am quivering and sweating, much worse than I did at that first Fellowship of Christian Athletes meeting all those years ago. Finally, I begin to talk.

Stephen, I need to share something with you. I haven't been

completely forthright with you. I am so afraid to tell you this, but I know that I need to.

Remember the babysitter and the sexual-abuse stuff?

Of course I do, he says.

The babysitter was not the only one.

I didn't think so. I'm glad you want to talk about it, Stephen says.

And so I begin. I tell him about the tennis ball and the garage and the teenage creep who forced himself on me and violated me, with power and with hate. I give him all the hideous details, moment by moment, feeling by feeling, violation by violation. Deeper and deeper into the story we go.

I tell him that even though the babysitter's abuse was repeated, this secret felt darker, more shameful, more damaging.

You sound angry. Hateful, Stephen says.

Yes, I'm angry.

With whom? The guy who abused you?

Yes.

Who else?

God. I am furious at God. I hate Him too.

What are you angry with God about? Stephen asks.

How could a loving God let this happen to me? How? Can you tell me that? I was only eight! Why didn't He do something? Why? I am shouting, and starting to cry.

The wound is raw and new again. I want to run. I want to die, but I know no matter what I do and how fast I run, I cannot escape. This kind of shame and pain no one can out run. It hunts you like a wolf. It's unrelenting. I have nothing left to do but walk into the pain, take it on.

Who else did you hate? Stephen asks.

I hated everything. Myself, my life. Everything. I start to

weep, and I cannot stop. I weep so hard I can barely get air and can't stop shaking. I weep more than I have in the last twenty years combined—no lie.

Stephen does the best thing he can do for me:

He lets me grieve.

He reminds me that I'm not alone.

You know, R.A., your God might just be big enough, loving enough, to take your hate, Stephen says. He pauses. That's yours to risk. That's faith: stepping past what you know, the shame and hurt, and into the mystery that love might be there for you. You are giving yourself and your children the greatest gift you could ever give them, because letting yourself face your story and feel all the pain you've run from is the only way you are going to be the free man you want to be, with the life you want to live.

After three of the most wrenching and wonderful hours of my life, we drive back to Nashville, the waning sunlight shining on the russet-colored hills. The seasons are changing. *I* am changing. The last secret is out.

MONDAY, AUGUST 15, 2011
San Diego

I walk back to the hotel after our 5–4 victory over the Padres tonight, a game that followed a yearlong pattern in which I pitch pretty well but not well enough to get the victory. I also continue my propensity to give up late home runs, in this case a two-run job to Will Venable in the seventh inning. I have eight starts left and my record is 5–11, my ERA 3.77. I aim to improve both before the year's out.

My story line is hardly the point tonight, though. Jason Isringhausen picks up his 300th career save and I am so thankful to be a part of it in a small way. For weeks I've been telling him that I would get the win the night he got his landmark save, because the old guys have to stick together. He went ahead and did it without me, and that leaves me with a feeling that's just a little bittersweet.

A part of me expects to come in tomorrow and see Izzy's locker empty. He has been grinding through injuries for a while—"a while" is baseballese for years and years—and has continually joked that when he gets 300 saves, he's out. However, the game holds a strange power over him, as it does for all of us. We think we can use it to an end of some sort and then walk away in peace. Baseball laughs at that notion, because it knows how hard it is to walk away from something you do well—knows how much we need the game, the lessons it teaches, the relationships it uncovers, and the truth it tells. Baseball also needs us, in a way, to pour into its history and its pedigree and to help create its lore, whether the names behind it are Ruth or

Mays or Mantle or Koufax or . . . Isringhausen. Izzy would wince if he knew I was putting him in that sentence, but his legacy is special in its own right, for it's a legacy of enduring pursuit of consistent contribution through a labyrinth of adversity. It has been fun to be his teammate and watch him interact with a game, watch him playfully dog all of us and wait for us to dog him back. When I walk to Petco Park tomorrow, I hope I'll see Izzy in his familiar place on the training table, getting his big, old, falling-apart body worked on, headphones on, iPad in hand. Either way, I know the game is better off having had him, and he is better off having had the game. And that is exactly the way it should be.

CHAPTER SEVENTEEN

RULE FIVE SURPRISE

Three hundred thousand dollars is a great salary. It's more than I've made in my previous five years combined, and almost a quarter of a million dollars more than I made as a Nashville Sound in 2007.

It might even be enough to stop me from getting on Anne's case if she buys another set of urns.

I've never been one to chase the almighty dollar, but with three kids and no guarantees I'll ever see the big leagues again, how can this salary not be seductive? So when I get a call from a man named Sebastian (John) Esposito in October 2007, I find myself in a muddle as wide as the Missouri.

John is a liaison to the Korean baseball league, a guy who assists Korean teams in finding American ballplayers who can help them win. He tells me that the Samsung Lions, based in Daegu, have made a $300K offer to me, and that another club, the Daejeon-based Hanwha Eagles, are also interested. I know nothing about Korean baseball, other than that it's on the upswing. I know nothing about

either team except that I had a Samsung DVD player once and it
worked well.

What I *do* know is that I've just had my best minor-league season. When will my leverage ever be better?

A few years earlier I wouldn't have even considered the idea of
playing in the Far East. But I am a different man, a more open man,
a man who has been humbled by his mistakes and strengthened by
his willingness to stand up and tell the truth. I have a rekindled
relationship with a merciful God, and more love and appreciation
for my wife than ever.

Anne and I talk it over. Baseball, and her husband, have dragged
her all over the place. I want her input. I value her input.

What do you think about spending five months of the year in
Korea? I ask. It means packing up the kids again and making the
biggest transition we've ever had to make as a family. Most of it will
fall on you, the way it always does.

Anne grew up traveling and grew up with three brothers. She is
adventurous and tough.

I'm open to it if you think it's the best career move, she says. I'm
sure the kids will adjust. It will probably be good for them, being
exposed to a whole different culture.

I begin to grow excited about the opportunity to make some real
money. I am leaning strongly to go to Daegu. I call Bo McKinnis,
who isn't just my friend and agent but somebody with a great gift
for taking emotions out of decisions and carefully assessing the
pros and cons. It's not commonplace for players to have as close a
relationship as Bo and I have. I tell him about the offer.

I think I want to take it, Bo.

There is a long silence on the other end of the line.

I don't think that is a good idea. You are coming off a great year. I anticipate you having some good interest here.

I know, Bo, but there aren't any guarantees over here. I was the PCL pitcher of the year and didn't even get a call-up. If that wasn't good enough, what is?

I realize that, but you have something very unique, and you are starting to figure it out. Korea, Taiwan, even Japan—those are places pitchers go to die. You need to realize if you take this money now and go play for the Samsung Lions or the Hanwha Eagles, the chances of you ever coming back here and playing in the big leagues are about zero.

I'll support you in whatever you decide is best, but I want you to think through all the ramifications.

Bo makes a good point: there will probably be no making it back to the majors. But I am not thinking about the future anymore. I'll be in my mid-thirties by next season. I am thinking about making as much money as I can make. And $300K this year—and probably another $300K next year if I do well and they re-up me—is probably not going to happen in the western hemisphere.

How can I turn my back on a possible $600K in Korea when I'm a $60,000 pitcher at home?

Bo and I decide to give it a day and talk again, but the meter is running; Esposito is asking that I give him an answer in forty-eight hours. Anne and I pray for God's will as we sort out the pros and cons. I am 80 percent sure I am heading for Daegu. I wonder if Rosetta Stone has a program in Korean. A day passes with no news. My cell phone vibrates and I see that it's Bo. I quickly pick up. I think about saying hello in Korean (*An-nyeong-ha-se-yo*) but I'm not sure Bo will appreciate my joke.

I've got some news for you. The Minnesota Twins, the Seattle Mariners, and the New York Mets are all interested in you. I don't have the particulars of their offers yet, but I will soon.

That's good news—very good, but I'm still praying on it, Bo. I have to give the Korean team my answer today, and I'll be honest: the guaranteed $300,000 is a nice financial blessing to have in a time when I need a nice financial blessing.

This is not what Bo wants to hear.

R.A., please trust me on this. You have gotten better every year with the knuckleball. There is real interest in you. Korea will be there whenever you want, but if you take it now, you will regret it. You are this close to busting through and making it. I'd hate to see you do something that you'll regret.

We hang up and I know decision time is at hand. I don't want to string Esposito along. The word "regret" keeps playing in my mind on an endless loop:

You will *regret* it.... I'd hate to see you do something that you'll *regret.*

Anne and I talk some more, and pray some more. Voice One and Voice Two are back once more:

VOICE ONE: *What's to decide? You've got to be pragmatic. Think of the family. You have one guarantee and it's in Korea. It's the only assurance you have that you'll make at least a year or two years' worth of decent money.*

VOICE TWO: *You have to believe in yourself. You have to aim high. You can take guaranteed money now, but how much money is that guarantee going to cost you down the line?*

VOICE ONE: *You are thirty-three years old and you haven't pitched in the big leagues in almost two full years. What Kool-Aid are you drinking, thinking teams are going to line-up to hand you a big-league uniform?*

VOICE TWO: *You are thirty-three years old but you are getting better and better at your craft. You are a knuckleballer, and knuckleballers pitch forever.*

VOICE ONE: *Be prudent.*

VOICE TWO: *Be brave.*

The voices have at it, until finally some clarity arrives. I believe it is God speaking to me, the way He did through the Holy Spirit the day I wanted to hurt Doug Melvin. This is what I hear in my mind: *You have lived your whole life as a survivor, doing what you need to get by, to flee from pain, to seek safety. Now I want more. I want much more. I don't want my life to be about settling. I don't want it to be about avoiding pain. I want it to be about pursuing joy.* Sure, Korea is safe, locked-up money. But to me, choosing Korea is choosing to settle. I would never find out how good I could be as a knuckleballer—never find out if I could, indeed, make it back from the six-home-run game.

I call John Esposito and tell him no, thanks.

I call Bo and tell him I'm staying and to get me a deal. I can feel him smiling on the other end of the line.

Bo talks to the Mets, the Mariners, and the Twins and works it hard, trying to find the best spot. The Twins are the most stable organization of the three, and seemingly the best shot to make it back to the big leagues. We decide the Twins are the way to go. Right after Thanksgiving 2007, I sign a minor-league deal that includes an invitation to big-league camp and a chance to make the big club.

It's the first time in a long time that I feel wanted.

Days later, the baseball winter meetings begin at the Opryland hotel in Nashville. It's an irresistibly short commute, so I venture over to meet Bill Smith, the general manager, and Rob Antony, his assistant, along with manager Ron Gardenhire. Granddaddy always told me it's a good idea to look your bosses in the eye to show them that you respect them but that you aren't scared of them.

I get on the elevator, and as I am ascending to their floor, I catch myself scripting something in my head to try to make a good first impression.

Stop it, I tell myself. *Be yourself. One time. Be yourself.*

I have spent the last fourteen months learning to live differently and to be authentic. This is a perfect opportunity to just be me.

I knock on the door and Rob answers. He takes me back to the conference area, where I find Gardenhire and Bill Smith and Terry Ryan, the former general manager, who is now a consultant.

Glad to have you aboard, Bill Smith says.

I shake hands all around and it becomes clear to me that I've stumbled into a delicate discussion. It turns out the Twins are deciding whether to trade their longtime ace, Johan Santana, to the Mets in exchange for a package of young players. It's almost trigger-pulling time and there seems to be a legitimate debate about what's best.

Go ahead and trade him, I say. I can pick up his slack.

Everybody laughs, taking my idle boast in the right spirit. I don't know where that came from but I am glad I am myself. I get out of there before I am any more of myself.

The next day Anne and I are driving to our couples counseling session, where we are learning to reconnect and enrich our relationship. This is also evidence of not wanting to settle: I don't want Anne and me to just get by as husband and wife. I want to have a passionate, joyful marriage. I notice that my phone is ringing and the caller is Maurice Patton, a reporter for the *Nashville Tennessean*.

Hey, R.A. So, how does it feel to be the newest member of the Seattle Mariners?

You mean the Twins? Yeah, it feels great. I feel like they will give me—

He stops me.

No, it's the Mariners. You didn't hear? They just took you in the Rule 5 draft. You are the oldest Rule 5 player since its inception, and I was curious to know your thoughts.

I don't say anything for a few seconds, but I am thinking: *I am what? I am a Mariner? I thought the Twins wanted me.*

That was fast. Did my Santana comment come back to bite me?

I tell Maurice I will call him back, and minutes later I hear from the Mariners, and it's true. The Rule 5 draft is a Major League Baseball provision that aims to prevent teams from stockpiling players in the minors when other clubs would be willing to give them a chance to play in the majors. Since I am not yet on the Twins' forty-man roster, I am eligible to be plucked—and that's what the Mariners do, paying $50,000 for me.

It's a positive sign that they like me enough to steal me from the Twins, but it's still a completely bewildering development. I was all geared up to be a Twin. I was already imaging myself in a Twins uniform, moving Anne and the kids to a new part of the country.

Now this. Could there possibly be any more plot twists in my baseball life?

I report to Mariners spring training in Peoria, Arizona, and have one of the best springs of my life. I pitch as both a starter and a reliever. They put me out there in every situation they can. My knuckleball holds up well, and I know it's dancing because Kenji Johjima, the Mariners catcher, catches about three of every ten knuckleballs I throw. The other seven hit him in the shin guards or the mask, or he chases them back to the screen. I encourage him to switch to the oversized glove that virtually all catchers use to catch the knuckleball. He's attached to his regular Mizuno, though, so knuckleballs keep going everywhere but in his glove.

I am among the top pitchers in the Cactus League in innings pitched and ERA that spring. I have one more appearance before opening day, against the Giants. I have my strongest outing yet, giving up a single hit in six innings and getting the victory. I leave the game as elated as I've been in a long time. It's been almost two years since the six-homer game, and now I can finally start my big-league career anew, in the great Northwest, pitching not to survive but to flourish, to be a craftsman with my knuckleball. I feel a wave of gratitude toward Bo McKinnis for talking me out of Korea, and toward Anne for always being there.

I tell her to book a flight for opening day.

I can't wait to share the moment with her in a whole new way, for I am becoming a whole new man.

Our last exhibition game is in Las Vegas against the Cubs. I find myself thinking about what the Mariners' clubhouse looks like and how nice it will be to have a locker there. There are still a few cuts to be made, and then we are off to Seattle. When the game ends, I pack my bag and give it to the clubhouse attendant. I put on a suit and am walking toward the team charter when I see Lee Pelekoudas, the assistant general manager, just ahead, waving as if he wants to flag me down.

He must be coming to congratulate me, I think.

R.A., I'm sorry to have to tell you this, but you didn't make the team.

My mouth literally drops open. I honestly think this must be a joke: Let's pull a prank on the guy and see how amusing his reaction is.

I am not amused. Lee can see I am not amused.

He says, I know you're disappointed, but I want you to know we like you a lot, so we made a trade to keep you. [Under Rule 5 regulations, clubs that lose a player can get that player back for $25,000 if the club that selected him doesn't put him on the big-league roster. The Twins bought me back, and then the Mariners traded a minor-league catcher, Jair Hernandez, in order to keep me.] We are keeping you on the forty-man roster. You just didn't make the opening-day roster.

Mouth still open. Getting dry now. Lee walks away.

Moments pass in silence, and I am angry. Why do I keep getting passed over? I pitched my butt off all last year and the Brewers never called me up. Now I pitch my butt off all spring, end it with a six-inning one-hitter, and am told I am not good enough. Is this more of the baseball-people-don't-trust-the-knuckleball crap?

What on earth do I have to do, God? I say to myself. I want to let God have it, when general manager Bill Bavasi comes over and attempts to console me. I let him have it instead.

You're mad, aren't you? he says.

You bet your butt I am mad.

You have a right to be mad. You pitched great. I'd be mad too. Just don't stay mad, because we are going to need you.

Slowly I start to calm down. I appreciate Bill's words, and though I am still confounded by the club's decision, I don't think he's feeding me a line of bull. I'm glad I am honest with my emotions. It's part of getting better.

I call Anne and tell her the news, and tell her not to come yet, because I am not on the big-league team.

I want to be with you no matter what team you're on, she says. So she flies up and we drive around Tacoma, home of the Mariners' Triple-A affiliate, the Rainiers. We find a little rental house up the hill from Puget Sound. It's a sweet place in an idyllic setting. Anne returns home, and when she comes back out with the kids, my mom flies with her to lend her a hand. My mom stays with us for the better part of a week. It is such a blessing to have her. She is doing anything and everything that's needed, and her patience and nurturing of the children has no bounds. Literally every day of my life, I feel more love and more gratitude for having my mother in my life.

APART FROM not being in the big leagues, Tacoma is a great place to pitch. The air is cool, the grass long, the fences tall. I lose my first couple of decisions, but I pitch deep into the games and we just don't score any runs. I hate losing, but my knuckleball is good and dependable.

The hitters' swings will tell you if your knuckleball is any good. That's the only feedback you need, Charlie always used to tell me. I am getting a lot of bad swings, and swings and misses. True to

Bavasi's word, the Mariners call me up in mid-April. I get to Seattle as soon as I can, driving as if the invitation had an expiration time. I am deliriously happy but privately paranoid.

What if this is another one of those deals like the time the Brewers asked me to join them in St. Louis, then sent me right back down?

It's a surreal feeling as I walk up to Safeco Field. I always wanted to believe I'd get back to the big leagues, but there's a small demon inside me that toils ceaselessly against hope, wanting to convince me that I am done, used up, that there is no recovering from the six-homer game, or my deeper past.

I have paid too much attention to the demon for too many years. I am done paying attention.

Piss off, I tell the demon.

After I get my uniform (number 41) and say hello to my new teammates, including Ichiro, Raul Ibañez, and Adrian Beltre, I shake hands with the manager, John McLaren, and the pitching coach, Mel Stottlemyre.

I knew you'd be here sooner rather than later, McLaren says.

You'll be in the bullpen tonight, R.A., Mel says.

I spend my first big-league practice in two years shagging flies in right field, in my new favorite American League park, which is friendly to pitchers and stunning to look at, with a giant retractable roof, and steel and iron latticework, and grass that is so verdant that it should have its own name: Safeco green. I savor every minute.

We're playing the Kansas City Royals, our starter Jarrod Washburn going against the Royals' Zack Greinke. At Safeco, a dark blue cinder-block wall separates the home bullpen from the visiting bullpen. Each inning I throw ten balls against the wall, monitoring the spin and feeling my release point. I am back in Uncle Ricky's gym, working on my pitch.

The game moves quickly. Greinke is cruising and Jarrod gives up three runs through six, and the Royals extend the lead to 5–1 in the top of the eighth. When the phone rings, I know what bullpen coach Norm Charlton is going to say before he even speaks:

You got the ninth.

Greinke throws another scoreless inning, and now it's time, and I am ready, more excited than nervous, fearless in Seattle. Hope is a powerful life force. As I warm up, I have no quivering leg or racing heart. I say a prayer to thank God not just for this opportunity but for the blessing to live in the moment fully.

David DeJesus is the first batter, a speedy guy with some pop in his bat. I fall behind 2–0, and then get him to pop out on a 3–2 fastball. I throw a good knuckleball to get ahead on Mark Grudziel-anek, the Royals' number two hitter, before getting him on a weak grounder with a fastball away.

The third hitter is one of their power guys, Mark Teahen. I like facing guys who have power, because they like to swing hard. A hard swing and a good knuckleball are the stuff of knuckleball pitcher dreams. I go up 0–2 on a couple of good knuckleballs and, on 1–2, throw a wicked knuckleball that seems to have its own gravitational pull, as if it stops in midair and starts back up again. It does this twice before Teahen swings. It's one of the best knuckleballs of my life.

Teahen misses it by almost a foot.

I walk off the field feeling as light and happy as you can feel when you are down four in the ninth. My one-inning reentry to the major leagues couldn't have gone any better. In the clubhouse afterward, a few writers ask me about how it feels to be back. I don't fake it: I tell the truth about how emotional it is and the hope I have in it. I fight back tears, and it's okay.

Forty-five minutes later, after a nice dinner in the clubhouse, I walk down the tunnel to the dugout and sit on the bench and take in the quiet afterglow of an empty stadium. A couple of grounds crew workers are tamping the mound and raking around the bases. In the twenty-four months since my previous big-league appearance, I almost lost my marriage, considered ending my life, nearly died in a river, and finally let go of my terrible secret. I began to be authentic and tell the truth; now, like the Safeco grounds crew, I am willing to rake through everything. In the soft, warming light of Safeco Field, I thank God for the gift of being here and then stop to take in the splendor of the scene before me, scanning from left-field foul pole to right-, a ballpark that looks like Oz, a peace growing inside me, along with a belief from somewhere that the best is yet to come.

THE WORLD-CHAMPION Red Sox come to town at the end of May, and for me that doesn't mean Manny and Ortiz or Dustin Pedroia. It means Tim Wakefield. He's the best knuckleballer in the game—and the only full-time one besides me. I get to the park early on Memorial Day afternoon and write a note to Tim, asking if we might get together and talk for a bit while he's in town. I give it to the clubhouse guy and he hand delivers it to Tim in the Red Sox clubhouse.

Meet me behind the plate in ten minutes, Tim says.

We talk for forty-five minutes. Tim is a warm and generous man, one of the nicest people in the game, and I take full advantage, firing questions at him the way I did with Charlie and with Coach

Forehand in my "Lapdog" days. I want to know about his grip, his nails, his tricks for killing spin. I want to know it all. I want to know about his psyche with the pitch, and his confidence.

Do you ever worry that one day you'll get out there and you just won't have it? About the pitch just deserting you? I ask.

No, he says. That never happens.

His certainty is scary. I envy him his self-conviction. I am still insecure with my knuckleball, fretting often about where I am with it, anxious that one day it's going to completely abandon me, flit away like a hummingbird, never to return.

Tim is throwing a bullpen today, and I ask if it's okay if I watch. He checks with John Farrell, the Sox pitching coach, and he says sure. Here's the knucklehead brotherhood in play again: there's no chance that an opposing pitcher, no matter how nice a guy, is going to invite me to watch how he grips and throws his split-fingered fastball or his slider. Those are state secrets.

Knuckleballers don't keep secrets. It's as if we have a greater mission beyond our own fortunes. And that mission is to pass it on, to keep the pitch alive. Maybe that's because we are so different, and the pitch is so different, but I think it has more to do with the fact that this is a pitch that almost all of us turn to in desperation. It is what enables us to keep pitching, stay in the big leagues, when everything else has failed. So we feel gratitude toward the pitch. It becomes way more than just a means to get an out.

It becomes a way of life.

Tim throws forty pitches in his bullpen. I study everything that he is doing. He is tremendously consistent with his pitch, and for me that is the biggest difference between us at this point. My best knuckleball is on par with his best knuckleball, but his so-so knuckleball is much better than my so-so knuckleball. He throws seven or eight out of ten knuckleballs that are really good. I am more in the six-to-seven range.

More than that, I learn from Tim that not every one has to be perfect. I drive myself batty trying to make every one perfect.

They just have to be good enough to get an out, Tim says. He makes a point of emphasizing the importance of arm path: bringing your arm through in the same way, down the center of your body, as if you were going to knock your pitching hand into your cup.

I thank Tim profusely when he's all done, and soon I am in my own bullpen, throwing my own knuckleball, trying to get better. Tim inspires me again two days later when he shuts us down over eight innings, giving up five hits and a single run, striking out eight and walking nobody. It is a masterful performance, but Erik Bedard, Brandon Morrow, and J. J. Putz are a little better, combining for a two-hit shutout. It is the perfect ending, as far as I am concerned. I can never root against my own team, even with Tim pitching, but I get the next best thing: a knuckleballer pitching brilliantly and dominating big-league hitters, and my team winning the game.

I HAVE MY BEST stretch of pitching as a knuckleballer over the next six weeks. I am getting ahead, changing speeds, throwing it with conviction, and when I put together a fourteen-inning scoreless streak out of the pen, I start to think I'm narrowing the gap between Tim and me. We fly to Toronto to take on the Blue Jays and McLaren calls on me in the bottom of the eighth in a 2–2 game. I strike out pinch hitter Brad Wilkerson to get started, then get Lyle Overbay and Marco Scutaro on groundouts.

In the bottom of the ninth, Scott Rolen comes up with the winning run at third. I get him to bounce out to force extra innings, and we win in ten on Miguel Cairo's suicide squeeze. I am the pitcher of record, and when Putz comes on and gets the save, I have my first big-league victory in almost three years.

J.J. hands me the ball, and I know exactly where it is going. It's going to the woman who captivated me when she was twelve, curled up in the den with her lion's-mane hair and homework. She's back in Nashville with our three kids, but I want her to feel included, to be part of this.

After the game, I take the ball back to my hotel room and write an inscription on it. I have a lot to say and a baseball is not even three inches in diameter. I write small:

Dearest Anne—

I wanted you to have this ball as a memento to keep.
It is the win I got vs. the Toronto Blue Jays on 6/9/08,
my first win since 2005. Let this ball communicate to
you how much I desire you to be a part of my life and
who I am authentically made to be. Accept this gift
as a celebration of living differently and being in the
moment together. You are so valuable to me and I am
honored that you would share my life with me and
let me be a part of yours. I cannot promise to love
you perfectly, but I can promise to give you who I am
fully and in earnest. You are cherished.

—R.A.

MONDAY, AUGUST 29, 2011
Citi Field

I feel for my catchers, because catching a knuckleball is one of the hardest and most thankless tasks in baseball. Josh Thole has made huge strides in the last two years in handling the job. This spring, a conversation with Doug Mirabelli, the guy who caught Tim Wakefield all those years in Boston, made all the difference.

Tonight, I throw seven shutout innings and strike out six against the Marlins, raising my record to 6–11. Josh had a fine game behind the plate.

Here is what it's like to catch me, in Josh's own words:

Catching a knuckleball is a different cat, for sure. They are the most mentally draining games of all, because you have to concentrate so hard and be so alert, just to try to get the thing to land in your glove. I use a glove called the Rawlings Spark that actually belongs to R.A. It's a women's softball catcher's glove, and about one third bigger than a regular catcher's glove. I can't even imagine trying to catch him with a regular glove. I'd be going back to the backstop every pitch.

R.A.'s knuckleball is so unpredictable, and can break so much so late, that it's almost like you have to surround the pitch more than catch it. Before I talked to Doug, I used to give R.A. a target, the way I do with conventional pitchers. When you do that, you have a tendency to have a stiff wrist and to reach out for pitches, which you can't do with the knuckleball. Doug told me to just keep the glove relaxed, kind of resting on your left knee. If you watch me catching R.A., you'll see now that I don't hold the glove up at all; it's down, like I'm not even expecting a pitch. That simple change has made all the difference because it makes it much easier to track and keep up with the flight of the ball.

The other change Doug suggested was to angle my body toward the second baseman. That clears my knees out of the way and eliminates lower-half movement, and leaves my glove hand closer to the plate, ready to snag the pitch when it's done breaking. These two changes have made a 100 percent difference for me.

Doug also was a great help with the mental aspect. He said that if you are catching the knuckleball, no matter how good you are, you are going to lead the league in passed balls. There's no way around it. Hearing that helped me relax and not get down on myself. The pitch is hard enough to catch without doing it when you are fighting yourself.

KNUCKLEBALLER'S NOTE: Josh did indeed lead the league with sixteen passed balls. But he had only two of them after July 25, so the Mirabelli wisdom clearly kicked in.

CHAPTER EIGHTEEN

GETTING MY PHIL

Three doors down from my locker in the Mariners clubhouse is the baseball home of Ichiro Suzuki. He is such a hit-making marvel, such a singular superstar, you need to use only his first name for everyone to know who you are talking about. I've spent my whole career seeking the secret of consistency. Is it repetition? Is it mind-set? Is it purely mechanics—and the ability to repeat them again and again?

Then I observe Ichiro, a wiry little top of a man, and realize it is easy: all you need is the hand-eye coordination of an athletic virtuoso; the precision of a Swiss watchmaker; and the drive and discipline of a Japanese martial artist, preparing for every game with utterly fanatical attention to routine and detail.

Ichiro racked up 200-plus hits in each of his first ten seasons, making a stupendous feat seem as inevitable as five o'clock traffic. He won ten straight Gold Gloves, won an MVP in his first year from Japan, and broke George Sisler's all-time single-season hit record when he knocked 262 hits in 2004. I was in the Rangers

bullpen when he broke the record, with a single up the middle off
Ryan Drese. Ichiro had three hits and a steal that night.

Just another workday.

Ichiro's routine is calibrated to the minute, from the time he gets
to the park every day to when he uses the bathroom before the
game. He takes the same amount of swings in the cage during batting practice. He eats the same pregame meal (a salmon rice ball)
at the same time (ninety minutes before game time). His stretching
routine is so thorough and intricate, you wonder if he moonlights
as a contortionist for Cirque du Soleil. He is such a perfectionist
that he refuses to do interviews in English, even though he can
speak it quite well. He's afraid he might get a word wrong, so he
always uses his interpreter. Ichiro's approach over 162 games never
varies. Nothing changes regardless of the results. The man is so
vigorously regimented that all you can do is simply surrender to the
fact that you can try to match his discipline, but you never will.

Ichiro inspires me with his preparation and motivates me to
ramp up my own readiness. I feel like it is working as the 2008
season hits its quarter pole. The key to good knuckleballing is
having the same feel for the pitch, over and over and over. That
means having the same grip on the ball, the same release, the same
follow-through. If anything is off even slightly, the ball is going to
rotate and your outings are going to be brief.

Though I'm working out of the pen, I feel that I've finally found
my niche at the big-league level. I have given up three runs in my
last twenty innings and walked only five, while striking out thirteen. I am feeling more confident than ever with the pitch. Being
hopeful is still something new for me. I am beginning to like the
concept.

On the charter flight back to Seattle from Toronto, I'm sitting near the back, listening to my headphones, reveling in my optimism, when I see Mel Stottlemyre, our pitching coach, coming down the aisle. It is not uncommon for coaches to wander to the back of the plane during the flight—a good time to process out what has been going right or wrong with one's performance.

Mel sits down in the seat next to me.

R.A., you've been throwing the ball well, and we want to start you next week against the Nationals, he says.

I gulp but try to disguise it.

Thanks, Mel. I appreciate that. Whatever the club needs is fine with me, I tell him.

We speak for a few minutes and Mel heads back to the front. I gulp again and look out the window and feel a stab of guilt, because I just told a lie to my pitching coach, another pitching coach who is one of the all-time good guys.

Here's the God's honest truth: I do not want to go into the Mariners' rotation. I don't want to change anything. I know it's a compliment that they want me to take on a bigger role, but my entire career has been a nonstop high-wire act—and I've fallen into the net too many times to count. I am finally in a place where I have a niche in the bullpen and I'm pitching effectively. I don't want to mess with it.

Why now? I say to myself.

It's not a feeling I can reveal to Mel or anybody else.

I am not proud of my lack of faith in myself, but the truth is that at this point in my journey my career feels about as sturdy as a house of toothpicks. You move one and the whole thing is going to crumble.

Three days go by and I start against the Nationals in Seattle. I get Cristian Guzmán and Elijah Dukes on weak grounders to start the game but then get nicked for a run, and nicked for six more in the second, the Nationals lighting me up like a Roman candle. I don't have good location, and the knuckleball just isn't dancing. By the time I leave, after recording 5 outs, I have given up 7 earned runs in 1⅓ innings.

So much for my scoreless streak.

My second start is another award winner. This time my lighting up is more like a bottle rocket, courtesy of the Florida Marlins, who score 5 runs off me in 3⅔ innings. I have now given up 12 runs in 5⅓ innings as a starter. My momentum has been trashed and I have no one to blame but myself. I pitch without conviction that I can throw my knuckleball for strikes, so the minute I fall behind I throw 85-mile-per-hour fastballs. I pitch with my mind racing, distracted, everywhere but in the moment. I pitch much the way I did in the six-home-run game against the Tigers, throwing it up there and hoping for the best. I thought I was beyond that. Apparently I'm not.

When will I ever get it?

I try to channel my inner Ichiro, but my consistency is still all over the place. Some days I emphatically trust the pitch and do great, and others I abandon it at the first sign of adversity, terrified to make a mistake. Because I have trouble committing to the knuckleball in 2–0, 3–1, and 3–2 counts, I wind up throwing fastballs and get into patterns.

I end up backing up a lot of bases.

I finish the year in the pen, and pitch just well enough to not get sent down. For the season, my ERA in the pen is under 3.0, and as a starter it is 6.72. I am a Jekyll and Hyde character, and in November the Mariners have seen enough and they non-tender me, which means "We don't want you anymore."

For the third time in my career, I am a free agent, and despite my ups and downs I believe I've shown enough in my good moments that somebody might want me, and the somebody turns out to be the Twins again. They sign me to a contract and extend a big-league invitation for spring training.

Before I get to camp, I decide that I need to see another therapist. This one is not for my head. It's for my pitch, and who better to consult on that front than Hall of Famer Phil Niekro? The late Dave Niehaus, my friend and the longtime Mariners' sportscaster, met Phil in Cooperstown in the middle of 2008 and mentioned that I'd like to meet with him and learn from him. Phil said, Anytime. Tell him to give me a call.

Anytime is now.

I call Phil and introduce myself.

I know who you are. I've seen you on TV a couple of times this year, he says.

We arrange for me to meet him in Atlanta next week at an indoor baseball facility near his home. It's the middle of January. I send him video ahead of time so he can get familiar with my mechanics.

Jeff Forehand, my buddy who is the coach at Lipscomb University, comes along to catch me.

Phil is sixty-nine years old and looks great, as if he could still baffle batters with his knuckler.

Let's get to work, he says. I have my laptop and I pop in one of the DVDs I sent him, one of the stronger games I had over the year.

I want to see one of your bad games, Phil says. We learn more from those.

I insert a new disc and Phil watches intently. Two line-drive base hits into my outing, Phil tells me to stop it.

Watch your hips, R.A., he says. You see them? You're losing so much finish by not firing your hips toward the plate, not getting your backside involved.

I see instantly what he is referring to. My right foot stays behind, as if glued to the rubber, robbing me of explosion toward the plate and the hand speed that comes with it. Obviously the knuckleball isn't a power pitch, so the point isn't to generate speed for the sake of speed. The point is that by firing the hips forward, bringing the body toward the plate in a single, tight motion, you keep your body properly aligned and greatly increase your chances of killing rotation and throwing a good, hard knuckleball with sharp, late movement—or finish, as we like to say.

Your knuckleball is lazy, Phil says. You need to give it energy.

We move to the indoor cages and a mound. I start throwing to Jeff, trying to implement what we talked about in the film room. I think about my hips and detaching my right foot from the rubber.

With every throw, I feel myself almost hop toward the plate, a sign that I am getting my hips involved. I feel myself coming toward the plate hard, with athletic power. The results are staggering. One after another, knuckleballs come out with no spin, dropping by the foot. Jeff, a good ballplayer, looks like a matador, waving at them as they flutter toward him.

That's the one, Phil says when I throw a knuckleball to his liking. I can't get back up on the mound fast enough after each throw. It feels great. I feel like I could throw for hours. Before I even get off the mound, I am full of gratitude, not just for Phil, but also for Charlie and Tim—for their expertise and their generosity of spirit. All three of them have made a point to open themselves up for me, to help a knuckleballer in need.

I'm part of a brotherhood, and the only prerequisite for admission is a passion for the pitch.

I gather my computer, my notebook, and my glove and pack everything up.

I can't thank you enough, Phil. This has just been a tremendous help. To have the chance to learn from someone like you is just priceless.

I have five hundred dollars in my pocket and try to give it to Phil. He looks insulted.

It's been my pleasure, R.A., he says. You are a good athlete, I can see that. Remember to be one on the mound as well. If you keep working on being an athlete and getting your hips involved, I think you're going to get where you want to go.

I will, Phil, thank you.

I drive north out of Atlanta on Interstate 75, feeling as if I've got an IV drip of adrenaline. I want to stop at every rest area and throw knuckleballs to Jeff. I want to stop at the Tennessee state line and throw more knuckleballs. I feel as if I've just been given the last big piece of a complicated puzzle, and now it all fits. Thanks to Charlie, I have the proper grip and the awareness of coming straight through the doorframe. Thanks to Tim Wakefield, I have the right arm path, releasing the ball and bringing my arm through toward my cup. Thanks to Phil, I'm firing my hips and exploding toward the plate, an action that is giving my ball a devastating finish before it gets to the plate.

You have an angry knuckleball, Phil says. It comes in so much harder than the way guys have historically thrown the pitch. That's a tremendous asset if you can harness it.

I spend the remaining days before spring training in the Lipscomb gymnasium, refining my delivery, doing all I can to make sure the puzzle pieces fit snugly together. The difference in the quality of my knuckleball is striking; I used to throw maybe three out of ten that had a big late break; now it is happening with almost everyone I throw properly. The only downside is nobody wants to catch me. Jeff is beaten up and doesn't want to do it anymore. A few college kids take turns, but lately when I show up with a glove and a bucket of balls, they suddenly have pressing commitments.

As I prepare to go to camp with my third organization in three years, the adrenaline drip is stronger than ever, and so is my belief that I can be something other than a mediocre major-league pitcher.

IN MY FIRST OFFICIAL minute as a member of the Minnesota Twins, I slip into an old habit. I walk in the clubhouse of their spring-training complex in Fort Myers, Florida, and immediately begin to scan the place for my locker and number. It's not because I want to know where to go. It's because I want to know what they think of me.

If you are lockering next to veteran guys—Joe Mauer or Justin Morneau, for instance—and have a number in the thirties or forties, that is the best possible news. If you are in a neighborhood with the bullpen catcher and the second-string batboy with a number 81 shirt in your locker, you're probably not going to need to shop for real estate.

It takes a little time, but I finally find my space—in a row with Joe Nathan and Francisco Liriano. My number is 39. This is welcome news, and spring unfolds auspiciously. In outing after outing, I am filling up the strike zone with as fierce a knuckleball as I have ever had. The puzzle is getting solved. I face the Orioles one afternoon in Sarasota, Florida. Brian Roberts, the Orioles second baseman is up. I throw him three knuckleballs and he misses all three—the last one so badly that the bat flies into the stands and he looks at the catcher and starts to giggle. (When knuckleballers get the giggle response—which really means *I am completely flummoxed and utterly embarrassed*—you know you're having a good day.) I start some games, and throw out of the pen some games, all with good results. I am hoping to show my versatility with the pitch. I finish the spring with 18 strikeouts in 17 innings, 4 walks, and a 2.02 ERA.

Camp is almost over and I still haven't heard anything. At my locker one morning, I get a tap on the shoulder from Rick Anderson, the Twins' pitching coach.

Gardy wants to see you in his office, Rick says. Gardy is Ron Gardenhire, the manager.

My heart shudders. Shoulder taps are not good this time of year. Skip-wants-to-see-you-in-his-office messages are even less good this time of year. I don't want to think about 2008, when I pitched my tail off for the Mariners and got sent to Tacoma, but how can I not? I want to hope for the best, but I'm not very good at that. Given my history of failure and disappointment, you can understand why.

You've pitched well. You left it all out there, I tell myself. *Don't jump to conclusions.*

I walk down the hallway to Gardy's office. It feels like one of those horror movies where the hallway seems like it's on a treadmill: you keep walking and you never get there.

I finally get there.

Have a seat, Gardy says.

I sit.

We all love the way you've thrown the ball this spring.

Oh, no.

Thanks, I say.

You've been solid or better than that in every appearance.

Not again.

I keep waiting for the "but." But it never comes.

You're on the team, R.A. Congratulations. Scott Baker is going to start the season on the DL, and we want you to start the fifth game of the year against the White Sox.

Thank you, Gardy. I do not jump up and down. I want to.

I stay behind in Fort Myers while the team flies to Minnesota, and pitch six innings in a minor-league game. Then I fly north to join the team. It's April 5 and opening day is tomorrow. It will be my fourth time on an opening-day roster, but my first since 2006. I feel euphoric, but I also feel dizzy from the unending ebb and flow of my career: I'm up. I'm down. Up. Down. Up and down again. Now I am up again, and I say a prayer to thank God for being such a real presence in my life and for giving me the strength to persevere. God knows me, hears me, disciplines me, and gives me over to my wicked self only to bring me back in a way that our relationship becomes more rich and robust.

Dear God, I am so grateful for the chance to live in the present unhindered by a past that has once haunted me. I am scared, but I am excited about my start on Friday. Thank You for this opportunity.

I want to add a postscript. I want to ask God for stability, to give me whatever I need to stay in the big leagues for a while... to allow me to have the one thing I have never had: a sustained run of success, a chance to be a truly valued member of a big-league pitching staff. I think of Hemingway and the final line of *The Sun Also Rises*:

"Isn't it pretty to think so?"

I don't pray for this. I don't want to be greedy.

THE START goes well in Chicago. It's thirty-nine degrees and the wind is gusting up to about twenty-five miles per hour, and it feels like I'm pitching in the Arctic Circle. But I get through five and get the victory over José Contreras, and the best part of it is that Anne and our daughters are in the stands (Eli is still too young to spend a night in the Arctic Circle). Anne is with me in this as never before, and even though our marriage is a work in progress and we have our issues to resolve, I am so grateful for her love and forgiveness, for knowing my secrets and shame and still loving me steadfastly. Gabriel and Lila look at me with such love in their eyes that I just keep praying to be a father worthy of this love. When I started the work with Stephen James, he told me something I've never forgotten.

If you aren't willing to face your demons—if you can't find the courage to take on your fear and hurt and anger—you might as well wrap them up with a bow and give them to your children. Because they will be carrying the same thing ... unless you are willing to do the work.

So I do the work. Every day, I do the work, and I am beginning to see big payoffs. Rich payoffs. Since I joined the Twins I have become close to Kevin Slowey, a fellow pitcher and Christian. We talk openly about our lives. I savor his friendship and I trust him with my thoughts and feelings. This is so completely new for me, being able to trust and open up to another man. The work is working. I know there is a long way to go yet, but experiencing the benefits of it gives me fresh fuel to get there, and seeing my children's faces is the greatest motivation of all. They didn't ask for my baggage and I am doing all I can to make sure they don't have to carry my baggage. They don't deserve to feel like they are a burden or a nuisance. Too often in the past I would be short with them and act put-upon around them, particularly before I had a start. They deserve to get my best, to be nurtured and to have their feelings validated. The work I am doing is helping me get beyond myself in ways I never have before, and to be a better father, a more joyful father.

I am a very grateful man for that.

Thank you for the blessing of my wife and children, Lord.

SCOTT BAKER returns from the DL and I go to the pen, which was the plan all along. I am pitching creditably, and if my knuckleball is not quite as sharp as it was in the spring, it is still coming out of my hand well. The Royals come to town to play a weekend series in early May. The big news for the Twins is that our all-star catcher, Joe Mauer, is coming off the disabled list and is ready to start the season.

The Saturday game is a wild affair, 7–7 in the top of the eleventh. Craig Breslow walks the bases loaded and Gardy comes out to get him and calls for me. It's a tough spot, made tougher because Joe has not caught me before. Honestly, I'm not sure if he has ever caught a knuckleball.

Gardy hands me the ball and says, Don't throw your knuckler in this situation. Work with your fastball and slider. We don't want Joe chasing it to the backstop and runners scoring, okay?

I am dumbfounded. Don't throw my knuckler? That's how I get people out. Throw my slider? Um, I don't even throw a slider. I look at Joe. He shrugs and runs back behind the plate. I am a little unsettled at this turn of events. I should know better at this stage of my career, but I let it get into my head. I go up 1–2 on the Royals' designated hitter, John Buck, but I am thinking way too much, feeling acute pressure to put my fastball in precise spots.

On the eighth pitch of the at-bat—all fastballs—I walk Buck, forcing in the go-ahead run. I want to scream. The one thing I couldn't do in that situation, walk the guy, I do. The Royals have the lead now without even getting a hit.

I get the next hitter, Alberto Collaspo, to ground out on a sinker, but David DeJesus singles in a run on another fastball and I have had enough. I call Joe out to the mound. Listen, Joe, I know you haven't caught me before, but I've got to throw my knuckleball. That's the reason I'm here.

Let it rip, Joe says. I'll be fine.

I hit Miguel Olivo with a knuckleball, and then get Tony Peña to ground out meekly to second to get out of the inning.

I don't get the loss, and don't even get the runs charged to me, since Breslow put them on, but I feel plenty responsible for us losing the game. I am decompressing, unhappily, at my locker when Gardy comes by.

I'm sorry I put you in that position. It wasn't fair to you, and I should've known better, he says.

Hey, Gardy, don't worry about it. It happens. I appreciate your apology.

I head off for the shower, impressed that Gardy would do this, own what he feels was his screwup. It's a glimpse into why he's such a good manager of people and why his players like to play for him so much. Gardy may have messed up tactically in this case, but did something infinitely harder when he came over to take full responsibility for it. I wonder how many managers would be secure enough, and grounded enough, to do such a thing.

My guess is: not many.

I appreciate it even more because I have had to take ownership of far more serious things in my life. I know how hard it is to
do, and I also know the redemptive power there is in being able
to do it. The longer I live, the more I come to believe that the ability to say the words "I'm sorry" is one of the greatest healing agents
in the world.

I RECOVER well from my Royals outing and pitch well for the rest
of the first half. In ten appearances in the month of June, I give up
only eight hits and one run, lowering my season ERA to 2.36 at the
beginning of July. I am on one of the best rolls of my life as a knuckleballer, with a pitch that is more consistent than ever, and that has
great finish. I feel as though I am really starting to synthesize all
that I've learned from Charlie, Phil, and Tim, and developing my
own personality with the pitch as well. Beyond that, I am getting
so many repetitions throwing it that it is becoming instinctual and
organic, with a repeatable delivery, which makes for a much higher
percentage of strikes.

I play catch virtually every day with either Kevin Slowey, my
best friend on the team, or Nate Dammann, the bullpen catcher.
They wind up chasing a bunch of knuckleballs that they can't catch,
affirmation to me that I am reaching a new level.

After I get back from the All-Star break, Kevin develops a wrist
injury and can't be a catch partner anymore. Nate gets other duties
assigned to him, so in the span of days I am stripped of my catchers.
The only guy who is left without a partner on the team is Joe Nathan, our star closer, whose catch partner has gotten claimed off
waivers.

Joe and I are friends, with an easy, cordial bond. We partner up after the break. The only problem for me is that it is Joe Nathan. Not that I'm intimidated. I just don't want our all-star closer to take a knuckleball on the knee or have to chase the thing into the far-flung crevasses of the Metrodome. So I start backing off my repetitions. I start worrying more about Joe's work than my own. I want to make sure he gets what he needs. I reduce the number of knuckleballs I throw by half during our pre-batting-practice catch time. I gradually start to lose my feel. I need my repetitions and I am not getting them. It's not Joe's fault. It's my own fault for not finding a way to get what I need.

Faster than you can say Wilbur Wood, I have regressed into the R.A. of a year or two before: a vastly worse pitcher. After the break, I get knocked around so badly, my ERA jumps to the fours, the low point probably coming in Anaheim against the Angels, who pummel me for 4 hits and 3 runs in $\frac{1}{3}$ of an inning. In early August, the Twins acquire Carl Pavano and need a spot on the roster.

Guess who gets elected to provide it?

I can't fathom it after the way I pitched in June and the run of success I had, but I am back in the minor leagues. I am a member of the Rochester Red Wings, one of the few minor-league teams I haven't played for, or so it feels. I go into the rotation and I get spanked around. I do not get a September call-up. It's my own doing, I know that, but it still feels as though the knuckleball naysayers out there—no small club—are much quicker to bury a knuckleballer compared with a regular pitcher. It's the same old refrain: How can you trust that pitch, or the people who throw it? It's too flaky, too flighty.

Too unreliable.

Am I making excuses? Am I ever going to get there?

Am I deluding myself?

I am so much more self-aware, so much healthier, than I've ever been before, with the work I've done on myself. Am I not seeing something here? Is this a great big blind spot I have, a mental blot as big as the mound itself? Am I in denial, like a drunk whose life is being ruined by alcohol but who insists the problem is everything *but* alcohol?

No, I do not think I am in denial. In my heart and soul, I believe I am getting progressively better as a knuckleball pitcher. I believe I can be a positive, contributing member of a big-league pitching staff. If you want to look at my history and argue otherwise, that's your prerogative. Go ahead. But I know my pitch and I know myself and I know I am getting better.

I just need one more chance. Will any team give me a chance?

My agent's phone rings. The caller is Omar Minaya from New York.

We're interested in talking to you about R. A. Dickey, Omar says.

Surrounded by crumpled water cups, wads of sunflower seeds, and jubilant Atlanta Braves, I sit in the dugout of Turner Field with one question: Why is this game so freakin' painful? It seems ludicrous that a simple game can make you hurt so much. It's not a hurt that comes from throwing 115 pitches, but the kind that comes when you pour your heart into a piece of work and then watch somebody come along and spray-paint it.

The Braves just beat me, 1–0, and are hugging and high-fiving everywhere I look. Soon the Braves will be gone and Styx will arrive for a postgame concert. The way I feel, I may stay in the dugout for the whole show, catatonic. I have just pitched three-hit ball and shut out the Braves into the eighth.

It earns me a pat on the backside from my manager and my thirteenth loss of the year. My ERA is 3.35.

I lose the game on a bouncing RBI single up the middle by the great Chipper Jones. I almost caught it. That makes the hurt even worse, and so does the fact that twice I failed to get a bunt down in key at-bats, a screwup that could've cost us the game. (I'm proud of being a competitive hitter and a dependable bunter. This failure is deeply frustrating.) But maybe the most irksome thing is that I missed on a 3–2 pitch and walked Martin Prado just ahead of Chipper. You can't walk a guy there. You just can't.

And I did, because I threw him a full-count knuckleball that stayed up.

There's an old baseball adage that you can't let yourself get beaten by anything but your best pitch—that you have to dance with the girl you bring. I bring Ms. Knuckleball to every party. Today she is a thing of beauty, dancing and sliding and flowing, the Brave men wanting her but not being able to catch her. Today she is also fickle. Earlier in my career I wouldn't have trusted my knuckleball in a 3-2 count and I would've thrown Prado a sinker, a much easier pitch to control. I can't do that now. I have to go at them with my best stuff or why even be out there at all? Maybe 90 percent of the time throwing the game I did will get you a win. Tonight it doesn't, because Tim Hudson was just a little better than me.

So I sit in the dugout with the cups and seeds and my regrets, thinking about my feeble bunts and my three strikeouts—the first time I have struck out three times in a game since eighth grade. I think about the strike I couldn't throw to Prado, and the strikes I couldn't throw to Jason Heyward, a .220 hitter, to lead off the same inning.

I am deep into this unhappy recap, watching workers set things up for Styx, when I look up to see Phil Niekro walking toward me. I haven't seen Phil since the offseason after 2008, when I went down to Atlanta to work with him. He was incredibly kind and helpful to me, and wouldn't accept a penny for his time. Just one knuckleballer helping another, big time.

I get up and shake his hand.

You had a great one today, Phil says. I'm sorry for you that it ended the way it did.

Thanks, Phil. There was a lot of you in that pitcher you saw out there today.

We talk for a few minutes about the day, the knuckleball, the

Braves. He is so affirming it can't help but take the edge off my ache. I begin to feel lighter, gladdened by the opportunities I've been given, the people like Phil and Charlie Hough who have invested in me, and the grace of God that has brought me to this place—a place where I can hold the disappointment of a moment along with the blessing of another chance.

Phil smiles as he turns to leave.

You need to come back down to see me so I can help you with your bunting, he says.

CHAPTER NINETEEN

CITI DWELLER

The Dickey Baseball Tour Across America arrives at its latest destination—Buffalo, New York—in April 2010. I don't want to count my number of stops, but I do know they've included the Dust Belt (Oklahoma City), the Coffee Belt (Seattle), and now the Snow Belt (Buffalo). And that's not even counting the Shuffleboard Belt (Port Charlotte, Florida). I find a two-bedroom apartment over a garage, a short ways out of town. I set up a card table for our kitchen table and go to Wal-Mart for our bedding—three inflatable mattresses that will be distributed thusly: a double for Anne and me, another double for our girls, Gabriel and Lila, and a single raft for Eli.

I have no idea how long we will be sleeping on these mattresses; I just blow them up and hope for the best.

I want to believe this is going to lead somewhere, but my new team—the New York Mets—is not making it easy. I signed with the Mets over the winter, mostly because I know Omar Minaya from our days in Texas and I felt his interest was sincere. He's tried to sign me for the past two years, so that has to mean something.

Omar tells me the fib that every team tells its free-agent pitchers—
"You're going to have a chance to make the rotation"—but that
doesn't do much to allay my anxiety when I get to camp and see all
the pitchers, squadrons of them, trying to make the team. Well, it
seems like squadrons of them; maybe two dozen. It's hard not to be
insecure about your chances of beating out everyone when you've
bounced around to as many Belts as I have. I am trying to forget
the body count and working on throwing the best knuckleball I can
throw when Dan Warthen, the pitching coach, stops by my locker
and, yes, taps me on the shoulder, a month into camp. I, of course,
know instantly that there are two scenarios that can play out here.

This could be a good, Gardenhire shoulder tap. Or it could be a
bad, John McLaren shoulder tap. I am rooting for the former.

Jerry wants to see you in his office, Dan tells me. Jerry is Jerry
Manuel, the Mets manager—the same Jerry Manuel who basically
called me the twelfth best pitcher on a twelve-man staff when I
came on in relief against his White Sox in 2001.

It is March 15. I've unpacked my bags in Port St. Lucie, but
the spring still has a while to run. Jerry doesn't waste any time, or
emotion.

We're sending you out to the minor-league side, he says. Go
down there and get your work in. We know you will be a professional.

I am the first player cut that spring. Not the second, or the third.
The first.

I console myself at the end of the day by filling up a little goody
bag from the ready supply of snacks and beverages that are in the
big-league clubhouse, heading home with pouches of trail mix and
a few bottles of chocolate milk and Gatorade. I may not be a major-
league pitcher in the Mets' eyes, but I am making sure I eat like one.

When I report to the minor-league complex, Terry Collins, who is running that department at the time, gives me more bad news.

There's a rule for all minor leaguers in the organization that no beards are allowed, Terry says.

I have had my beard for six years. I am fond of my beard. I'm not going to let it interfere with my livelihood, but the rule seems inane.

Are you serious? I ask.

Yes, I am.

There's no exemption for a thirty-five-year-old man with a wife and three kids?

No, I'm sorry, R.A. There's not.

So I gather Gabriel, Lila, and Eli around, and we go on the porch of my Port St. Lucie rental house, and we make a family project out of shaving Daddy's beard. Everybody gets a turn with the clippers and gets to take a whack out of my lovely, luxurious growth. I'm fit to be a Met organizational player now, but as I rub my bare chin for the first time since 2004, I am wondering anew what the heck I am doing and where this is all going. How long am I going to keep dragging Anne and the kids around the country so I can chase this increasingly far-fetched dream? I know I've asked this question before. More than once. But really, where does it stop? No horn is going to sound, and no clock is going to tick down to zero. It's on me to decide, and I just don't have any clarity about it.

Is it fair to keep doing this? Is it financially foolish? Perseverance is fine and all, but isn't there a time when you have to stop messing around with your grip and be a grown-up?

Yes there is. One morning, I find myself making a call to Lipscomb University and get a nice admissions officer on the phone.

I tell her my name is R. A. Dickey and I am hoping she can answer a few questions for me. I tell her I attended the University of Tennessee some years ago and left school about a year short of getting my degree in English literature. My GPA was over 3.0, so I don't think that's going to be an issue. I think I may want to transfer to Lipscomb so I can finish my studies. I ask her how we can set this in motion.

It's really quite a simple process, the admissions officer says. We just need to get a copy of your transcript from Tennessee and, assuming all the credits are transferrable, we can see where you stand and then get things moving. Depending on departmental requirements, you may not even need a full year of credits.

I thank her for her time and make a note to call Tennessee to get my transcript. My emergent plan is to be an English teacher, but obviously I am not getting hired without a college degree, at least. I remember what a positive impact Miss Brewer at MBA had on me. It's exciting to imagine myself in a high school classroom, teaching English. With a beard.

I think about what it would be like to be an undergraduate again, fourteen years after I stopped my studies to be a pro ballplayer. I wonder what it will be like to be buying books by Tolstoy instead of throwing knuckleballs by Tulowitzki.

I love literature. But it's hard to even comprehend.

So the classroom is not for now—not yet. The mound is still my office, and I know how the business in the office is conducted. If I get my work done and done well in Buffalo, maybe I'll get a shot at working at company headquarters in New York City. But will I? Will I really get a fair shot if I do well? From what I hear, Omar and Jerry need the club to have a strong showing to keep their jobs; are they going to entrust their futures to a geriatric knuckleballer who has twenty-two career victories and seems to have been knocking around baseball since the Eisenhower administration?

I pray about it, often, and keep working on fitting the puzzle pieces together and being as consistent as I can. In some ways getting sent out early is a blessing, because it means I am going to get lots of work—which is exactly what I need.

After having a bit of a rough go against the Scranton/Wilkes-Barre Yankees in my first start in Buffalo, I pitch into the eighth inning or beyond in my next three starts and am feeling very good. My next start is against the Durham Bulls, the best-hitting team in the International League. It's a brutally cold night, the wind whipping furiously off of Lake Erie. Only three hundred people are in the stands.

Fernando Perez, a switch-hitting outfielder, leads off the game for Durham. I go up 0–2 and float a knuckleball toward the plate. He gets under it and pops it weakly over second base. It plops in for a single.

I retire the next twenty-seven hitters in order. A perfect game, with one mulligan.

I've never had another game quite like it, and not many others have, either. Whoever heard of twenty-eight up, twenty-seven down? I throw only three or four fastballs out of ninety pitches. The knuckleballs have some crazy finish to them, dropping like rocks in a pond. I strike out six, walk nobody, missing the strike zone only twenty-two times over nine innings. Ken Oberkfell, the Buffalo Bisons manager who has been around baseball for more than three decades, tells the press afterward that it may have been the most dominant pitching performance he has ever seen. He played on teams with guys like Mike Scott and a young Tom Glavine, so that is saying something. The club owners reward us with a steak dinner the following night, but the prize I really want is a one-way ticket to Citi Field.

Five weeks into the season, my record is 4–2, my ERA 2.23. I have struck out thirty-seven and walked eight. I wonder if the Mets are paying attention. I'm in the apartment on the air mattress when Oberkfell calls my cell phone. Anne and the kids haven't arrived from Nashville yet because school is still in session. Stephen James has just come up for a visit, and I'm eager to engage him in long talks about God, fatherhood, and living well in the moment.

Sit tight, the Mets might be making a move, Oberkfell says.

Okay, I will. Thanks. I tell Stephen the good news, though it might mean our visit will be cut short.

Ten hours later, I don't have to sit tight anymore, because the Mets want me to join them in Atlanta. The next thing I know, I am throwing in the outfield of Turner Field to Dave Racaniello, the bullpen catcher, with Dan Warthen observing. I am not pitching a game in Atlanta; the Mets just want to see me throw and figure out what they've got. I don't need any more than that for the hope to kick in in a big way. I want more than anything to share it with Anne, and I get to, because she arranges for the kids to stay with her parents and she drives down to Atlanta for a night to meet me and to celebrate this opportunity. Who knows how many more of these will be coming? Who's to say I won't be in a Lipscomb University classroom three months from now? Anne and I both know I am running out of road, and we want to embrace it with all we have. It's a tender time we share, praying together with thanks for the possibilities ahead as we sit on the edge of a bed in a hotel room.

I fly ahead of the team to Washington so I can get a full night's rest. Dan Warthen apparently liked what he saw, because I am

starting the first game of our series against the Nationals in Nationals Park. I walk into the visitor's clubhouse and the equipment
manager hands me a gray road jersey with number 43 on the back.
All I want to do is pitch and find a baseball home. Three hours
before my first game as a New York Met, I am acutely aware of how
much I yearn for stability, to put down roots in a team and be a
completely trustworthy performer, not a 4A guy who can pitch like
Mr. Dependable one night and Lady Gaga the next.

After eating my pregame turkey sandwich in the players' lounge,
I look at video of the Nationals with Dan, then spend some quiet
time in prayer at my locker. I contemplate the fresh start ahead of
me and suddenly all the old doubts and fears are coming at me,
sweeping in like a storm on the prairie. They are coming hard, pelt-
ing me with familiar negativity:

*Do you know how much pressure there is on you tonight? You
know that if you stink, you are right back in Buffalo, don't you?
What if you are as brutal as you were that night against the Tigers?
How many more teams are going to give you a chance? Why don't
you just admit that this is your fifth organization in five years and
nothing is going to change just because your uniform does?*

It is an insidious assault, but here's the switch: I don't let it rock
me anymore or rule me anymore. Because of the work I've done in
counseling, I know that just because a bird of prey may fly into my
head, I don't have to let it build a nest. I can look at it and say,
"There's that bird again," and not give it any power. I can recog-
nize that every athlete in the world has these fears and doubts, and
those that say they don't are liars. The trick that the best athletes
have mastered is that they don't let the birds set up nests. They have
the anxious thoughts and feelings and let them go, brushing them
off the way an umpire brushes off home plate.

One thing I know for sure is that when I take the mound in Nationals Park, I want none of this noise. I want to be fully present with my pitch, the way I learned to be after I came out of the Missouri.

Thanks be to You, God, for giving me another opportunity. I do not take it for granted. Thank You for letting me hold on to hope and to keep pursuing what I believe is within my reach: the chance to be a trustworthy big-league pitcher at last. Please, Lord, let this time be different. Let my family and me flourish here, and belong here. I want to belong so badly, Lord. Please let me perform the way I know that I can. Whatever Your plans are for me, I know that You will care for me and love me and provide me with the strength I need to do Your will. In Jesus' name, Amen.

When I pray, I am not just talking to God. I am deepening my relationship with Him. To me, prayer is not a me-driven, goal-driven endeavor, something I turn to when I really need to pitch a dominant game or get out of a tight spot or a personal crisis. I've never prayed to God and said, "Lord, please let me strike out Albert Pujols four times tonight." Nor will I ever do that. God is not a genie in a bottle that you rub when you want something. He is the ever-present, ever-loving Father, the guiding Spirit of my life, my Light and my Truth. He has a plan for me; I believe that as much as I believe anything in my whole life, and even if I don't end up flourishing in New York or proving myself to be a trustworthy big-league pitcher, I know that's because He has something else in store for me, and whatever that is, I know that I will be at peace.

THE FIRST BATTER I face in my Mets career is Nyjer Morgan, the Nationals' left-handed center fielder. I go up 1–2 on him and throw a knuckleball away and he tries to surprise me, squaring around and bunting, lofting a little pop by the third-base line. I never figured he'd bunt with two strikes to lead off the game, but I get a good break on the ball and sprint off the mound. It's dropping fast and I don't know if I can get there. I know the only shot I have is a headlong dive. So that's what I do, leaving my feet and laying myself out.

I make a sprawling catch by the third-base line. One out.

It is the perfect way to start. I love to field my position. I love being an athlete. I'd rather make a play like that than strike a guy out on three pitches.

After setting down the Nationals without a hit through three innings, I get a lead when Angel Pagan hits an inside-the-park home run in the top of the fourth, but the Nationals break through on three singles, a walk, and a sacrifice fly to score twice in the bottom of the inning.

In the fifth now, I make an ill-advised 2-2 pitch to Livan Hernandez, a very good hitting pitcher, throwing a fastball that he slaps into left for a single, and then I walk Morgan. With two on and nobody out, I am faced with the most pivotal at-bat of the game. A hit or two here and the floodgates open, and I probably don't get out of the fifth—and may be back on the inflatable mattresses in the Snow Belt.

Cristian Guzmán, Washington's second baseman, steps in. I expect him to bunt. We all expect him to bunt, so the corners are playing in tight. I get ahead 0-1 and, surprisingly, he doesn't square. Maybe he doesn't think he can get a bunt down on my knuckleball; I don't know. On my second pitch I throw a good, spinless knuckleball that is up a bit but packs some late drop. Guzmán swings away and loops it into center. It looks for sure like it's going to fall. Pagan charges hard, keeps charging, and reaches down. He makes a gorgeous shoestring catch. Both runners think the ball is going to drop and take off. Angel hurries to get the ball to second but in his haste he launches it way over José Reyes's head, beyond the mound, which I have vacated to back up the plate. Catcher Henry Blanco alertly charges the rolling ball and fires to Reyes at second. Reyes throws to Ike Davis at first for one of the oddest triple plays ever recorded.

An inning later, I get Pudge Rodríguez, my former Texas teammate, to hit into a weak, 6–4–3 double play. I come off the mound fired up, and Dan pats my back and says, "Good job." My night is done. I wind up with a no-decision in a 5–3 loss, but I'm heartened that I'd given the Mets a quality start my first time out: two runs in six innings.

My first start at home comes six days later, against the Phillies. Anne and the kids come up to New York for the occasion, and we are all shoehorned into a hotel room near Times Square. I am thrilled to have them with me, but I am also very conscious of getting rest and being completely focused, and having three kids who are under nine in a hotel room, while fun, is not necessarily conducive to concentration. I am too cheap to spring for another room at $250 a night. So we stay crammed in. The morning of the game, Anne wants to go tourist on me and take the kids to Rockefeller Center and take in the view from the top.

I am completely against it. But I am outvoted.

We'll walk around a bit and come right back, Anne says. It will be easy and fun and won't take away from your preparation, she says. It turns out not to be too much fun, and definitely not easy. There are lines everywhere. We can't get a cab. The kids get squirmy and cranky. I am the crankiest of all. I carry our four-year-old son,

Eli, back to the hotel on my shoulders, worried that I may be ticketed back to the minors in Buffalo because of a sightseeing outing.

I say good-bye to the troops and catch the number seven subway line to Citi Field. The train trip helps me decompress from our relaxing day in New York. I gradually get fully into my game mindset, and by the time I am at the park, I am tunneled in. I go out and deliver again, pitching six shutout innings for my first National League victory. For the next month I pitch better than I have in my entire big-league career. I pitch from ahead, and pitch aggressively, bringing the best knuckleball I can muster on every pitch. In an almost surreal groove, I am so concentrated on each pitch that it's as if it is going to be the last pitch of my life. Nothing can faze me.

After almost a week in the Times Square hotel, I find out that Shawn Green, the former Met, has a condo in Greenwich, Connecticut, that we can stay in. We move in but nobody tells the management company, I guess, because not long after we arrive, the power is cut. We live in the dark, and the midsummer swelter, for five days. We buy a Styrofoam cooler and load it with ice for the perishables, and get by with flashlights and candles. We could've moved somewhere else, gotten a hotel, but we just stick it out. I don't conduct a poll, but I figure I'm probably the only pitcher in all of baseball who goes home to a dark house and reads by candlelight after ball games. What can I tell you? I like adventure. Maybe I subconsciously wanted to relive my nomadic days when I slept in vacant houses, I don't know. Whatever the draw is, the powerless interlude has no impact on my pitching. I remain locked in. After I shut down the Tigers on 4 hits over 8 innings to run my record to 6–0 in late June, I become, in my own quirky way, a New York story—an old knuckleballing guy with a Tennessee twang and a missing body part.

Who is this weirdo?

People keep waiting for me to revert to my retread form, for the league to catch up to me. They view me as a trick-pitch purveyor who can't truly be counted upon. I've got a career ERA of almost 5.00, after all. Wait until he finds his true level again, and get ready to duck.

None of this surprises me, and none of it offends me. All it does do is make me want to change people's minds. I want to change their minds about how they think about the knuckleball . . . and how they think about me. Without being preachy or pedantic about it, I want to show them the degree to which change is possible. I mean, just take a look at me. Once I was a hypercompetitive kid who threw in the mid-nineties and made muscular pitching his modus operandi. Now I am a hypercompetitive grown-up who maxes out in the mid-eighties and dares you to get a good piece of a flaky, fluttering ball I'm throwing with my fingernails.

Once I kept secrets and hid and ran from the truth and ran from intimacy. Now I am about as close as you can get to being an open book, feeling called by God to tell the truth and be authentic and love my wife and children with everything this imperfect man can summon.

Once I lived in almost terminal shame, knowing why but never wanting to unpack it. Now I live in God's mercy and I want to unpack everything, no matter how messy and hurtful it can be. (The unpacking, ultimately, includes this book.)

Do you think that it's a coincidence that when I was finally able to stop hiding as a human being, I also stopped hiding as a pitcher?

I don't.

Our season ends with a 3–0 victory over the Reds. What a ride it has been. Not quite a peaceful trip through the countryside. More like a turbulent spin aboard an old, rickety roller coaster straight out of the state fairgrounds, circa 1949.

When you look at it in its totality, the New York Mets' 2011 season was really more like a miniseries than 162 games worth of baseball. We were brutal early, good for a nice stretch in the middle, and then fell off late. With a slew of injuries to key players, we brought kids like Lucas Duda and Justin Turner up from Buffalo and everybody battled hard, and in doing so honored our manager, Terry Collins, who never lost his intensity and never let us use injuries as an excuse. We were scrappy overachievers who hung around the periphery of the wild-card race much longer than most people figured. And then at the very end, the final game, the whole drama was entirely wrapped around our best and most dynamic player, José Reyes.

I want to tell you a few things about José. He's not only a terrific teammate and one of the most gifted players I've ever been around, he's also probably the game's greatest single energy source. His exuberance and energy are unmatched, and so is his ability to win games with his glove, his bat, and his legs. In the first 81 games, he hits .352 with 30 stolen bases and 15 triples, and plays superbly at shortstop. It is as supernatural a performance over time as I've ever seen.

Then José hurt his hamstring and went on the DL, came back, and went on the DL again, and the air went totally out of the Mets balloon. He couldn't run the same way, couldn't dominate with his speed, wasn't close to being the same player. He had only one more triple the rest of the season. About all he could still do was try to win the batting title, which brings us to the last day.

José and Ryan Braun of the Brewers battled it out right to game number 162. José led off that final game with a bunt single, raising his average to .337, then took himself out when he reached first, peeling off so quickly that latecomers or people who went to get a soda missed him altogether. José's .337 average did, in fact, win him the first batting title in Mets history, but it came bundled with an avalanche of criticism and near hysteria that went on for days.

Was it selfish and cowardly to take himself out of the game, just so he wouldn't risk the title by perhaps making a few outs? Didn't he owe something more to Mets fans who paid good money to see him—in perhaps his final game as a Met, with his free agency pending?

The whole thing was very unfortunate, and to my mind, could've been handled better by everybody. At the very least, I would've loved to have seen José go out to short for the top of the second. Terry, who I believe did as great a job this year as any manager I've ever been around (our 77–85 record doesn't come close to doing him justice), could've replaced him then and he would've gotten a huge ovation, I'm sure. If nothing else, his exit wouldn't have been so sudden and jarring. It would've been a more fitting departure for a player who truly leaves it all out on the field.

Personally, I would've liked to have seen José play the whole game. He's a guy who hates to sit—goes nuts when he has to sit—so to take himself out, even in a meaningless game, is contrary to his ethos as a ballplayer. I hate to see his stellar play all year sullied by the way it ended, to hear people say that he backed into the title. I appreciate the fact that the batting title was important to him, and don't begrudge him that or judge him for it. We're all entitled to our own goals. I know how hard he works and how much he punishes his body, every day. I also know how much it ate him to have his legs, the lifeblood of his game, break down again, as they have before. To see a man who gives so much of himself, who plays with such passion, being a spectator as the final innings of the season came and went just doesn't seem to be the right image. I would've much preferred to see him flying around second with braids flapping and sliding head-first into third.

Now, that would've been a much more fitting ending for José Reyes.

CHAPTER TWENTY

FINGERNAILS IN FLUSHING

I am on my way to Nationals Park, on the D.C. Metro. It's Saturday on July Fourth weekend. The subway car is teeming with red-clad fans wearing Nationals T-shirts and jerseys, a smattering of Ryan Zimmerman's number 11 shirts and a slew of Stephen Strasburg's number 37 shirts. I sit in the middle of the car and listen to the fans banter. I hear a little boy, maybe eight years old, on his way to his first ball game, talking excitedly to his father, firing questions to his father about Strasburg—and why wouldn't he? He is the most heralded pitching prospect in baseball in years, a kid who has single-handedly injected fascination into a long-moribund franchise, with his 100-mile-per-hour fastball and ridiculous curve.

I am eager to see him myself, because I am pitching against him today.

It is a matchup of almost absurd contrasts, young guy versus old guy, fireballer versus flutterballer, Anointed One versus Anonymous One. It is a match of an F-18 fighter jet against a butterfly. Every great story needs to have tension, and this baseball narrative should have it in abundance.

I am pretending to read *Life of Pi* by Yann Martel, but I am really listening to the talk in the subway car. Nobody has any idea who I am—one of the perks of journeyman stature. I hear my name a dozen or more times. It is a surreal experience, knowing I'll be one of the protagonists in the drama in two hours or so, surrounded by people who will be attending the drama. I am not far from a guy who is reading the *Wall Street Journal*. I look closer and see an article and a cartoon on the sports page, under the heading "Rocket Boy vs. The Baffler." It depicts Stephen Strasburg (aka Rocket Boy) as an airborne superhero in full costume, complete with chiseled physique and otherworldly powers and baseballs blazing out of his right hand. It depicts me (The Baffler) as a much less imposing figure, on the ground, with a question mark on my chest and base-balls floating all about.

I almost laugh out loud. *The Baffler*. I love it.

"It's amazing that one guy can throw 100 [miles per hour] and the other can throw 75 and they can both be really good at what they do," David Wright says in the article.

The crowd in Nationals Park is close to forty thousand, almost triple the size of the turnout in my first start with the Mets, five weeks earlier. They are not there to see The Baffler.

We score on Jason Bay's RBI double in the top of the first, and as I take the mound I am enthralled by the moment, and the challenge ahead. I relish that there is all this buzz around Strasburg, and that I am no more relevant than the right-field peanut vendor. I don't look like Stephen Strasburg. I don't throw like Stephen Strasburg, and I am certainly not as wealthy as Stephen Strasburg, but I sure am ready to compete with him.

And I do precisely that.

Strasburg goes 5 innings and gives up 4 hits and 2 runs. I go 7 innings and give up 6 hits and 2 unearned runs. Neither of us gets a decision, and the Nationals rally for 4 runs in the final 2 innings to win, 6–5. I've done my job, and done it well. I wish I had kept the cartoon.

We are ten games over .500 (47–37) and just two games behind the Phillies in the National League East in early July, but we start to fade after the all-star break and we can never quite arrest it, though I still feel good about how hard I am competing and the results I'm getting. On August 13, the Phillies come to Citi Field, and to me it is our last and best chance to get back in the race. I am coming off my worst start of the year, against these same Phillies, in which I lasted just 3 innings and gave up 8 hits and 4 earned runs in Citizens Bank Park. I wasn't quite as bad as the line sounds—there were some untimely bleeders and bloopers in there—but my team gave me a two-run lead against Roy Halladay in the first and I couldn't take care of it, and that's on me.

Now we have our rivals again, and when I get to the ballpark on Friday afternoon and start to get ready, I am in a surprisingly good place. I'm not panicky because I had a misstep the last time out. I am not losing any sort of faith in my knuckleball, or letting birds of prey even think about setting up their nest. Every year I've thrown the knuckleball, it has gotten better. It has gotten more consistent, with more finish, so consequently I have more confidence in it. In 2008 in Seattle, about 65 percent of my pitches were knuckleballs. In 2009, in Minnesota, about 75 percent were knuckleballs.

This year I am throwing knuckleballs 85 percent of the time, which is how it should be. It is, after all, my best pitch, my best chance to win. I'm also effectively changing speeds, throwing knuckleballs as slow as sixty-nine miles per hour and as hard as eighty-one. I choose to focus on my body of work with the Mets, and not one shabby start in Citizens Bank Park.

There is a blank canvas before me tonight, I tell myself. *It's up to me to paint it, to dab enough nasty knuckleballs in enough good spots to make it come together. If I work the brush with full conviction, maybe I can make it a masterpiece.*

I thank God for where I am now, for this shift in perspective that is allowing me to purge the unhappy memories of my previous start and take the mound tonight as a free man. My opponent is Cole Hamels. It won't be easy.

Hamels and I match zeroes through five. I am in one of my best places of the season, the best since the twenty-eight-up, twenty-seven-down game. I get through the fourth inning in nine pitches and have yet to give up a hit. In the fifth, Jayson Werth, the Phillies right-fielder, leads off. Werth has had some success against me and he's a dangerous guy. The count runs full after I throw five straight knuckleballs. I look in for the sign and Henry Blanco, my catcher, calls for a fastball.

I work fast. I like to get the ball and get back on the rubber and fire away again. But now I take a step back and look in again at Henry. I don't know why he has called for a fastball. I don't agree with it. If Werth sits on it, the scoreless tie could be gone in a millisecond.

I shake him off, but Henry puts down the fastball sign again. In my typical start, there are only three or four times a game when a catcher's pitch-calling skill comes into play and we deviate from the knuckleball-intensive game plan. This is one of them. Henry is an astute guy and he must see something in how Werth is holding his hands or how he has moved up in the box to try to get the knuckle-ball early. I trust him.

I wind up and deliver what Henry wants: a fastball on the outer half of the plate—a defrost pitch, as I call it, because you throw slow, slow, slow, slow, and then you heat it up in a hurry. Werth is completely defrosted. So surprised that he locks up and doesn't move a muscle. Strike three.

One out.

Next I get Shane Victorino swinging on a knuckleball, and get Brian Schneider to ground out weakly. I am more than halfway through and still have a no-hitter, but we're not doing anything against Hamels, either. I get the first out in the sixth and then Hamels steps in and I start him off with a knuckleball. He lines it into right for a single, and that's the end of my no-hit fantasies. The Citi Field crowd recognizes me with a warm ovation. It's a nice gesture, but I have much work yet to do. I get Jimmy Rollins to ground out and retire Placido Polanco on a long fly to center.

In the bottom of the sixth, Carlos Beltrán hits an RBI double to give us a 1–0 lead. I need to make it hold up. I am determined to make it hold up. I get through the middle of the order on eight pitches in the seventh, and need only nine more to get three fly-ball outs in the eighth. We go down so fast in the bottom of the eighth that I almost feel as though I never left the mound.

I have a strange epiphany as I warm up for the ninth, three outs away from a one-hit shutout. There's something different about this start, and now I know what: for the first time in my big-league career, I feel dominant. The way I'm controlling the pitch, the consistency of my feel and my release point, the sharpness of its movement—it's all making for a pitch that is just a beast to get a good piece of.

Domonic Brown is first up, pinch-hitting for Hamels. On an 0–1 pitch he grounds out to short. Rollins comes up and I go up a strike on him and then he grounds out to Ike Davis at first.

Now it's Polanco, the last man between me and a shutout of the National League champions. The fans are standing and clapping. Polanco takes a knuckleball for a strike and I go up 0–1 again. I wind again and throw a knuckleball that darts away from him. He swings and hits it off the end of the bat, a harmless fly to right field. Jeff Francoeur squeezes it, and my day at the office—and my first shutout in seven years—is complete.

Henry Blanco and the rest of the team rush up to congratulate me, and the Citi Field crowd stands in appreciation. I don't do well with being celebrated. I've always wanted to resist it or at least deflect it somehow, probably because of all the shame I've dragged around all these years, and not feeling entitled. But I'm getting better at it, and can at least take in some of the praise. More than anything, I feel grateful for the opportunity God gave me to shine and for feeling as though I just might belong here.

As I walk through the tunnel into the clubhouse, I have a flashback to my only other major-league shutout, in Comerica Park against the Tigers. I was pitching for the Rangers and Alex Rodriguez was the shortstop. When ARod came up to congratulate me afterward, he said, You have me to thank for that.

What do you mean? I asked.

I called every pitch from shortstop, ARod said, explaining that he relayed signs to our catcher that day, Einar Diaz.

Well, thank you, I told ARod.

The next time out, I gave up six hits and six earned runs in a 9–2 loss to the Royals.

I asked ARod after the game if I had him to thank for that too.

No, I didn't call the pitches tonight, he said.

WE STAY OVER .500 until the middle of September before a 5–10 finish in the final fifteen games consigns us to fourth place in the National League East and a 79–83 record. Even without a pennant race, I am more intense with my starts than ever before, because I know I'm pitching for a contract—and my future. I've been a vagabond for a long time and I'm ready for it to stop. The only way that happens is if I prove to the Mets that I'm someone they need to bring back. And I accomplish that by finishing strong, and treating every start as if it were my own personal game seven, no matter what the standings say.

My last start of the year is against the Milwaukee Brewers, in the second game of a doubleheader at Citi Field. I go 7 strong innings, give up 6 hits and 1 run, and lose. I finish the year with an 11–9 record and a 2.84 ERA. It's the most victories I've had in a season, and the lowest ERA I've had in a season by far. I want to believe it's ample justification for the Mets to re-up me for a year through the arbitration process, but when talks begin between Bo McKinnis and the Mets, it quickly becomes clear that a two-year agreement is within reach. I wind up agreeing to a deal for $7.8 million over two years. There is only one downside to it.

It means I have to get a physical, my first full baseball physical since the one I had with Dr. Conway in 1996—the one that launched me on the road to orthopedic infamy, and cost me my first-round offer.

This time the physical is with Dr. Struan Coleman at the Hospital for Special Surgery in New York. I couldn't have been more anxious that morning if I'd spent it dodging taxicabs in midtown.

I don't like my history with physicals.

It's going to be okay. There's absolutely nothing wrong with you, Bo McKinnis reassures me. It's going to be routine.

Bo joins me at the hospital and stays for the ninety minutes it takes Dr. Coleman to check out my arm. I have an MRI and a variety of other tests. I want to believe it's going to be fine, but didn't I think that in 1996?

Yes, I did.

I thank Dr. Coleman, and Bo and I go on our way. A few hours later, Sandy Alderson calls Bo.

Everything checked out fine, Sandy says, so I'll get the contract out to you to sign.

Bo calls me right away.

You passed the physical and now it's time to sign your contract, Bo tells me.

I feel immediate and immense relief. Finally, I can begin to appreciate the financial security I'm about to have. I may be well short of the Jeter/ARod income bracket, but the contract I'm about to sign is ten times the amount that I lost when the Rangers pulled their offer. It seems miraculous to me, the grace of God at work in my life again.

And with a fourth child on the way in spring training, the timing is propitious.

Still, for me, the greatest payoff of all is to be wanted. I don't have to go shopping for a new club or go through a dog and pony show to convince somebody that I am better than my numbers. I don't have to prove anything—because I've already done it, across 174 innings and 27 starts. And that means that, for the first time in fifteen years, I do not have to go to spring training to audition for a job.

I already have a job.

I belong.

For now, anyway, I've changed not only the perception that I am nothing but a 4A pitcher but also the perception that you can't trust the knuckleball or the people who throw them. This is exactly what I've been praying for for years. I wouldn't pretend to know how God works, why things happen the way they do. I just know that God is good, and He has blessed me abundantly.

Nashville, Tennessee

Toward the end of the 2011 season, as the batting race moved toward its conclusion, I wore a bold silk-screened workout T-shirt with José Reyes's picture on the front. I wanted to show José how much I was pulling for him. The shirt did its job well, but it must be retired now, because as sad as I am about it, José is no longer the New York Mets' shortstop. He is now playing that position for the Miami Marlins, a club with a new name, a new ballpark, a new manager, a new $106 million leadoff hitter, and apparently new access to a pile of money.

It hurts a ton to lose a talent like José. It hurts even more to lose him to a division rival.

I can't say that I am surprised about it, though. With the club's financial issues and the money José figured to command, I thought all along that we were long shots to keep him. When I found out the Marlins started courting him at 12:01 a.m. on the first day he was officially on the market, I became less optimistic still. Everybody wants to feel wanted, and although I don't doubt that Sandy Alderson would've loved to have held on to José, I also don't doubt that the Marlins' full-throttle courtship helped seal the deal.

As I write this, Ruben Tejada is slated to be our shortstop. He's a promising young player who did a lot of good things last year, and I believe he's going to be a solid big-league player. But I don't expect him to be José Reyes, and nobody else should, either. That would be expecting me to be Roy Halladay.

A player with José's talent comes along once every twenty-

five years, if that often. There are legitimate questions about his durability and about the prudence of giving a six-year deal to a twenty-nine-year-old shortstop whose game is built around speed. Is there a chance that the Marlins will wind up regretting the deal? Sure there is. That takes nothing from the kind of player the Marlins are getting: a one-man energy plant and a breathtaking athlete.

I could give you fifty José Reyes highlights in the two years we were teammates, but one that comes to mind first occurred on my opening-day start at Citi Field last April, against the Nationals. In the top of the fifth, with the bases loaded, Rick Ankiel hit a missile up the middle that looked headed into center field for a two-run single. José moved quickly to his left, snared the ball, touched second, and threw to first for the double play. End of threat. End of inning. José made this play all the time, and made it look easy. He probably saved me ten runs last year all by himself.

Players come and go so often in baseball that you get used to saying good-bye. Kevin Slowey, Mark Teixeira, Joe Nathan, Carlos Beltrán . . . I could go on and on about the players who I really enjoyed being teammates with who I wound up saying good-bye to. Now José Reyes, as good a two-way shortstop as I've ever seen, is added to the list. I wish him all the best when he's not playing the New York Mets.

CHAPTER TWENTY-ONE

UNBROKEN MOMENTS

A parking spot. As of February 15, 2011, I have my very own parking spot. It's hard to believe that this is revving my engine the way it is, but what can I tell you? Number 43 is written on the asphalt between two white lines that are fifteen feet long and ten feet apart. The lines don't just demarcate any space. They demarcate *my* space. I am not far from Frankie Rodriguez's number 62 and his black Lamborghini, a high-end neighborhood to be in in the Digital Domain players' lot in Port St. Lucie, Florida.

It took the better part of two decades, but I have my own big-league space. I ride a bicycle to the park most days, but that is completely irrelevant. I have a place that is mine. I am not a guy just passing through or living on the minor-league fringe. I belong. What a wonderful concept.

Right from the start, this year isn't about surviving for me. It's about wanting more. It's about thriving, and being trustworthy. This is where my journey is taking me. I want to prove that I am trustworthy not just as a pitcher but also as a husband and a father and a believer, and one has everything to do with the others. Because if I have it in me to be fully present in one realm of my life, I know it will overflow into the other realms. The only way to prove it is by showing up every day and being someone who is worthy of trust.

Trust is a big issue around the Mets, for reasons that go far beyond one pitcher's search for himself. The club has an acclaimed new general manager, Sandy Alderson, and well-regarded new manager, Terry Collins, but the blaring headlines all spring long are about the Mets supposedly being on the brink of financial ruin after being scammed out of hundreds of millions of dollars by the jailed Ponzi king Bernie Madoff. Beyond that, the trustee in charge of the Madoff case is suing Mets ownership for hundreds of millions more on the belief that the Mets owners, Fred Wilpon and Saul Katz, should've been suspicious about their rate of return. The wreckage Madoff left behind is unfathomable—lives ruined, families wiped out, one of his own sons taking his own life—but neither the scandal nor its possible impact on the Mets is ever broached to us, the players, not even with a drive-by, "Just keep doing your job, guys" sort of comment.

We hear nothing, and because ballplayers are traditionally good at sticking their heads in the sand anyway, the matter doesn't infiltrate our daily lives in the least. We don't ponder what the Wilpons knew when we stretch, and we don't discuss the loan the club got from Major League Baseball to meet their short-term expenses. We're deep in our diamond-shaped cocoon. It doesn't mean we're all a bunch of spoiled brats; it just means that our little palm-treed corner of paradise is not easily wobbled, even though some black ballplayer humor—which is as old as the game itself—surfaces from time to time:

Maybe we'll be staying at Motel 6s on the road this year.

I hope they didn't have our per diem money with Bernie.

Is it true David Wright's going to be piloting our charter?

I want to believe that the truth will come out, but until it does, I am going to put my energy into my own truth-seeking . . . and continue to work on my knuckler.

NOT HAVING TO PITCH my way onto the team makes an even bigger difference than I thought it would. It frees me up to experiment with some things, one of which is a superslow knuckleball. I throw most of my knuckleballs between 75 and 80 miles per hour, though I can bump it up into the low eighties if I want. Dan Warthen and I agree that if hitters have to be on the lookout for the same pitch at 58 or 60, it might be an effective weapon. The challenge is getting the release down without telegraphing it so I have the element of surprise in my favor. It takes me several weeks to get comfortable enough with it to the point that I can use it in a game.

When we break camp and drive south to Miami to get 2011 started, I'm a pitcher with deeply conflicted feelings. On the one hand, I'm pumped to start the third game of the season. On the other hand, I have enough fear and anxiety to fill the Grand Ole Opry. It's the usual garbage in my head, fears that I won't be good enough, that I am destined to implode and that I'll be back in Buffalo by nightfall. (Not that worrying is an original Dickey concept: "The pressure never lets up. Doesn't matter what you did yesterday. That's history. It's tomorrow that counts. So you worry all the time. It never ends. Lord, baseball is a worrying thing." That's a quote from Stan Coveleski, a Hall of Famer.)

But there's an extra overlay this year, and that is feeling the pressure of proving myself worthy of my new contract. I warned myself not to do this, but here I am doing it anyway, feeling the need to justify the Mets' investment. While I'm at it, I also feel pressure to stuff socks in the mouths of all the baseball pundits who think my success in 2010 was a fluke and that I am destined to go back to my proper journeyman place.

I sit on my hotel bed in Miami and do some self-directed therapy, reminding myself that fears do not rule me and only have power over me if I let them. I'm done with locking fear away, running from it as if I were a fugitive. All that does is feed the monster and make me more fearful. Once you can accept that everybody has fear and realize that you are not alone with it, it takes the venom right out of it. You stop thinking there is something horribly wrong with you. So as I prepare to face the Marlins at Sun Life Stadium, I am not looking to eliminate the fear so much as look at it honestly and walk well with it.

I pray before I go to bed, thanking God again for His steadfastness:

When I take the mound tomorrow, God, please let me compete as a man with the faith and self-awareness to rise above whatever fear I might have and put everything I have into every pitch I throw.

I take the mound in a good place. The noise in my head is a nonfactor. I pitch six innings, give up no earned runs, and strike out seven. The wind swirls for most of the game, so I use my hard knuckleball more than usual, because it doesn't get blown around so much. We win, 9–2, and after I meet with the press, I take some time to decompress by thanking God for giving me the faculties and gifts to be able to do what I do, for I truly love it, and thanking Him for providing me with the wisdom to not give my fears any voice or power, freeing me up to embrace this moment fully.

I wanted a sense of belonging, and I couldn't ask for more of it:

the Mets have configured the rotation so that I start the home opener at Citi Field against the Nationals, an incredible honor. When I am introduced before the game, I get one of the loudest ovations of any player. When you've had more boos than cheers in your career, you notice big ovations, believe me. It's forty-five degrees and raw, but my knuckleball is moving all over the place as I warm up. It's a beautiful day for baseball.

After getting two quick outs in the top of the first, I throw an 80-mile-per-hour knuckleball to Ryan Zimmerman, and the moment it leaves my hand I know there is a problem. I have broken the nail of my right index finger. The pressure of the nail against the horsehide causes the nail to split. This is not a good thing to happen to a knuckleball pitcher. It is, in fact, a horrible thing to happen to a knuckleball pitcher. Everything I do starts with the nails that grip the ball. If the nails aren't right, I can't grip the ball right, and bad things ensue. The count is 2–2, and I don't want to risk breaking the nail worse, so I come back and throw one of my new, super-slow, 59-mile-per-hour numbers up there.

Zimmerman is ahead of it by a half hour. He misses by so much, he laughs.

I do not laugh.

I go in the dugout and work feverishly on my nail. Mike Herbst, our assistant trainer, keeps my nail-repair kit in his trainers' box. He hands me my glass nail file and I try to even it out. I apply a hardening agent called Trind Nail Repair that my mother-in-law gave me. I can dab on Trind until Bernie Madoff gets out of jail and it's not going to address the central issue: the broken nail is too short to allow me to grip my knuckleball.

Trouble, big.

I go back out for the second and get two fly-ball outs, but Rick

Ankiel singles and then I walk the next two hitters on five pitches apiece. I've never broken a nail during a game before. I have almost no clue where the ball is going. I am trying to gut through it but I have that old familiar feeling that I am going out there with a pea shooter. For me to throw a knuckleball without the nail on my index finger is like a quarterback trying to throw a pass without his pinkie. The bases are loaded and I go up 0–2 on the opposing pitcher, Jordan Zimmermann. One pitch away from getting out of it, I throw a mediocre knuckleball and Zimmermann drives it into right for a two-run single. I am furious at myself, at the situation. When I get to the bench at the end of the inning, I slam my glove into the dugout wall.

I have such high expectations for this start, and can't believe what is happening to it. I walk three more guys, one with the bases loaded, and leave the game after five. We lose, 6–2, and I am completely humbled and deflated.

Opening day. Check.

Huge ovation. Check.

Broken nail. Checkmate.

I don't even make it into the sixth inning. It makes me sick.

I spend the days ahead obsessing over my busted nail. I take calcium supplements. I apply Trind frequently with a little applicator brush. Two days before my next start, the nail is growing nicely and I do my scheduled bullpen. About halfway through a seventy-pitch session, I throw a knuckleball and the nail splits again. Blood spurts all over my right hand.

This time the split is all the way down into the nail bed.

Now I am in a real bind. I've got basically no nail and know if I go out there against the Rockies in such a condition, I'm going to get raked. I tell Dan Warthen that I need to get to a nail salon ASAP. The words aren't out of my mouth when I think about how ridiculous they sound. I try to imagine Clayton Kershaw or Justin Verlander rushing up to their pitching coaches and saying, "I got an emergency. I need to make an emergency run to a nail joint."

I try to imagine them asking their trainers to keep a nail kit with them at all times, one that includes all of the indispensable tools of the knuckleballing trade: a glass file (metal files can leave jagged edges), Trind, superglue, a tube of acrylic, and a buffer.

I can't.

What are you waiting for? Dan says.

I ask Dan not to tell Terry or anybody else, because I don't want people getting worked up about it.

A few minutes later I am heading to the parking lot with Theresa Corderi, one of our cooks. She knows the neighborhood and she knows nails. She takes me to a little place on College Point Boulevard called Pink Nails. It's run by Korean ladies and I am the only ballplayer on the premises. For seven bucks (tip included), a guy applies acrylic to my one busted nail. I do not get a discount for being in full uniform. The acrylic seems to take well. Theresa and I hustle back to the ballpark. As we pull in, Jeff Wilpon, the Mets' chief operating officer, is walking in just ahead of me. I pray that he doesn't turn around and see me arriving at the ballpark ten minutes before game time. I wonder if I can get a note from the people at Pink Nails if I need backup. It doesn't come to that. Jeff keeps walking.

So do I.

My nail holds up okay against the Rockies two days later, but that's about all that holds up. Every time out, it seems, something gets fouled up. Balls find gaps. I surrender home runs at terrible times. The games when I pitch well and the team plays well never seem to align.

I go into my ninth start of the year, in Houston, with a 1–5 record and a 4.50 ERA. I am embarrassed by the numbers next to my name. Here's my chance to do something about it. Domed stadiums are usually good for knuckleballs. I feel good warming up, though often the bullpen warm-up doesn't correlate at all to how you fare throwing real pitches to real hitters. I had a great knuckleball in the pen the night I gave up six homers to the Tigers, after all.

Michael Bourn leads off for the Astros. He mashes the third pitch of the game, a 2–0 fastball, for a triple to right center. It is not the start I want, and it swiftly gets much worse. With one out, Hunter Pence singles. Carlos Lee singles. I give up three more hits to the next three hitters. The Astros are being smart, shortening up and taking me the other way. I feel like I'm in the center of a merry-go-round, and it feels awful.

I'm down four runs after an inning, and the only good that comes of the outing is that I plead with Terry Collins to keep me in the game, let me at least eat some innings and save the bullpen. I wind up pitching into the sixth, and by game's end I am the not-very-proud owner of a 1–5 record and a 5.08 ERA.

I walk off thinking of the pitching wisdom I once heard from Greg Maddux, who said, "The best pitchers have a short-term memory and a bulletproof confidence."

I am trying to keep mine short. It is not easy. I am frustrated beyond belief, not just because of my horrible record, but because I know I'm close to being effective, because my knuckleball is moving well. It just seems that there a few bad pitches at inopportune times, and a few too many counts where I'm falling behind. Close, unfortunately, doesn't count.

A few minutes after I walk into the clubhouse following the game, I turn on my phone and see a text from Anne. "Hey, babe," she begins. She goes on to write lovingly about her faith in me. She attaches two adorable photos of Van, our seven-week-old boy. He is wearing a baseball hat in one of them. The media is waiting to talk to me about my debacle, and no doubt a raft of stories are forthcoming about my fairy dust running out. Let them write whatever they want and skewer me in a hundred different ways. Anne and I continue to work on our marriage but I am overcome with gratitude for her and for all the ways God has blessed us. Somehow, even as I stand at my locker after a wretched performance, I feel stronger and more real and more centered than I ever have, my roots reaching farther and farther into the earth. I trust that I am close to turning things around on the mound. Life is good. Life is rich. And God is so merciful. A rocky start in a baseball game cannot change any of that.

BASEBALL CAN BE a brutal, bottom-line business. Your failures are right there on the scoreboard, illuminated, in-your-face proof of what a slug you are, whether it's a .182 batting average or, say, a 5.08 ERA. Then the numbers go viral on the Internet, making for more fun, giving everybody and their aunt Bessie a chance to weigh in on your epic deficiencies. I'm pretty good at not taking it personally and not paying attention to the dirges. Much worse for me is what those shabby numbers mean: that I haven't been someone my team can count on. Say whatever else you want about an ERA of 5.08, but to me it drills down to not giving my team much of a chance to win. Of course, there are variables beyond my control that might inflate the number of runs I give up, like outfield misadventures and bloops that fall in, but all that stuff tends to even out. More even than my won-lost record, I care about my ERA; if you gave me a choice between being 12–10 with a 4.25 ERA and 10–12 with a 2.75 ERA, I'll take the latter, not because I don't want my team to win as many games as possible, but because if I have an ERA of under 3.00 it means in the long run we're going to win a lot more games than if I'm giving up an extra run and a half.

So I'm in ERA-reduction mode, trying to get back to respectability even as we try to recover from a brutal April and scrap our way into contention with the Phillies and Braves. My next time out after Houston, I beat the Yankees at Yankee Stadium, giving up four hits and a run over six innings, and then we go to Chicago to play the Cubs. I am ready to turn my season around right here, right now, and I rack up two quick scoreless innings to start.

Pitching to Kosuke Fukudome with two outs and two on in the third inning of a scoreless game, I get him to hit a roller toward second. I break off the mound to cover first. I am halfway there when it feels as if somebody drove a railroad spike through my right arch. I do a face plant on the Wrigley infield. I am in major pain, the most I've ever felt on a ball field. I know my day is done. The question is, how much worse is it than that? I fear the worst but try to put a good face on it for Sandy Alderson, who has made the trip with us.

Don't count me out for my next start. I'm a quick healer, I tell him.

It's getaway day, so we fly home to New York that night. I don't even bother going home or to a hotel; I just put down my crutch and grab a cot in the Citi Field trainer's room and sleep there. I have an appointment to see a foot specialist at the Hospital for Special Surgery in the morning. His name is Dr. Jonathan Deland, chief of the hospital's foot and ankle center. He has deep-set eyes and thin lips and a direct, agreeable manner. I go for an MRI and then we meet in his examining room.

How does it look?

You've got a partial tear of the plantar fascia, a band of tissue that runs along the bottom of your foot, he explains.

How do you treat it? When can I get back and pitch with it?

We treat this symptomatically. It depends on the severity and your tolerance for pain, he says.

When Jonathon Niese or Dillon Gee or any other young guy asks me for advice, one of the first things I always say is: Don't ever go on the disabled list if you can avoid it. I've seen people get Wally Pipped more times than I can count. Don't give them a chance to Wally Pipp you.

As I sit on the examining table, I am remembering my own advice. The last thing I want is to give the Mets any reason to look someplace else for a starting pitcher, or to put me on the DL. Pain I can deal with. I'm not going to do anything idiotic, but I am good with pain. The doctor pokes and prods.

Does this hurt? he asks. I shake my head. Then he moves down my foot a bit and presses hard. How about this?

No, not much, I say every time he asks. I am lying. I am an accomplished liar when it comes to staying on the field. In a game against the Cardinals a bit later in the season, David Freese hits me in the neck with a line drive. I pick the ball up and throw him out at first to end the inning. In the dugout tunnel, Ray Ramirez, our trainer, checks me out and asks me: Did that get you? I am positive I will be out of the game if he knows I took a line drive in the neck.

No, it got a piece of my glove. I'm fine, I say.

Ray goes and checks the replay, but it's not definitive; it looks as if I did get my glove up. I skate, and stay in the game.

Dr. Deland keeps probing. I keep telling him it doesn't hurt. I am thinking about my next start. It is all I am thinking about. Pain? What pain?

For the next few days I get almost round-the-clock treatment from Ray. He gives me ultrasound and heat and ice and a whirlpool. Rohan Baichu, our massage therapist, goes at the underside of my right foot hard. It hurts a ton, but I don't say a word. My foot feels much better after he's done. The treatments are working. Three days later, I tell Dan Warthen I want to have my usual bullpen session. He's surprised but likes the way I am throwing the ball.

I need to see you field your position, he says. He rolls a series of balls out to see how well I can get off the mound. I get off the mound okay. Not great, but okay. He asks how it feels, and I lie again.

I'm good to go, I tell him.

Five days after going splat on the Wrigley grass, I have convinced the Mets I am ready for my next start, against the Pirates at Citi Field. I ask Ray for an injection of Toradol, a painkiller and anti-inflammatory, an hour before first pitch. I've never taken anything stronger than Advil before getting on the mound, but my foot is still barking at me and I know I need a little help. I get the shot in the butt, and it makes a big difference.

I don't make another start the rest of the year without Toradol.

Against the Pirates, I fight through the pain for the first inning but then the Toradol kicks in. I take a two-hit shutout and a 1–0 lead into the eighth, only to see it dissolve on a two-out, two-run single by Neil Walker. I strike out a career-high 10 hitters and throw 81 strikes and only 27 balls.

I take the loss and fall to 2–6. It's not the outcome I had in mind, but I feel good about the effort and I think the Mets feel good about it too.

The effort, it occurs to me later that night, is really what matters the most, isn't it? Outcomes can get completely convoluted, buffeted by all manner of forces and factors. You honor yourself and your game when you pour all you have into it, when you live in the athletic moment. I will never have the weaponry of Tim Lincecum or CC Sabathia, but I can give just as much of myself. I can compete as hard, or harder. It's the lesson Uncle Ricky kept pounding into me as a kid: the mental is to the physical as four is to one.

Without putting it so succinctly, my mother taught me the same thing, and I appreciate her more every day for it.

My mother is one of the toughest and most resilient people I know, and one of the best. More by deed than word, she taught me that you do not pout or mope or pass blame when things don't go your way. If you have a problem, you find a solution. If you make a mistake, you look in the mirror.

If your car breaks down after picking up your toddler from day care and you get attacked by a dog as you walk to get help, you make sure the baby is safe and you keep walking.

My mom, Leslie, has walked through so much in her life. She grew up with abuse and alcoholism, became a teenage mother, had a marriage end, worked two jobs to get by, suffered from alcoholism and could only guess what a healthy, loving family life looked like, and wouldn't think she deserved it if she found it. She spent two decades walking on eggshells, especially after five o'clock, when Granddaddy started drinking and friends knew not to come over.

My mom would always be the peacemaker, no matter what it took. One night when Granddaddy was raging and screaming at my mom's brother Bob, the two of them wound up in a scuffle, fists and foul language flying, and my mother jumped on Granddaddy's back to try to get him to stop, because that was and is her way, always keeping on, always wanting to make things better for everybody else. In time she got around to caring for herself in the same way, pursuing recovery, getting counseling, and starting to change the harsh, self-critical tapes that had been playing in her head her whole life. My mom bounced around emotionally for much of the time I was bouncing around the minors, but she never stopped giving or fighting for the right thing. When I asked her to write about some of her reflections on her life and mine for this book, she wrote two thousand powerful, honest, and profoundly loving words, including these:

"I really thought you didn't like me or were ashamed of me, so I always watched you from what seemed like a distance as you got older... but I was always so proud of you...."

When I was thirteen, I walked out on my mother and ripped her heart out. I walked back in after I got my own help and faced my own demons. Now we are as close as a mother and son can be, both of us taking the risk that that necessarily entails. Now she brings love and light into our home every week, helping, giving, loving her grandchildren, loving all of us. Now I cannot imagine my life without her. After I got hurt in Chicago, she saw an interview with me and called to say, "You spoke so eloquently it made me very proud." The pride goes both ways.

I have not had the same sort of breakthrough with my father. There is so much that remains unspoken, a chasm that I do not pretend to understand, one that has widened as the years have passed. It makes me sad and makes me long for something more. I love my father and want to share the closeness we once had. I have prayed for that for years, and pray that in some way this book will help achieve that.

PRINCE FIELDER is at the plate, coiled in wait, a man mountain with a helmet, a nose guard disguised as a first baseman. He's one of the best power hitters in the game, a guy I love competing against. It's the top of the second inning at Citi Field. The knuckleball is usually a great weapon against most big swingers, but Prince is a bit different because he has power to all fields, and can wait on the ball well. He takes a knuckleball for a strike, and I come back with another one that misses. I throw another knuckleball and he fouls it off, and then the same—a knuckleball that he fouls off. He's ready to battle me; I can see it and feel it—that this is going fifteen rounds. He's not cutting back on his swing, but moving his hands quickly to fend off whatever I am coming up with. Five times in a row I go at him with good, diving knuckleballs, and he gets a piece of every one.

After each pitch, I think about whether it's time to mix it up and throw Prince a fastball. As a pitcher, I never want to be predictable, or get into a rut with my pitch patterns. My goal is to always keep the hitter guessing, wondering. Of course he knows I am going to be throwing knuckleballs most of the time. But will it be the slow one or the fast one or the medium one? Or will I try to sneak a fastball by him while he's sitting in the knuckler?

You don't want the hitter comfortable, or sure about what's coming.

The at-bat is now into its eighth pitch. I look in to Josh Thole, my catcher, and we're staying the course. I come through Charlie's doorframe and push forward with my hips, getting them fully involved, the way Phil wants me to. I look to throw the pitch with my arm path bisecting my body, the way Tim advises, and throw it one baseball width above Josh's mask, my usual guidepost, because that gives the ball plenty of room to drop and still be a strike. I throw one of the two or three best knuckleballs of my whole life, a ball that plunges eighteen inches, down and in.

I am sure I've got him.

Fielder fouls it off.

I am stunned. I have no idea how he gets a piece of it. Somehow he is able to drop his hands and flick the bat forward, dribbling a ball toward the dugout. He looks out at me and then at the ump and shakes his head, as if to say, "That was a nasty pitch, man."

The count is still 1-2. It feels as if he's been in the box for fifteen minutes. On the ninth pitch of the at-bat, after eight straight knuckleballs, Josh calls for a fastball. Josh's instincts are that Fielder's seen so many good knuckleballs in this at-bat and is so locked into them that he won't expect anything but another one. I agree wholeheartedly. It's time to defrost him.

I wind and fire, an 87-mile-per-hour fastball, a little up and a little in.

Fielder is not expecting it. It ties him up. He manages to tip it, but not enough. The ball settles into Josh's glove.

Strike three.

Fielder glares at me and then smiles as he walks back to the Brewers' dugout. I smile, too, if only on the inside. We both know that it may be the only 87-mile-per-hour fastball that will beat him the entire year. It's one of my most gratifying moments of the season, going mano-a-mano with one of the best hitters alive, and prevailing.

Four innings later, Fielder is back in the box, and he gets some payback, grounding an RBI single up the middle. It's a good pitch that he does well to get the bat on. I can do nothing but credit him with a good piece of hitting. The duels with Prince Fielder that day remind me why I love what I do so much. There's nothing like it. It's what I will miss the most when I'm not playing anymore.

BASEBALL, FOR ME, is a game of managing regrets. You are always going to have regrets; they are as much a part of baseball as home plate. As a pitcher, I may regret that I was afraid to throw my knuckleball when I was behind in the count. I may regret that I didn't change speeds, or was too predictable in my pitch sequence, or that I didn't anticipate that an opposing pitcher would be sitting on a fastball. If you let your regrets linger, they will devour you. Remember Greg Maddux's words: You need a short memory. You manage your regrets by letting them go, taking them to the curb as if they were the trash.

You manage them by forgetting them as soon as the ball leaves your hand, or leaves the park, and turn 100 percent of your intensity and your competitiveness to the next pitch. It's the only pitch you can throw, after all.

As the 2011 season winds down, I feel good about my body of work and how I've managed my regrets, and there were no shortage of them. I regret my lack of feel for my knuckleball early on, my propensity for giving up home runs in big spots, my putrid start that had me staring at an ERA over 5.00. I could easily have let these things turn my season into a train wreck, but I managed them well. In the twenty-four starts I've made since I left Houston, I have won only six times, but I've pitched to an ERA of just over 2.60—one of the best ERAs in the league over that span. I have a streak of eleven straight quality starts, dating to July.

Now I have one more, my last start of the season, in the first game of a doubleheader. It's at Citi Field, against the Phillies. The Phillies have the division locked up and we have the off-season locked up, so theoretically the game means nothing.

It means plenty to me.

After I have the season's last shot of Toradol in my rear end—I will not miss those things—I sit at my locker in the back right corner of the clubhouse, Chris Capuano at the locker to my left, Jonathon Niese to my right. I am not one to get overly nostalgic, but I am wistful about the season being over. I'm about to turn thirty-seven years old, and even though my knuckleballing mentors all pitched well into their forties, I know I'm a lot closer to the end of my career than the beginning, and there's unmistakable sadness in that. I'm proud of how we as a team battled this year, and how hard we played, no matter that there were plenty of times when we literally had more Buffalo Bisons on the field than New York Mets. I understand management's decision to trade Francisco Rodriguez and Carlos Beltrán from a business standpoint, but, from a competitor's standpoint, to lose two of your best players when you are on the periphery of the pennant race is tough to stomach, and I'm proud that we persevered through that too. From his first meeting with us in the spring, Terry Collins set a positive, professional tone and managed to be honest and forthright without burying people and losing people. He's just a tremendous leader of men.

So I'm sad the season is almost finished, but I am determined to finish it well. Isn't that what people remember the most? How you finish?

God, you've blessed me in so many ways this year, and I am so grateful for that. As I prepare to take the ball for the last time this year, please help me to be trustworthy one more time and to be in the moment every pitch, to glorify You in everything I do. Amen.

Fifty minutes before game time, I take an eight-minute Jacuzzi, then a five-minute shower. I say another prayer and head out to the bullpen a half hour before first pitch. I run a few sprints in the outfield. When I finish, I stand in front of Dan and he flips two balls into the air simultaneously, and I catch them. I do this before every start, bar none. I like to keep a very specific routine before I pitch, because it helps lock me in for the competition to come. I choose one of the two baseballs I've caught, and then I start to throw, first on the outfield grass, from thirty feet, then in the bullpen. I throw fifteen fastballs, then three cutters, three changeups, and twenty knuckleballs. I always end with knuckleballs. This is my routine and I don't deviate from it.

JIMMY ROLLINS LEADS OFF for the Phillies. I throw two knuckleballs to go up 0–2, then follow up with my slowpoke, 61 miles per hour. He freezes. Strike three. I retire the side in order and do the same in the second and third. In the fourth, Rollins lines out to second, and the Phillies go down in order again. By the time I get John Mayberry Jr. to hit a foul pop, I've faced fifteen Phillies and retired fifteen Phillies.

The crowd cheers as I walk off. Whenever I have a no-hitter

through five, I always make note of it. Obviously there is no guarantee, but when you are more than halfway through, well, you know you've got a shot.

When I had the one-hitter against the Phillies in 2010, it was in the sixth inning that Cole Hamels, my adversary again today, broke it up. I don't forget that when I go out for the sixth inning again. Carlos Ruiz, the Phillies' catcher, leads off. I quickly go up 0–2, but he works the count full. I throw three straight knucklers that he fouls off, and then I throw ball four. It doesn't miss by much, but it misses. The perfect game is over. I have huge regrets losing a perfect game this way, but I can't dwell on them, not if I want to keep going. I get the next two guys and now Rollins is up again. On the 1–1 pitch, he belts a knuckleball that sits up and drives it deep to right, way back. Nick Evans retreats to the track and gets turned around and somehow makes a tumbling catch on the warning track. The crowd goes berserk. I punch the air.

It's still alive. Thank you, Nick.

The Mets have never had a no-hitter in their fifty seasons of baseball, a span of nearly eight thousand games, one of the more bizarre and inexplicable streaks in the history of the game. Everybody in the ballpark knows it, including the pitcher. With Nick's play in right and the knuckleball I have going, I allow myself to think this could be the day. I follow my regular routine in between innings. I drink some water, towel off, and take a little walk. Hamels retires us in order, so the game remains scoreless and I am right back out there, facing Placido Polanco.

Polanco grounds out to open the seventh, and next up is Shane Victorino, a switch-hitter who has taken to batting right-handed against me after having almost no success left-handed. I fire a knuckleball for a strike, then he takes one for 1–1. I get the ball back from catcher Mike Nickeas and go right back at Victorino with one more knuckleball. It feels good leaving my hand, but it doesn't have much dive to it. Victorino turns on it and crushes a line drive to left. Nobody is catching this one. It goes for a double. The crowd stands and cheers me, and they stand for a good while.

I look up at the ballpark around me. I am having my usual resistance to being celebrated, but my awareness of it is helping me get better at accepting it. I stand on the Citi Field mound and feel good and strong. I don't have to hide under the stands because people want to salute me and I don't feel worthy of it. That's ancient stuff. *You don't live there anymore,* I think. *You live here.* So I just stand there and listen and tell myself: *It's okay to let these fans applaud you.*

It is perfectly okay.

I give myself a few more moments to be sad about losing the no-hitter, then turn my attention to Ryan Howard. On my first offering, Howard bounces a ball up the middle, scoring Victorino. Two batters, two hits, and faster than you can say Tom Candiotti, the no-hitter and shutout are both gone. I am on the hook for a loss, and really sad about it.

On the bench in the dugout, I know I'm done if we get a man on, because I'm up fourth this inning. With two outs, pinch hitter Val Pascucci, just up from the minors, drives a home run over the left-field fence to tie the game. The dugout instantly fires up, euphoric that we've finally broken through and that the game is tied. Terry calls me back and Ronny Paulino pinch-hits for me and grounds out. I am relieved that I at least won't get my fourteenth loss.

David Wright hits a double in the bottom of the eighth, scoring Ruben Tejada with the game-winning run. We win the second game too.

After the sweep, I walk back to my hotel room along a dark and desolate Queens street, elevated subway tracks overhead and Grand Central Parkway underneath. The trains clack. The cars rush. I wonder who all these people are and where they are going. I keep walking. I know for once where I am going, and know that it is God who is guiding me there.

In my hotel room, I call Anne to check in and see how things are at home, and then I write in my journal about the finish of my fifteenth season of professional baseball, and the quiet joy I get from knowing that I was trustworthy, and that I belonged. I write, too, about conquering fears and managing regrets and letting myself live in the present—not just on the mound, but everywhere; about learning to not worry about the next week or month or year, but rather to put all my energy into living the next five minutes well.

If I keep living the next five minutes well, I know I'll be exactly where I'm supposed to be.

Finally I say a prayer of thanks to God for taking a broken man and making him whole, for being my Redeemer, graciously giving me a second chance as a pitcher, as a husband and father, and as a Christian man. I know my journey is nowhere near complete. The point isn't to arrive. The point is to seek, to walk humbly with God, to keep walking and keep believing even though you know there will be times when you make mistakes and feel lost. You keep seeking the path, and He will show you the way.

Thank you, merciful God, for all these blessings and more, for giving me the courage to stop hiding, and the courage to find a new way.

I turn out the light. I close my eyes. I have hope.

SUMMITS

The year of 2012 isn't two weeks old and already I've learned a memorable life lesson: Altitude sickness is nasty stuff. I find this out 18,500 feet over Africa, on a climb up Mount Kilimanjaro. We knew altitude sickness could hit us at anytime. We also knew that it could end our ascent if we got a bad case of it—not that there is any such thing as a good case. The symptoms slam into me on a treacherous and steep stretch of trail, half as wide as a base path. We are making our final push to the top. I start feeling faint. My mind is cloudy and my stomach is in revolt, not quite the same way it would be if I'd eaten a bad clam, but not happy, either. Everywhere I look I see darting flashes of light, as if I were at the hub of a strobe-light show. My body feels as if it is in an alien universe. I promised myself, and Anne, before I left that I wouldn't pull another Missouri River stunt and be an idiot, pushing myself to the brink of death.

Remember that promise, I tell myself.

It is about five degrees and the wind is cutting into us like a scythe. My iPod is frozen, so I have to find other ways to take my mind off how I feel. I think about the kids and what they are doing back home. I think about the charity we are raising money for, Bombay Teen Challenge, and the good that can come of it. I start running through National League East lineups, batter by batter, trying to figure out how I am going to go after Giancarlo Stanton and Carlos Ruiz and the rest, my own game of fantasy baseball at almost four miles above sea level.

I finish with the lineups and still feel shaky. Much as I hate to do it, seven hours into the day's climb, I ask our guide, Joshua, if we can stop. I sit down on a rock on the side of the trail, hoping the symptoms will abate. Joshua hands me a hot cup of tea. I reach for it but am so wobbly my hand doesn't come within six inches of the cup. I feel my innards convulse. I reach again and hardly get any closer. I ask him to go into my backpack and hand me a Diamox, my altitude-sickness medication. I chew the tablet so it gets into my bloodstream faster. Joshua puts the cup right into my hand, and I take a sip of tea. I ask God for strength. After a few minutes I feel a bit better, the fog lifting, the nausea receding.

I stand up and take a trial step, then another. I hate to come out of games because of injury. I am the same way on mountains.

I am good to go.

It's only a few hundred feet to Stella Point, Joshua tells us in a buoyant voice, referring to the last landing area before the final push to Uhuru, the peak of Kilimanjaro. I don't know how my climbing colleagues, Kevin Slowey and Dave Racaniello, feel, but to me this is better than the Gipper speech.

I can do a few hundred feet, I tell myself. I climb on. We get to Stella Point and after Dave gets a blast of oxygen from Joshua, we keep on pushing, one tremulous foot after another. Now we're within three hundred feet of Uhuru, then two hundred, then one hundred. The sky looks so close. It seems to get lighter with each step. My adrenaline surges. Altitude sickness? What altitude sickness? My cleated boots crunch into the icy path, step after step, and I want to get there so badly I almost want to sprint. I keep my head down, my focus on my feet, and in a minute I take one more step and look up and realize there is no more path to climb.

We are here. We are at the summit, 19,340 feet over Africa, bathed in the orange light of daybreak, the most breathtaking dawn I have ever seen. In case we weren't sure of our whereabouts, a big brown sign with yellow letters—a little tacky, to be honest—welcomes us:

CONGRATULATIONS!
YOU ARE NOW AT UHURU PEAK

I am overwhelmed in that moment by God's goodness, and by His majesty. I thank Him for this journey and for all His blessings, and try to take in the immensity of the world before me, but I can't. I somehow feel smaller than I have ever felt in my life, but it's not only okay. It is intoxicating. It is as if God is speaking to me, and His message is clear:

This world is much, much bigger than you.

BY THE TIME I get back down to sea level, and Port St. Lucie, I am not thinking much about majesty or sunrises. I have a much more basic issue before me, one that consumes me from the time I wake up until the time I go to sleep.

Am I going to be a pariah in my own clubhouse? Are my team-mates going to be repulsed by my brokenness and not want to have anything to do with me?

On March 29, I publish a memoir that reveals secrets I've kept my whole career and most of my life. I write about being a victim of sexual abuse, about lies I told and images I tried to perpetu-ate. I tell the whole truth about my shame and my flaws and my sins. I don't do it because I want to sell a bunch of books or make headlines. I do it because I need to. I do it because I want to be authentic, because I know it will help me and think it can help other people who might be running from their own past and their own baggage.

In the weeks before publication, the Mets' organization is wor-ried that I might take shots at them and tell unseemly tales from the locker room. I assure them that the only one I throw under the bus is myself. The day before the book is released, Jay Horwitz, the Mets' VP of public relations, distributes copies to the beat writers who cover the team. Stories start posting on the Internet. *Sports Illustrated* publishes a piece, along with a short excerpt. ESPN airs a segment on me. Much of the focus, not surprisingly, is on the abuse.

Now it is all out there and there's no turning back, I tell myself.

I walk into the clubhouse the next morning, deeply anxious about what the response might be. I try not to be self-conscious. It is a lost cause. I say good morning to a few guys and head to my locker and start to get changed, and it seems like any other day. Nothing is different. I'm not getting strange looks that I pick up on. Dillon Gee, one locker over, greets me warmly and doesn't ask to relocate. I feel tremendous relief. Maybe the days ahead will be dif-ferent, but for now, normalcy is beyond my hopes. A few minutes later, I run into the Mets' owner, Fred Wilpon, in the clubhouse. Fred is not a guy you see in there very often. He moves close to me, in a way he never has before. He gives me a hug and cups my chin · in his hand.

This is a story that needs to be told and I'm very proud of you for telling it, he says.

Thank you, Fred, I say.

I MAKE MY FIRST start in the second game of the year, against the Braves at Citi Field. It's a Saturday afternoon. Johan Santana had been superb on opening day, in his first start back from major arm surgery. It gives the whole club a big emotional boost, and now I want to keep it going. But here comes the negative voice again, pounding on me:

You know what's going to happen if you aren't any good today, if you don't get off to a strong start this season? I'll tell you what's going to happen. People are going to write that it's because of the book. They're going to say that you are distracted. That you've opened your life up to intense scrutiny and can't deal with it. That you should've waited until you retired to search for your authenticity. So you better be on your game, or this whole career rejuvenation is going to disappear faster than those homers the Detroit Tigers hit off you to start 2006.

Remember how I felt compelled to justify my new contract in the spring of 2011? Here I am again, consumed with proving myself once more. I get to the park late in the morning. I ask God for strength and the clarity to block out all the noise in my head and pour everything into the moment.

Throw the best knuckleball you can. Get the ball back from Josh

Thole, and then throw another one. This is my mantra. The outing goes serviceably well. I give up five hits and two runs in six innings. Though I walk four batters—not good—I pitch around trouble effectively, except for the two-run homer Martin Prado knocks off me in the fifth. We win, 4–2, and everybody goes home happy.

In my next start against Cliff Lee and the Phillies, I have a 4–1 lead in the top of the fifth. I come up to the plate and hit a dribbler to Jimmy Rollins at short. I am busting it down the line when I feel a strong tug in the lower part of my abdomen. I get thrown out, but my bigger concern is the tug. I am pretty sure I have torn a muscle but don't tell anybody about it. The muscle hurts; adrenaline overrides it. I pitch seven innings and give up one run and we win again. After the game I tell Ray Ramirez, our trainer, what happened. He looks at it and confirms my self-diagnosis. The injury lingers the whole year, but it's nothing I can't deal with, with a little help from Toradol, the same anti-inflammatory and painkiller I used for almost all of 2011. The Toradol shots become part of my routine for the rest of the season.

I get lit up in my next start in Atlanta, where it is raining so hard it feels as if I am throwing water balloons, but I win three of my next four starts to go to 5–1, and by the time we get to Pittsburgh for my start against the Pirates in late May at PNC, I not only have the book worries behind me, I also have a new-fangled variation on my knuckleball.

Dan Warthen and I have been working on finding a way to throw a knuckler that gives the illusion of rising as it gets to the plate. It really just stays on the same plane, but if guys are missing it, I don't care what it does. I don't change my grip at all, just shorten my stride and try to stay under the ball a little more. It gives the hitters one more thing to think about and makes the pitch that much harder to track. The early returns against the Pirates are striking. I give up one run in seven innings and strike out eleven and don't walk anybody. I can't tell you for sure how many times guys swing and miss at the pseudo-riser, but I *am* sure I am going to keep throwing it.

I strike out ten more and walk just one in my next start, pitching no-run, three-hit ball into the eighth inning against the Padres, and by now there's no doubt that I am pitching the best baseball of my life. And probably the single biggest reason for it is that I am controlling my knuckleball to a degree I wasn't sure was possible, given the capricious soul of the pitch. I have spent most of two months living ahead in the count. Against the Pirates, I threw 89 pitches, 68 of them strikes. When you are always around the plate, it changes the whole balance of the at-bat. Hitters can't go up there and say, "I'm going to wait until I get a better count, and make him throw me something I can hit." Now they wait and suddenly they're looking at an 0–2 hole. It changes everything, puts me in command. It is an exhilarating feeling to have, and the exhilaration seems to be spreading all around the club.

The Cardinals come into Citi Field on the first of June, and the New York Mets are 28–23 and one of the surprises of the National League. Johan is on the mound, and he's been pitching great. We go up 2–0 in the fourth. Johan strikes out two guys in the fifth and gets Rafael Furcal to line out and the Cardinals are still without a hit. In the sixth the Cardinals go down in order, with no small amount of help from third-base umpire Adrian Johnson, who calls a Carlos Beltrán bouncer down the third-base line foul, even though replays prove it to be fair. Beltrán winds up tapping out to third. The buzz in the ballpark is building with each out. Everybody in the park knows the Mets have never had a no-hitter in their fifty-year existence, one of the great and mysterious quirks that baseball seems to specialize in. Could this be the night?

Kirk Nieuwenhuis crushes a three-run homer off Cardinals' starter Adam Wainwright and now we're up 5–0. With one out in the seventh, Yadier Molina rips a line drive to deep left. Mike Baxter races back to the track. The ball is a laser. Baxter keeps sprinting. As he nears the wall he stretches out his left arm. He snares the ball in his webbing and then crashes into the W of the W.B. Mason sign on the left field wall. He collapses in a heap. The ball is still in his glove. It is one of the great clutch catches I've ever seen. The place is going nuts now. So is the dugout. Mike, it turns out, dislocated his shoulder on the play and would be out for a couple of months, sacrificing his body for a pitcher chasing history.

By the time the ninth inning comes around, I can't even look. I have a towel over my head in the dugout. I will let the crowd tell me what's going on.

Matt Holliday swings at the first pitch of the inning and lines out to center. Allen Craig hits a short fly to left. One out to go now. The crowd is on its feet. Up steps David Freese, MVP of the 2011 World Series. The count goes full. My towel is still in place. Johan throws a sinking changeup. Freese swings, and he misses, and Citi Field explodes in noise. As soon as I hear it, I snap the towel off and charge the mound, along with everybody else in the dugout.

It's an unforgettable moment for the franchise and for my teammate, a champion of a competitor. It is only later, when the euphoria abates a bit, that I realize I have to follow this act, on the same mound, eighteen hours later. It's a daunting thought. Old fears try to fire up and start trouble, inflaming self-doubt. I work hard on not paying attention. I do not pitch a no-hitter, but I do shut out the Cardinals on seven hits. I strike out nine and walk nobody. I throw

100 pitches, 73 of them strikes. My record is 8–1. Who knew I was just getting started?

In my next three starts, I give up no earned runs. I pitch back-to-back one-hitters against the Rays and the Orioles, striking out twenty-five and walking two. My streak of scoreless innings pushes past forty and my record goes to 11–1. Suddenly, happily, my pitching world is spinning into an orbit that is usually the domain of Cy Young winners and Hall of Famers.

Nobody can believe what I am doing. Few can fathom that a knuckleball pitcher—the only one left after Tim Wakefield's retirement—is leading the league in strikeouts. Writers keep asking me how I am able to control a famously unruly pitch, how I am getting such results. I do not want to engage in excruciating analysis. Truly, I do not want to do any analysis at all. I want to keep the mind-set I had as I neared the summit of Kilimanjaro and literally lived my life one step at a time. Now I am living one pitch at a time. I have been getting progressively better at throwing the knuckleball. I am throwing it at different speeds, different elevations, throwing most everything for strikes. I can't say with certainty that I knew this was coming, but I will tell you this: I knew I was getting better with my knuckleball every year, and now, in 2012, I am in a whole new place altogether.

What is there not to like about that?

In late June, we play the Yankees on ESPN's *Sunday Night Baseball*, CC Sabathia vs. R.A. Dickey, Yankee ace vs. Met upstart, The Big Man vs. The Baffler. I have not given up an earned run since the Pirates game. The streak is a cool thing and I hope it goes to a 100 innings, but it also weighs on my mind all the time, with all the fuss, the constant questions about Orel Hershiser's record of 59 scoreless innings. For a guy who has spent his whole professional life being overlooked, it's a little overwhelming. Part of me wishes I could find a way to keep pitching at this level, but do it without the attention.

That, alas, is not how it works.

Neither CC nor I am very good that night. My streak ends when my old buddy, Mark Teixeira, hits a sacrifice fly in the third, and then Nick Swisher socks a three-run homer off me. I give up five runs in six innings, but we rally to take me off the hook for the loss, and I can't wait to get the ball again in five days, against the Dodgers in L.A., where I am back in form, pitching three-hit, scoreless ball over eight innings and striking out ten. My record is now 12–1 and two days later I get awakened by a phone call in my hotel room at 9:00 a.m.

The caller is our general manager, Sandy Alderson.

Congratulations. You were voted to the All-Star team. You deserve it, Sandy says.

I take a minute to digest the words and wrap my head around this honor. There aren't many first-time All-Stars who are thirty-seven years old. I never doubted I could be good, but to get this sort of affirmation means so much. There is a tempest in New York for a spell when manager Tony La Russa picks Matt Cain to start the game over me, but this is not something that costs me any sleep. Sure, I want to start. I believe that with a 12–1 record and a 2.40 ERA I have the credentials to start, but this is not going to spoil the experience of going to Kansas City and being a part of the greatest assemblage of baseball players in the world, and sharing it with Anne and the kids, the six of us packed into one hotel room. Let the mayhem begin.

I get one of the biggest cheers when I am introduced before the game. When La Russa calls for me to pitch the bottom of the sixth,

I run in from the pen and I listen to the cheers and smell the grass and the field looks brighter and greener than any I have ever seen. I look to where Anne and the kids and my mom are sitting. I feel as if I'm on stage at a Broadway musical. The show lasts fifteen pitches. Every one of them is delicious. I end by getting Miguel Cabrera, a man bound for a Triple Crown, to hit into a 6–4–3 double play. I walk off the mound and think: *Only God could write this narrative.*

THINGS UNRAVEL FOR THE Mets in the second half of the season, and gloom gathers around Citi Field as we sink in the standings. I just want to honor my craft and glorify God and keep throwing the best knuckleballs I can. I'm not as dominant as I was in the first half, but when I shut out the Marlins to close out August, I am 17–4, and determined to get to 20. I split my next four decisions and go to the Citi Field mound for my last home start of the year with a record of 19–6. It is September 27. The opponent is the Pirates, the team that I unveiled the pseudo-riser against, back in May. More than 31,000 fans show up for a Thursday afternoon date, a remarkable turnout for a late-season game with no larger meaning. It lifts me up, thinking that many of these people are in the park just to support me. I give up two runs early but our bats rally and when David Wright, who has been just tremendous all year, crushes a three-run homer, I have a 6–3 lead in the bottom of the fifth. I record five straight outs on strikeouts in one stretch. After I get Andrew McCutchen on a deep fly to center to end the seventh, I'm sure I'm done for the day, but Terry says he wants me to go out for the eighth. So I go out for the eighth. I strike out Garrett Jones and Pedro Alvarez.

I have nothing left. Terry has the bullpen ready. When I walk

Travis Snider after an eight-pitch battle, Terry emerges from the dugout. I've thrown 128 pitches, given up nine hits, and struck out thirteen. The crowd has been chanting my name intermittently throughout the game. Now they are standing as I walk toward the dugout, pouring so much emotion and affection into me it's almost palpable.

I tip my hat but wish I could do more. I want to remember this moment forever, and I will. I watch the rest of the game in the dugout, except I don't really watch. I just peek from time to time, because I can't bear it.

The bullpen wobbles and the score narrows to 6–5. Bobby Parnell comes in with one gone in the ninth. He gets Josh Harrison to bounce out. One out to go. The hitter is Jose Tabata, the leftfielder. On a 1–0 count, I hear a crack of the bat. I am still only peeking. Tabata drives a liner to right. Mike Baxter, the man who saved Johan's no-hitter, doesn't have to crash into anything. He tracks the ball and locks it into his glove and the roar that goes up in Citi Field is louder than anything I've heard since we were in the race, months before.

I am a 20-game winner. I run out of the dugout to thank Bobby for the save, to thank and hug everybody.

I finish the greatest season of my life with a record of 20–6, and a 2.73 ERA. I lead the league in innings (233 $^2/_3$) and strikeouts (230). (This is as good a place as any to apologize for the misstatement on page 1, where I write that I will never lead the league in strikeouts. My bad.) I also have more complete games (five) and shutouts (three) than any National League starter. All that remains now is to find out whether my performance is deemed worthy of a Cy Young Award by the Baseball Writers' Association of America. Gio Gonzalez of the Nationals won one more game than I did. The

Dodgers' Clayton Kershaw, the 2011 Cy Young winner, had a better ERA and batting-average against. I hear all sorts of arguments, people dicing numbers every which way. I don't do any of that. I make up my mind that I am not going to morph into a sabermetrician to evaluate my chances. I want to be honored, of course, because it means I will have been judged the best at what I do, and who doesn't want to be the best? But why get my mind spinning while I wait?

The results are announced in the early evening of November 14. I am home in Nashville. A satellite TV truck is in the driveway, ready to record my reaction. Jack O'Connell, secretary-treasurer of the BBWAA, takes the podium on the MLB Network and carries an envelope. Now I know how actors feel on Oscar night. Jack begins by talking about history being made tonight, and before I even hear my name, I know. I know I am the 2012 National League Cy Young Award winner. In fifty-six years of voting, no knuckleball pitcher has ever won a Cy Young, in either league. Until now. I try to take it all in, embrace this moment. I think about all the people who have loved me and believed in me who made this possible. I think again of the power of hope. I began the year on an African summit and I am ending it on a baseball summit. I like the symmetry. God is good.

ACKNOWLEDGMENTS

Ten weeks before this book was published, I climbed to the summit of Mount Kilimanjaro, more than 19,000 feet above the African continent. It was a life-changing journey for me, not just because I felt as though I could see forever, but because being on Uhuru Peak at dawn's first light filled me with rapture for God and the majesty of His world.

In the course of my ascent with companions Kevin Slowey and Dave Racaniello, I had to overcome nausea, altitude sickness, extreme fatigue, and fierce and unrelenting wind and cold. It was so worth it, for reaching such a peak filled me with profound reflection and gratitude, both for my life and for the life story you have just read.

It was spring of 2008, early in my season with the Seattle Mariners, when I first felt called to write a book about my life. I use the word "called" because I literally felt something outside myself tell me to start writing. Whether the voice was God's or my own creative psyche, I can't say for sure. Probably it was a mixture of both. I started writing on an inflatable mattress in a rental apartment in

Tacoma, Washington, and soon became so terrified by the process, and what I was putting down in my notebook, that I stopped and didn't pick it up for two years, when it became clear to me that God really did want me to tell my story—and tell every aspect of it.

I was given a gift during those two years. A few men emerged in my life who helped me deal with the fear and affirmed to me that I had a story worth sharing, no matter how painful the process might be. Thank you, Stephen James, not only for giving me the courage to face my past but for teaching me how to seek truth and grow towards being an authentic man. Carter Crenshaw, our pastor at Nashville's West End Community Church, was a spiritual rock and the same loving, loyal, godly friend he has been for years. Jason Robbins was an equally steadfast friend and constant source of encouragement. Michael Karounos helped shape the vision for my story and cared enough to tell me the truth even when it was hard to hear.

Thanks, too, to my friend Mike Jones, who offered fresh eyes and valuable editorial input; to George Vecsey of *The New York Times;* and to Teri Thompson, executive sports editor of the New York *Daily News*. George wrote a column about me in the *Times* at the end of the 2010 season, and subsequently referred me to Esther Newberg, his literary agent, who, with Teri's help, partnered me with Wayne Coffey. Esther took an immediate liking to the project, even though I annoyed her to no end by insisting on calling her "ma'am." She warned me that she might drop the project if I didn't drop the "ma'ams," so I did, and then Esther did what she does best—finding the perfect landing spot for the book—with David Rosenthal's new Penguin imprint, Blue Rider Press.

David was a believer in the book from the start. He was unwavering in encouraging me to write the book I wanted to write, and despite being an ardent Mets fan, he never once leaned on me to rip anybody. The whole Blue Rider team—Aileen Boyle, Sarah Hochman, Gregg Kulick, Linda Rosenberg, Garrett McGrath, David Chesanow, and Dick Heffernan and his superlative sales group—matched my enthusiasm and believed in this first-time author from the outset.

I don't think "thank you" is strong enough to express my gratitude to Wayne Coffey, who is much more than a writer to me. He is an answer to prayer. His writing expertise and wise tutelage allowed me to give my story a voice. Our countless hours together—whether on the phone or at venues ranging from Nashville to Citi Field to Port St. Lucie to various National League cities—produced much more than a narrative-shaping dialogue. They transformed a working relationship into a friendship that has been more valuable to me than even the pages that we pored over. I'd also like to express my gratitude to the other Coffey people, especially Wayne's wife, Denise Willi, a national tennis champion whose patience throughout this process was even more stout than her forehand. Alexandra, Sean, and Samantha Coffey have become three of my most loyal fans, and I appreciate them, too, just as I appreciate Frank Coffey, who taught Wayne how to play center field back in the day, for his invaluable editorial input.

All I can say about my mom is that I am blessed to be her son, for she is as courageous and loving and good-hearted as any person on this earth. I love you, Mom. To Billy and Lynn Caldwell, and Uncle Ricky, thank you for all your love and for always being there, and to my sister, Jane, and her daughters, Abby and Kaitlyn, love and blessings to you for being in my life. To my dad, you taught me and gave me so much in my early years, and I love you for that. It is my prayer that renewed closeness and honesty will be in our future.

Much thanks to Susan Waynick for her love and provision in my early years.

Will, Ben, and Bo Bartholomew are the three best brothers-in-law a man could have—the brothers I never had—and Sam and Vicki Bartholomew are the patriarch and matriarch of a wonderful Christian family. A special thanks to Bo, whose selfless friendship was always a motivation for me to relentlessly pursue a relationship with Jesus Christ.

Finally, I'd like to thank my wife, Anne, and our children, Gabriel, Lila, Eli, and Van. They had to be without a husband/father for more than a year while I spent my days either playing baseball or writing. They rarely complained while I gave them much less than they deserved. You are the greatest treasures of my life. To Anne, thank you for loving me in the middle of the darkest hours of my life. Your love for me when I couldn't stand myself saved my life, and I will never forget that. You stayed by me and stood with me and more than anyone, helped me to have hope and to heed the words of Thomas Merton, author of my favorite prayer:

My Lord God, I have no idea where I am going. I do not see the road ahead of me. I cannot know for certain where it will end. Nor do I really know myself, and the fact that I think I am following your will does not mean that I am actually doing so. But I believe that the desire to please you does in fact please you. And I hope I have that desire in all that I am doing. I hope that I will never do anything apart from that desire. And I know that if I do this you will lead me by the right road though I may know nothing about it. Therefore I will trust you always though I may seem to be lost and in the shadow of death. I will not fear, for you are ever with me, and you will never leave me to face my perils alone.

INDEX